ICWMC 2021

The Seventeenth International Conference on Wireless and Mobile Communications

July 18 – 22, 2021

Nice, France

ICWMC 2021 Editors

Xuesong Cai, Aalborg University, Denmark
José Rodríguez-Piñeiro, Tongji University, China
Rony Kumer Saha, KDDI Research, Inc., Japan
Cosmin Dini, IARIA, USA/EU

Printed from e-media with permission by:

Curran Associates, Inc.
57 Morehouse Lane
Red Hook, NY 12571

Some format issues inherent in the e-media version may also appear in this print version.

Printed with permission by Curran Associates, Inc. (2023)

International Academy, Research, and Industry Association (IARIA)
412 Derby Way
Wilmington, DE 19810

Phone: (408) 893-6407
Fax: (408) 527-6351

petre@iaria.org

Additional copies of this publication are available from:

Curran Associates, Inc.
57 Morehouse Lane
Red Hook, NY 12571 USA
Phone: 845-758-0400
Fax: 845-758-2633
Email: curran@proceedings.com
Web: www.proceedings.com

Table of Contents

Affordable Quality of Service Assessment for Cellular-Connected UAV Communications 1
Hong Zhu, Jose Rodriguez-Pineiro, Tomas Dominguez-Bolano, Xuesong Cai, and Xuefeng Yin

Communications for Massive UAV Scenarios 8
Uwe-Carsten Fiebig

A High-Accuracy DOA-Based Localization Method: UAV Virtual Multiantenna Array 10
Jianqiao Cheng, Ke Guan, and Francois Quitin

Characterizing the Small-Scale Fading for Low Altitude UAV Channels 16
Xuesong Cai, Jian Song, Jose Rodriguez-Pineiro, Preben Mogensen, and Fredrik Tufvesson

Bounded Path-Loss Model for UAV-to-UAV Communications 20
Jian Song, Xuesong Cai, Lam-Thanh Tu, and Preben E. Mogensen

Comparison of Techno-Economic Solutions for 5G Networks and Beyond 22
Christos Bouras, Fotios Kaisoudis, and Anastasia Kollia

Keep it Flat (KiF): Resource Management in Integrated Cloud-Fog Networks 28
Neam Farroukh, Mohamed Nassar, Shady Elbassuoni, and Haidar Safa

Dynamic and Opportunistic Millimeter-Wave Spectrum Access in 5G New Radio Multi-Operator Cognitive Radio Networks 35
Rony Kumer Saha

On Operating 5G New Radio Indoor Small Cells in the 60 GHz Unlicensed Band 38
Rony Kumer Saha

Use of Augmented Reality (AR) and Virtual Reality (VR) to Address Four of the "National Academy of Engineering Grand Challenges for Engineering in the 21st Century" 44
Bibhav Bhattarai and Daniela Marghitu

A Direction of Arrival Machine Learning Approach for Beamforming in 6G 54
Anabel Reyes Carballeira, Abel Rodriguez Medel, and Jose Marcos Camara Brito

Taking into Account Children Accurate Weights During Parent Selection Process in RPL to Wxtend WSN Lifetime 60
Doda Afoussatou Rollande Sanou, Yelemou Tiguiane, Hamadoun Tall, and Mahamadi Boulou

On Achieving High Capacity using Small Cells in Multistory Buildings: A Review 65
Rony Kumer Saha

ICWMC 2021

Forward

The Seventeenth International Conference on Wireless and Mobile Communications (ICWMC 2021) continued a series of events on advanced wireless technologies, wireless networking, and wireless applications.

ICWMC 2021 addressed wireless related topics concerning integration of latest technological advances to realize mobile and ubiquitous service environments for advanced applications and services in wireless networks. Mobility and wireless, special services and lessons learnt from particular deployment complemented the traditional wireless topics.

We take here the opportunity to warmly thank all the members of the ICWMC 2021 technical program committee, as well as all the reviewers. The creation of such a high quality conference program would not have been possible without their involvement. We also kindly thank all the authors who dedicated much of their time and effort to contribute to ICWMC 2021. We truly believe that, thanks to all these efforts, the final conference program consisted of top quality contributions. We also thank the members of the ICWMC 2021 organizing committee for their help in handling the logistics of this event.

ICWMC 2021 Chairs

ICWMC 2021 Steering Committee
Dragana Krstic, University of Niš, Serbia
Rajat Kumar Kochhar, Ericsson, Sweden
Magnus Jonsson, Halmstad University, Sweden

ICWMC 2021 Industry/Research Advisory Committee
Sivakumar Sivaramakrishnan, vToggle Ltd., New Zealand
Christian Makaya, IBM T.J. Watson Research Center, USA
David Navarro, Ecole Centrale de Lyon, France
Carl James Debono, University of Malta, Malta

ICWMC 2021 Publicity Chair
Mar Parra, Universitat Politecnica de Valencia, Spain
Alvaro Liebana, Universitat Politecnica de Valencia, Spain

ICWMC 2021
Committee

ICWMC 2021 Steering Committee

Dragana Krstic, University of Niš, Serbia
Rajat Kumar Kochhar, Ericsson, Sweden
Magnus Jonsson, Halmstad University, Sweden

ICWMC 2021 Industry/Research Advisory Committee

Sivakumar Sivaramakrishnan, vToggle Ltd., New Zealand
Christian Makaya, IBM T.J. Watson Research Center, USA
David Navarro, Ecole Centrale de Lyon, France
Carl James Debono, University of Malta, Malta

ICWMC 2021 Publicity Chair

Mar Parra, Universitat Politecnica de Valencia, Spain
Alvaro Liebana, Universitat Politecnica de Valencia, Spain

ICWMC 2021 Technical Program Committee

Mohamed Abid, University of Gabes, Tunisia
Afrand Agah, West Chester University of Pennsylvania, USA
Iness Ahriz, CNAM, France
Wafa Akkari, University of Manouba, Tunisia
Ali Kadhum M. Al-Quraby, University of Babylon, Iraq
Diego Alberto Godoy, Universidad Gastón Dachary, Argentina
Adel Aldalbahi, King Faisal University, Saudi Arabia
Rashid Ali, Sejong University, Seoul, Republic of Korea
Adda Ali-Pacha, University of Sciences and Technology of Oran, Algeria
Karine Amis, IMT Atlantique, France
Tran Hai Anh, Hanoi University of Science and Technology (HUST), Vietnam
Antonio Arena, University of Pisa, Italy
Kamran Arshad, Ajman University, UAE
Radu Arsinte, Technical University of Cluj-Napoca, Romania
Salih Safa Bacanli, University of Central Florida, USA
Corey E. Baker, University of Kentucky, USA
Diego Orlando Barragan Guerrero, Universidad Técnica Particular de Loja, Ecuador / ETS, Canada
Paolo Barsocchi, ISTI (Institute of Information Science and Technologies) | Italian National Research Council (C.N.R.), Pisa, Italy
Jordi Mongay Batalla, Institute of Telecommunications | Warsaw University of Technology, Poland
Hadda Ben Elhadj, SM@RTS | Higher Institute of Informatics | Monastir University, Tunisia
Sonia Ben Rejeb, Higher Institute of Computer Science (ISI) - Higher School of Communications of Tunis (SUPCOM), Tunisia
Djamila Bendouda, Ecole Nationale Supérieur de Technologie, Algeria
Driss Benhaddou, University of Houston, USA
Vincent Beroulle, Grenoble INP, France
Robert Bestak, Czech Technical University in Prague, Czech Republic

Yousaf Bin Zikria, Yeungnam University, South Korea
Abdelmadjid Bouabdallah, University of Technology of Compiegne, France
Ridha Bouallegue, Higher School of Communications of Tunis "Sup'Com", Tunisia
Christos Bouras, University of Patras, Greece
Ines Bousnina, Tunisia Polytechnic School - University of Carthage, Tunisia
Brik Bouziane, Eurecom School, France
Maurizio Bozzi, University of Pavia, Italy
An Braeken, Vrije Universiteit Brussel, Belgium
Ibtissem Brahmi, University of Sfax, Tunisia
Marcos F. Caetano, University of Brasilia, Brazil
Jun Cai, Concordia University, Montreal, Canada
Xuesong Cai, Aalborg University, Denmark
Rodrigo Campos Bortoletto, Federal Institute of Education, Science and Technology of São Paulo - IFSP, Brazil
Eric Castelli, CNRS / Laboratoire LIG, Grenoble, France
Riccardo Colella, National Research Council of Italy, Italy
Nicolae Crisan, Technical University of Cluj-Napoca, Romania
Saber Dakhli, University of Carthage, Tunisia
Luca Davoli, University of Parma, Italy
Enrico Del Re, University of Florence and CNIT, Italy
Sandesh Dhawaskar Sathyanarayana, University of Colorado Boulder, USA
Ding-Zhu Du, The University of Texas at Dallas, USA
Jalel Dziri, National Engineering School of Tunis, Tunisia
Mohamed Elhadad, VEDECOM, France
Ahmed Fakhfakh, University of Sfax, Tunisia
Fairouz Fakhfakh, Universiy of Sfax, Tunisia
Faten Fakhfakh, National School of Engineering of Sfax, Tunisia
Souhir Feki, University of Carthage, Tunisia
Miguel Franklin de Castro, Federal University of Ceará, Brazil
Mounir Frikha, Higher School of Communications of Tunis (SUPCOM), Tunisia
Marco Furini, University of Modena and Reggio Emilia, Italy
Krishna C. Garikipati, Niantic Inc., USA
Jordi Garcia, CRAAX Lab - UPC BarcelonaTech, Spain
Abderrahmen Guermazi, Higher Institute of Technological Studies | National School of Engineers of Sfax | University of Sfax, Tunisia
Xiang Gui, Massey University, New Zealand
Habib Hamam, Université de Moncton, Canada
Abdelaziz Hamdi, ISITCOM | University of Sousse, Tunisia
Hicham Hammouchi, International University of Rabat (UIR), Rabat, Morocco
Wibowo Hardjawana, University of Sydney, Australia
Rym Hicheri, University of Agder (UiA), Norway
Ali Kadhum Idrees, University of Babylon, Iraq
Muhammad Ali Imran, University of Glasgow, UK
Terje Jensen, Telenor, Norway
Wassim Jerbi, Higher Institute of Technological Studies | University of Sfax, Tunisia
Zakia Jellali, Higher School of Communication of Tunis (SUP'COM) | University of Carthage, Tunisia
Magnus Jonsson, Halmstad University, Sweden
Geethu Joseph, Syracuse University, USA

Georgios Kambourakis, University of the Aegean, Greece
Madhan Raj Kanagarathinam, Samsung R&D Institute, India
Lutful Karim, Seneca College of Applied Arts and Technology, Toronto / Moncton University, Canada
Suleman Khan, Northumbria University, Newcastle, UK
Wooseong Kim, Gachon University, S. Korea
Rajat Kochhar, Ericsson, Sweden
Peng-Yong Kong, Khalifa University, United Arab Emirates
Dragana Krstic, University of Niš, Serbia
Michel Kulhandjian, University of Ottawa, Canada
Vimal Kumar, University of Waikato, New Zealand
Souad Labghough, Mohammed V University in Rabat, Morocco
Mohamed Lamine Lamali, Univ. Bordeaux | LaBRI, France
Mohamed Latrach, ESEO / IETR - University of Rennes 1, France
SuKyoung Lee, Yonsei University, Seoul, South Korea
Ilhem Lengliz, Military Academy | HANALAB, Tunisia
Deyu Lin, Nanchang University, China
Eirini Liotou, National and Kapodistrian University of Athens, Greece
Jia Liu, Dalian University of Technology, China
Jian Liu, University of Tennessee, Knoxville, USA
Yueliang Liu, China University of Petroleum (East China), China
Maximilian Luebke, Friedrich-Alexander University Erlangen-Nürnberg, Germany
Stephane Maag, Institut Mines Telecom / Telecom SudParis, France
Tianle Mai, Beijing University of Posts and Telecommunications, China
Amel Meddeb Makhlouf, NTS'COM (New Technologies for System Communications) | ENET'COM (High School of Engineering in Electronics and Communications), Tunisia
D. Manivannan, University of Kentucky, USA
Hend Marouane, Sfax University, Tunisia
Aref Meddeb, University of Sousse, Tunisia
Hamid Menouar, Qatar Mobility Innovations Center (QMIC), Qatar
Sofien Mhatli, ISI Kef | University of Jandouba, Tunisia
Fabien Mieyeville, University of Lyon | Université Claude Bernard Lyon 1 | CNRS, France
Farshad Miramirkhani, Isik University, Istanbul, Turkey
Makoto Miyake, M-TEC Co. Ltd. | Mitsubishi Electric Corporation, Japan
Mohammad Moltafet, University of Oulu, Finland
Mohamed M. A. Moustafa, Egyptian Russian University, Egypt
Tathagata Mukherjee, The University of Alabama in Huntsville, USA
Sami Myllymäki, University of Oulu, Finland
Assia Naja, International University of Rabat, Morocco
Sameh Najeh, Higher school of Communication (Sup'Com) of Tunis, Tunisia
Leïla Najjar, Higher School of Communication of Tunis (SUP'COM), Tunisia
Giovanni Nardini, University of Pisa, Italy
Leila Nasraoui, National School of Computer Sciences (ENSI) | University of Manouba, Tunisia
Nejah Nasri, National Engineering School of Sfax (ENIS_LETI_Tunisia), Tunisia
Idrissa Ndiaye, Université Cheikh Anta Diop, Senegal
Armielle Ngaffo, Mediatron Laboratory, Tunisia
Maciej Nikodem, Wroclaw University of Science and Technology, Poland
Boubakr Nour, Beijing Institute of Technology, China

Ekaterina Pakulova, Institute of Computer Science and Information Security of the Southern Federal University, Russia
Tudor Palade, Technical University of Cluj-Napoca, Romania
Travis Peters, Montana State University, USA
Paulo Pinto, Universidade Nova de Lisboa, Portugal
Michele Polese, Institute for the Wireless Internet of Things | Northeastern University, USA
Adib Rastegarnia, Purdue University, USA
Heena Rathore, University of Texas, USA
Muhammad Atif Ur Rehman, Hongik University, South Korea
Éric Renault, ESIEE Paris, France
Francesca Righetti, University of Pisa, Italy
Miguel Rodríguez-Pérez, University of Vigo, Spain
Elisa Rojas, University of Alcala, Spain
Haidar Safa, American University of Beirut, Lebanon
Hajer Saidi, National Engineering School of Sfax, Tunisia
Fahad Salamh, Purdue University, USA
David Sánchez-Rodríguez, University of Las Palmas de Gran Canaria, Spain
José Santa, Technical University of Cartagena, Spain
Vladica Sark, IHP GmbH - Leibniz Institut für innovative Mikroelektronik, Germany
Adérito Seixas, Universidade Fernando Pessoa, Porto, Portugal
Stavros N. Shiaeles, Plymouth University, UK
Soulayma Smirani, National Engineering School of Tunis (ENIT) | University of Tunis El Manar, Tunisia
Animesh Srivastava, Google, USA
Álvaro Suárez Sarmiento, Universidad de Las Palmas de Gran Canaria, Spain
Fatma Tansu Hocanın, Cyprus International University, Lefkosa, TRNC
Rui Teng, Advanced Telecommunications Research Institute International, Japan
Hitesh Tewari, Trinity College Dublin, Ireland
Varese Salvador Timóteo, Universidade Estadual de Campinas - UNICAMP, Brazil
Hajer Tounsi, Ecole Supérieure des Communications de Tunis, Tunisia
Florian Tschorsch, Technical University of Berlin, Germany
Eirini Eleni Tsiropoulou, University of New Mexico, USA
Sudhanshu Tyagi,Thapar Institute of Engineering & Technology | Deemed University, India
Rehmat Ullah, Hongik University, South Korea
Véronique Vèque, Université Paris-Saclay, France
Abdul Wahab, Queen Mary University of London, UK
Lei Wang, University of Connecticut, USA
Xianzhi Wang, University of Technology Sydney, Australia
You-Chiun Wang, National Sun Yat-sen University, Taiwan
Ulf Witkowski, South Westphalia University of Applied Sciences, Germany
Ouri Wolfson, University of Illinois at Chicago / University of Illinois at Urbana Champaign, USA
Diane Woodbridge, University of San Francisco, USA
Abid Yaqoob, Insight Centre for Data Analytics | Dublin City University, Ireland
Syeda Kanwal Zaidi, Massey University, New Zealand
Sherali Zeadally, University of Kentucky, USA
Huanle Zhang, University of California, Davis, USA
Rafik Zitouni, ECE Paris, France
Karim Zkik, International University of Rabat, Morocco

Copyright Information

For your reference, this is the text governing the copyright release for material published by IARIA.

The copyright release is a transfer of publication rights, which allows IARIA and its partners to drive the dissemination of the published material. This allows IARIA to give articles increased visibility via distribution, inclusion in libraries, and arrangements for submission to indexes.

I, the undersigned, declare that the article is original, and that I represent the authors of this article in the copyright release matters. If this work has been done as work-for-hire, I have obtained all necessary clearances to execute a copyright release. I hereby irrevocably transfer exclusive copyright for this material to IARIA. I give IARIA permission or reproduce the work in any media format such as, but not limited to, print, digital, or electronic. I give IARIA permission to distribute the materials without restriction to any institutions or individuals. I give IARIA permission to submit the work for inclusion in article repositories as IARIA sees fit.

I, the undersigned, declare that to the best of my knowledge, the article is does not contain libelous or otherwise unlawful contents or invading the right of privacy or infringing on a proprietary right.

Following the copyright release, any circulated version of the article must bear the copyright notice and any header and footer information that IARIA applies to the published article.

IARIA grants royalty-free permission to the authors to disseminate the work, under the above provisions, for any academic, commercial, or industrial use. IARIA grants royalty-free permission to any individuals or institutions to make the article available electronically, online, or in print.

IARIA acknowledges that rights to any algorithm, process, procedure, apparatus, or articles of manufacture remain with the authors and their employers.

I, the undersigned, understand that IARIA will not be liable, in contract, tort (including, without limitation, negligence), pre-contract or other representations (other than fraudulent misrepresentations) or otherwise in connection with the publication of my work.

Exception to the above is made for work-for-hire performed while employed by the government. In that case, copyright to the material remains with the said government. The rightful owners (authors and government entity) grant unlimited and unrestricted permission to IARIA, IARIA's contractors, and IARIA's partners to further distribute the work.

Affordable Quality of Service Assessment for Cellular-Connected UAV Communications

Hong Zhu*, José Rodríguez-Piñeiro*, Tomás Domínguez-Bolaño†, Xuesong Cai‡§, Xuefeng Yin*
*College of Electronics and Information Engineering, Tongji University, Shanghai, China,
{zhuhong0120,j.rpineiro,yinxuefeng}@tongji.edu.cn
†CITIC Research Center & Department of Computer Engineering, University of A Coruña, Spain, tomas.bolano@udc.es
‡Department of Electronic Systems, Aalborg University, Aalborg, 9220, Denmark, xuc@es.aau.dk
§Department of Electrical and Information Technology, Lund University, 22100 Lund, Sweeden, xuesong.cai@eit.lth.se

Abstract—**In recent years, Unmanned Aerial Vehicles (UAVs) have been used extensively in military and civilian fields, making the research on cellular-connected UAVs a popular topic for Fifth Generation (5G) and beyond communications. In order to support the increasing amount of applications, it is essential to evaluate the performance of UAV communications. In this work, the end-to-end delay, packet success rate, and throughput of Air-to-Ground (A2G) communications are evaluated based on a realistic channel model obtained from measurements. The measurement campaign, conducted in a suburban environment, includes both Line-of-Sight (LoS) and Obstructed Line-of-Sight (OLoS) scenarios. From the results, it can be seen that architectural elements close to the flight route can severely decrease the communications performance even when the visibility between the Base Station (BS) and the UAV is permanently ensured. Moreover, we have shown that the Quality of Service (QoS) requirements for critical communications proposed by 3rd Generation Partnership Project (3GPP) can be fulfilled by establishing a threshold on the received Signal to Interference and Noise Ratio (SINR). This way, the SINR can be used as a condensed performance metric for the design of safe flight routes for critical communications for UAVs.**

Keywords- ***A2G communications; critical communications; end-to-end delay; QoS requirements; UAV.***

I. Introduction

In recent years, there has been a explosion of Unmanned Aerial Vehicle (UAV) military and civilian applications, such as assistance in surveillance and rescue missions, logistics service, and aerial photography. All these applications get benefited by the high mobility, flexibility, affordable price, and extended service life of UAVs [1]. For most of the UAV applications, a connection between the UAV and a terrestrial Base Station (BS) is usually required. Different services can rely on this Air-to-Ground (A2G) communication link, such as data or video transmission from the UAV to the ground or the onboard reception of control signals from a terrestrial commander [2]. Due to this, the application of Fifth Generation (5G) communications for UAVs has attracted a considerable amount of interest. Therefore, it is essential to judge whether the terrestrial commercial stations can satisfy the requirements of UAV communications.

According to the 3rd Generation Partnership Project (3GPP), the Quality of Service (QoS) requirements (including availability, end-to-end delay, and throughput requirements) for the UAV communications can be classified into two types depending on the communication nature: payload-oriented, and critical [3]. Comparing these two kinds of communications, the reliability and latency requirements are more stringent for critical communications since they transmit safety and control-related messages. As a consequence, it becomes of utmost importance to evaluate the performance of A2G communications in terms of the end-to-end delay and the network availability (i.e., the probability that the QoS of users can be satisfied [4]).

Several approaches [4]–[6] have been proposed in the literature to evaluate the performance of UAV communications. She et al. [4] characterized the latency, reliability, and network availability of UAV communications by deriving the decoding error probability and studying two optimization problems to minimize the total bandwidth and maximize the network availability for Ultra-Reliable Low-Latency Communications (URLLC). An iterative algorithm was proposed in [5] to optimize the UAV deployments by obtaining the minimum average transmission power under given constraints of maximum latency and block error probability. Horani et al. [6] provided models on both air-to-ground and ground-to-ground scenarios to characterize the end-to-end latency taking into account the queuing delay, which depends on the amount of users who are multiplexed on the same radio resources.

It can be seen that the above-mentioned approaches are solely focused on theoretical analysis considering the propagation delay, bandwidth, transmission power, or processing time, and do not provide empirical validation. Our previous work [7] evaluated the throughput of A2G communications based on a realistic (measurement-based) channel model, and in [8] we considered the joint evaluation of the end-to-end delay, availability and throughput with measurement-based results for the first time. However, only purely Line-of-Sight (LoS) scenarios were considered in these works.

In this work, we extend our previous studies [7] [8] to Obstructed Line-of-Sight (OLoS) scenarios and show the influence of the propagation environment elements in the communications performance. We evaluate the end-to-end delay, packet success rate, and throughput performance of the A2G communications for low height UAVs. It is noteworthy that we employ a realistic channel model based on measurements in a suburban environment, not only for the LoS propagation conditions but also in the OLoS ones. The effect of the

Hybrid Automatic Repeat reQuest (HARQ) techniques and retransmission mechanisms were considered, implying the implementation of both the forward link and feedback link for the simulations. The obtained results demonstrate that the architectural elements of the environment may have a significant influence on the UAV communications performance, which is also severely affected by the distance between the BS and the UAV. The provided results of latency, reliability, and throughput constitute a basis for the planning of the network deployments and flight routes for different UAV-based services, especially for those requiring critical communications. However, note that the results consider only the physical layer of the communication system [9], since upper layers will be dependent on the specific application or deployment under consideration.

The rest of the paper is organized as follows: Firstly, Section II describes the details of the measurement campaign and the construction of the channel model. Then, Section III contrastively analyzes the results of performance, in terms of availability, latency and throughput, for both a LoS scenario and an OLoS scenario. Finally, Section IV summarizes the main achievements of this work.

II. Measurement Campaign and Channel Model

In this section, we detail the process of analyzing the performance of the UAV communications by means of simulations with a measurement-based channel model. The measurement campaign used to obtain the channel model is described in Section II-A. The channel model definition and the signals processing are detailed in Section II-B. Finally, the required concepts on HARQ techniques are described in Section II-C.

A. Measurement Environment and Equipment

The measurement campaign was performed in a suburban environment at the Jiading Campus of the Tongji University (Shanghai, China). The environment includes rivers, trees, roads and buildings between 15 m and 70 m high. The two scenarios considered, namely the LoS and the OLoS, are described in detail in [10] and respectively imaged in Figures 1a and 1b. The LoS scenario consists of a straight flight in the absence of large obstacles, whereas in the OLoS scenario the UAV flies over a low building and close to high ones. The figures include the representation of the flight routes and the position of the BS, located about 20 m far away from the starting point of the flight routes, being its (latitude, longitude) coordinates (31.2873872°, 121.2040907°). The coordinates of the starting point for both flight routes expressed as (latitude, longitude) are (31.287433°, 121.204179°); the coordinates of the end point of the flight routes for the LoS and OLoS scenarios are (31.284102°, 121.208412°) and (31.288310°, 121.208793°), respectively. Representative buildings are also marked in the figures. The flight height is 15 m and the speed of the UAV is about 5 m/s in both scenarios.

As depicted in Figure 1c, the measurement equipment consists of two parts, the ground part and the air part. The ground part is fixed on a lift at the height of 15 meters and works as a transmitter. The air part, acting as a receiver, consists of an UAV equipped with a quasi-omnidirectional antenna, another Universal Software Radio Peripheral (USRP) N-210 used to received signals, a GPS-disciplined oscillator, a small computer to collect the data from the USRP and a router to control the small computer. More specifically, the central carrier frequency of the measurement is 2.5 GHz with a bandwidth of 15.36 MHz, which is similar to the commercial Long Term Evolution (LTE) deployments of the measurement area. Note that the wireless local area network (WLAN) connection used to control the small computer on the UAV from the ground causes no interference to the measurements since it works in the frequency band of 2.4 GHz.

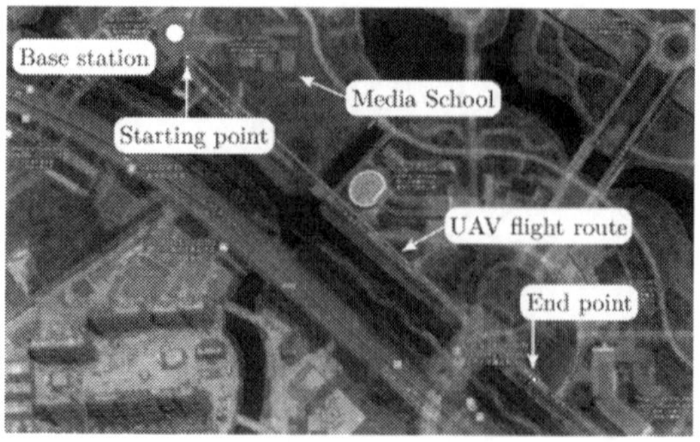

(a) Measurement environment (LoS scenario).

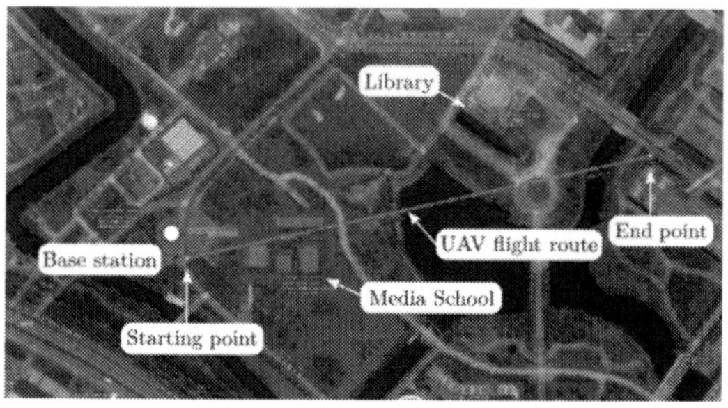

(b) Measurement environment (OLoS scenario).

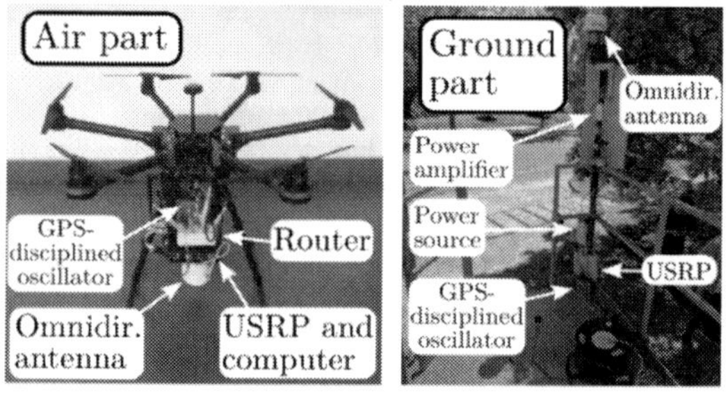

(c) Measurement sounder (air and ground parts).

Figure 1. Measurement scenarios and sounder.

B. Signal Processing and Channel Model

For the generation and processing of signals, the "GTEC 5G Simulator" [11], an open development whose source code (together with that of the "GTEC Testbed") is publicly available under the GPLv3 license at [12], was used. The GTEC 5G Simulator includes the necessary modules to configure the transmit signals and process the acquired samples. What is more, the functionalities of the "GTEC 5G Simulator" include, but are not limited to, channel estimation, interpolation and equalization, as well as signal synchronization in time and frequency domain. In addition, the sounding signal is an Orthogonal Frequency-Division Multiplexing (OFDM) signal with a frame structure similar to that of downlink LTE structure. After acquiring the OFDM frames, the Space-Alternating Generalized Expectation-maximization (SAGE) algorithm [13], integrated in the "GTEC 5G Simulator", was used to extract the channel Multipath Components (MPCs). Each snapshot, regarded as a set of consecutive samples from the received signal used to estimate the MPCs, is approximately 10 ms long. For the m-th snapshot, the channel impulse response can be expressed as [10]

$$h_m(t,\tau) = \sum_{l=1}^{L} \alpha_{m,l}\delta(\tau - \tau_{m,l})e^{j2\pi\nu_{m,l}t} \tag{1}$$

where t is the time variable, τ is the delay variable, and $\alpha_{m,l}$, $\tau_{m,l}$, and $\nu_{m,l}$ are the complex amplitude, delay, and Doppler frequency for the l-th MPC of m-th snapshot, respectively. $\delta(\cdot)$ denotes the channel impulse function (Dirac delta) and L is the amount of MPCs per snapshot. According to our observations [10] [14], $L = 15$ paths are sufficient to capture all the MPCs of the received signal in our measurements. Note that, as shown in [15], $\alpha_{m,l}$, $\tau_{m,l}$, and $\nu_{m,l}$ are approximately constant for each snapshot since the UAV flies at low speed (around 5 m/s).

The estimated channel snapshots are used to simulate the transmission of LTE signals according to the 10 MHz bandwidth downlink LTE profile [16] and further obtain the results of the communication performance, including the end-to-end delay, the packet success rate and the throughput. In time domain, the i-th received LTE subframe can be expressed as [8]

$$y_i(t) = x_i(t) * h_m(t,\tau) + n(t) \tag{2}$$

where $x_i(t)$ represents the i-th transmitted LTE subframe, $*$ is time-varying convolution operator, m is the number of snapshot corresponding to the time of simulation for the i-th subframe, and $n(t)$ is Additive White Gaussian Noise (AWGN).

In order to match the measured channel in our simulation, the AWGN power is adjusted to fit the measured Signal to Interference and Noise Ratio (SINR), calculated as in [17]. The comparison between the simulated and measured SINR is shown in Figures 2a and 2b for LoS and OLoS scenarios, respectively. In these two figures, the X-axis is the horizontal distance defined as the distance between the UAV and the BS projected on the ground, and the Y-axis is the SINR in dB. The simulated SINR is displayed as a solid blue curve whereas the measured SINR is displayed as dotted orange curve. As shown in the figures, the trend and absolute values of the simulated SINR are consistent in general. A slight deviation between the simulated and measured SINR values can be appreciated for the lowest SINR values due to the limited sensibility of the receiver.

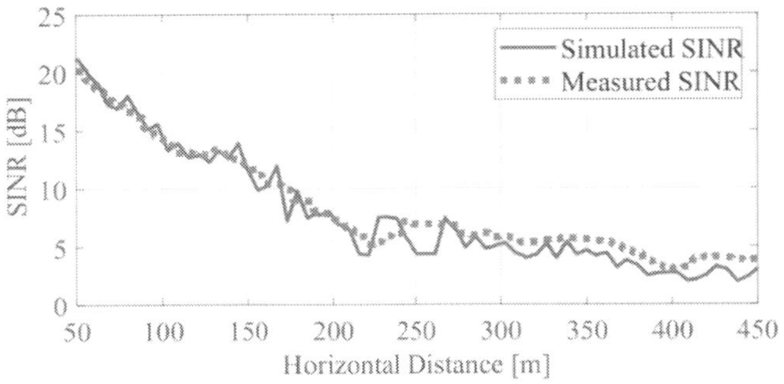

(a) Simulated and measured SINR in LoS scenario.

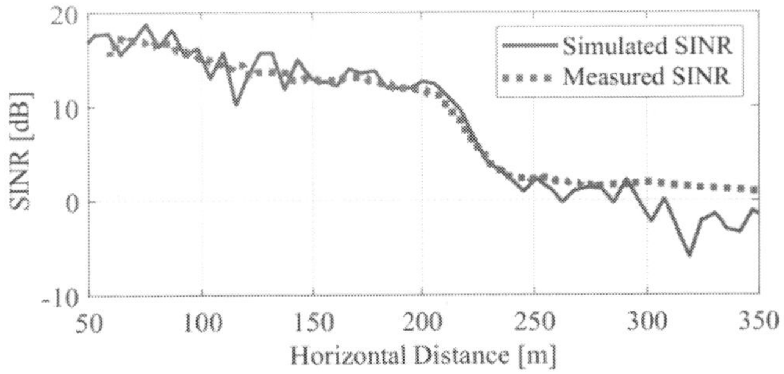

(b) Simulated and measured SINR in OLoS scenario.

Figure 2. Simulated and measured SINR for both scenarios.

C. Retransmission Mechanisms in LTE

After generating the transmit signals and obtaining the channel model, we simulate the transmission of LTE signals. In order to calculate the end-to-end delay, the LTE packet retransmission mechanisms need to be considered. According to the LTE standard, each received packet is checked for errors by means of a Cyclic Redundancy Check (CRC) [18]. If a CRC error is detected at reception, then probably a retransmission of a packet will be requested. For each retransmission of a packet, a different Redundancy Version (RV) value will be used, hence the RV sequence can be used to represent the number of transmissions of each packet. More specifically, when the receiver gets a new packet with errors, it first tries to correct the errors using a HARQ technique, which combines both Forward Error Correction (FEC) and Automatic Repeat reQuest (ARQ) [19]. If there are no remaining errors in the packet after the correction, the receiver will send a positive acknowledgement (ACK) to the transmitter. In contrast, if the errors can not be corrected completely, a negative acknowledgement (NACK) will be sent to the transmitter and the packet will be retransmitted [16, Section 9.3.4].

As defined in LTE, at most 8 HARQ processes operate simultaneously [16, Section 10.3.2.5]. In other words, the ACKs/NACKs corresponding to 8 packets are processed in parallel despite the fact that the transmitter sends one single packet at a time. Note that the reception of the ACK/NACK reply at the transmitter is not instantaneous, but implies both a propagation delay as well some processing time at the receiver, hence several data packets are handled by the transmitter simultaneously. Furthermore, the sequence of operation of the HARQ processes is random and hence, the order of transmissions of packets cannot be predicted [16, Section 10.3.2.5]. This way, in order to calculate the end-to-end delay per packet, we track the RV value for each of the 8 HARQ process, which is consistent with the LTE standard definition [16, Section 10.3.2.5].

When errors remain after the operation of a HARQ process, a retransmission is requested and the number of transmissions will increase in one unit until a maximum of 4. When the RV is 4 and there are still uncorrected errors, the packet will be dropped as specified by the LTE standard [16, Section 10.3.2.5]. However, when there are no remaining errors for a HARQ process within the first 4 transmission attempts, the packet is assumed to be received correctly and an ACK is sent back to the transmitter. This way, for each packet, the end-to-end delay is defined as the time instant when it was received correctly minus the time instant when it was transmitted for the first time. Note that only the LTE physical layer is considered in this work and hence, we did not consider additional delays introduced by higher levels of the communication system [9], which may be different for different applications.

III. RESULTS

This section shows the obtained results, including the simulated SINR, number of transmissions per packet, packet success rate, end-to-end delay and throughput. By comparing the obtained values with the constraints specified by the 3GPP in [3], we can judge whether terrestrial deployments enables critical communications for UAVs.

A. Simulated SINR

The simulated SINR, obtained as in [17], varies with the horizontal distance between the UAV and the BS for both LoS and OLoS scenarios, as shown in Figure 3. It can be seen that the SINR for the LoS scenario is higher than 0 dB for all the flight distances and it decays with the horizontal distance with an approximately steady trend. For the OLoS scenario, the SINR decay is also steady from 50 m to 200 m. At around 200–250 m, a sharp decrease in the SINR occurs, caused by the building labeled as "Media School" in Figures 1a and 1b. Note that the height of the building is around 5 m lower than the flight altitude, and hence, even if the UAV is always visually reachable from the BS, the building has a great impact in the transmission of the signals, leading to OLoS propagation conditions. For flight distances larger than 300 m, the SINR becomes lower than 0 dB for the OLoS scenario.

B. Number of Transmissions Attempts per Packet

Figure 4 shows the number of transmissions per packet versus the horizontal distance. For convenience, a 1 s moving average was applied. From the results, it can be seen that a

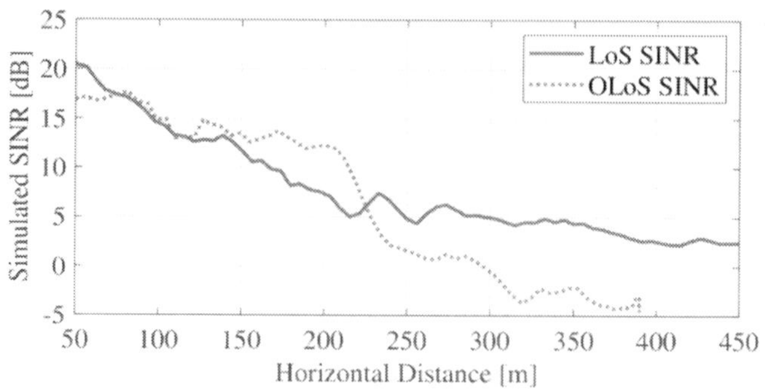

Figure 3. Simulated SINR for the LoS and OLoS scenarios.

single attempt can lead to the successful transmission during the early part of the flights for both LoS and OLoS scenarios. As the horizontal distance gets larger, an increasing number of transmissions is needed, since the number of transmission attempts per packet is limited to 4, according to the LTE standard [16, Section 10.3.2.5]. The increase of the number of transmission attempts for the OLoS scenario is abrupt when the horizontal distance is around 200–250 m, due to the decrease of SINR caused by the building labeled as "Media School" in Figures 1a and 1b. It can also be seen that for horizontal distances larger than 250 m, the packets require 4 transmission attempts with high probability.

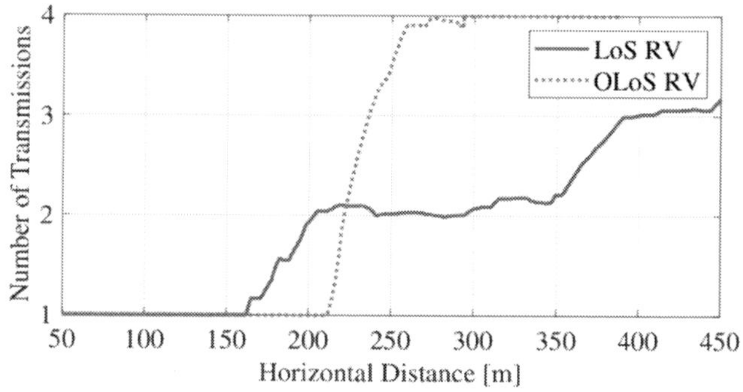

Figure 4. Average number of transmissions attempts per packet for the LoS and OLoS scenarios.

C. Packet Success Rate

Figure 5 shows the comparison of the packet success rate, obtained by using an average window of length 1 s, w.r.t the horizonal distance for the LoS and OLoS scenarios. For the LoS scenario the packet success rate is 100 % during the whole flight. However, for the OLoS scenario, the packet success rate is 100 % at the beginning of the flight, and it starts to decrease after reaching a horizontal distance of about 230 m. Finally, it drops rapidly to 0 % at about 300 m. It can be seen, by recalling the results on Figure 3, that the decrease in packet success rate is well correlated with that on the SINR. We can also observe that, combining the results of Figures 4 and 5, the number of packet transmission attempts for horizontal distances larger than 300 m (for the OLoS scenario) is always

4. This means that, for the OLoS scenario, when the horizontal distance is larger than 300 m, all the packets are transmitted incorrectly even after 4 attempts.

It can be seen that an architectural element of the environment (the building labeled as "Media School" in Figures 1a and 1b in our case), even still allowing visual contact between the BS and the UAV, can cause a sudden decrease of the packet success rate. According to the constraints specified by the 3GPP in [3], the reliability requirements for UAV communications state that the packet error rate shall be lower than 0.1 % for critical communications. Therefore, for satisfying this criterion, the horizontal distance should be limited to approximately 230 m for the OLoS scenario, whereas the constraints are always fulfilled for the LoS scenario. More importantly, it can be seen that a SINR larger than 0 dB can be a good indicator for the fulfillment of the reliability requirements for critical UAV communications stated by the 3GPP [3].

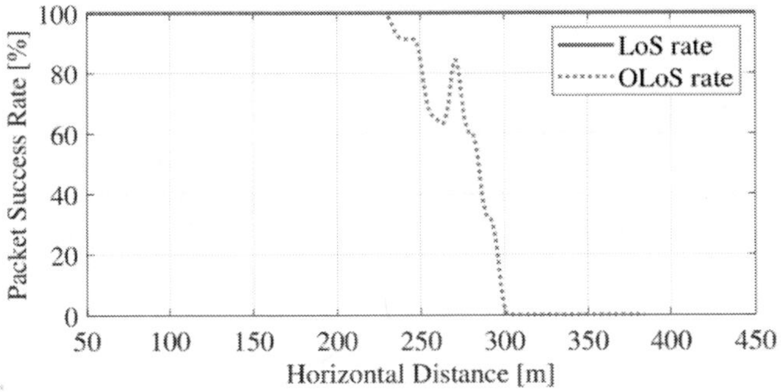

Figure 5. Packet success rate for the LoS and OLoS scenarios.

D. End-to-end Delay

As shown before, when the SINR decreases to around 0 dB, no packets will be received successfully. Figures 6a and 6b show for the LoS and OLoS scenarios, respectively, the instantaneous end-to-end delay per transmitted packet w.r.t. the horizontal distance, including the processing time at the receiver [16, Section 10.3.2.5]. In the figures, each blue dot corresponds to the delay for a specific packet. The minimum delay values correspond to the cases in which the packets are transmitted successfully at the first attempt. When the SINR decreases, the delay per packet starts to increase due to the need of performing several transmission attempts. Note that since the packets are processed on a 1 ms time basis at the BS, the values of end-to-end delay are almost discrete, being the propagation delay negligible. The specific discrete values are affected not only by the number of transmission attempts per packet, but also by the random ordering of the the HARQ processes. Finally, as indicated in Section II-C, the packets with remaining errors after 4 transmission attempts will be dropped, hence the maximum value of the end-to-end delay is limited. The specific upper limit of the delay value can change based on the HARQ ordering strategy followed by the BS. For our simulations, it is 36 ms.

Figure 6c represents the comparison of the end-to-end delay for the LoS and OLoS scenarios. For convenience, a 1 s moving average was applied. The growth rate of the delay for the OLoS scenario when the horizontal distance is 200–250 m is greatly larger than that of LoS scenario due to the presence of the building labeled as "Media School" in Figures 1a and 1b, which is consistent with the results of packet success rate shown in Figure 5. The end-to-end delay is crucial for critical communications, which require to deliver the packets on time. In particular, an end-to-end delay within 50 ms is required for critical communications, according to the constraints specified by the 3GPP in [3]. It can be seen that this constraint is fulfilled for all the packets successfully delivered.

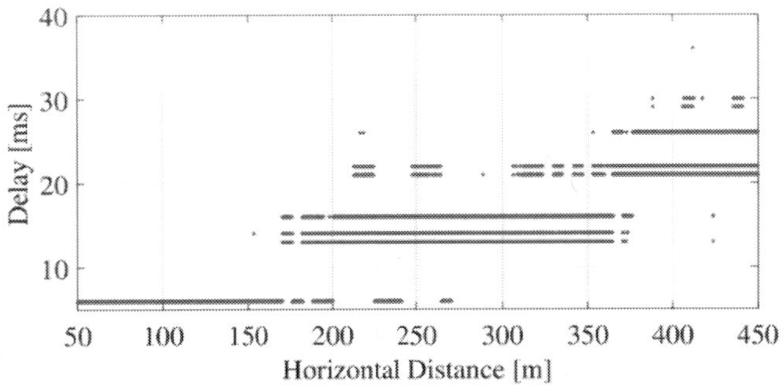

(a) Instantaneous end-to-end delay for the LoS scenario.

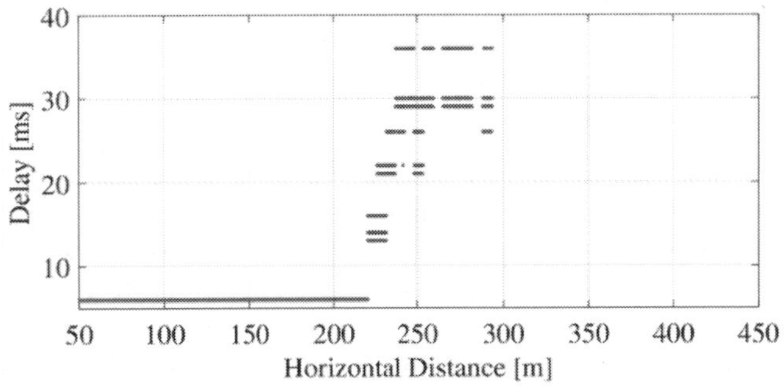

(b) Instantaneous end-to-end delay for the OLoS scenario.

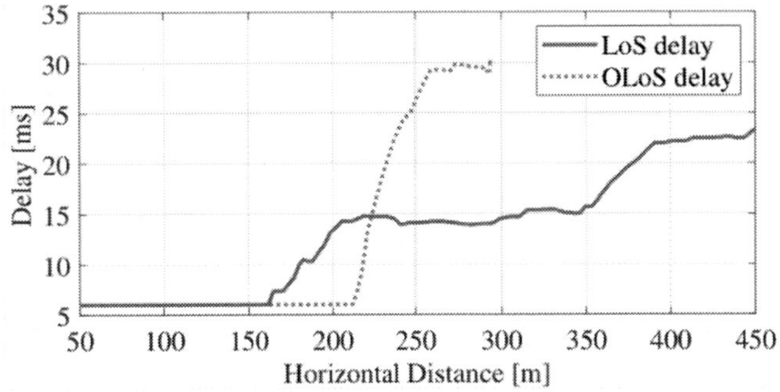

(c) Average end-to-end delay for the LoS and OLoS scenarios.

Figure 6. End-to-end delay for the LoS and OLoS scenarios.

E. Throughput

Figure 7 shows the throughput w.r.t. the horizontal distance between the BS and the UAV for the LoS and OLoS scenarios, respectively. For convenience, a 1 s moving average was applied. The maximum throughput value is 12.8 Mbps for both scenarios, corresponding to the case in which all the packets are successfully received at the first transmission attempt. The minimum throughput value for the LoS scenario is about 4 Mbps, whereas for the OLoS scenario the throughput decays to 0 Mbps after approximately 300 m, since no successful packets are transmitted (see Section III-C). As expected, the decrease of the throughput is well correlated with the increase of the number of transmission attempts per packet, the decrease of packet success rate, and the increase of end-to-end delay (Figures 4, 5 and 6c, respectively). However, according to the constraints specified by the 3GPP in [3, Table 5.1-1], the required data rate for critical communications is relatively low, just 60–100 Kbps, which is always reached for the distances in which most of the packets are transmitted successfully.

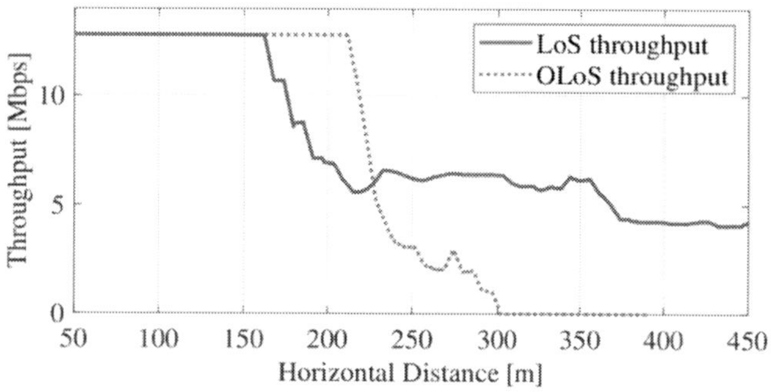

Figure 7. Throughput comparison for both scenarios

IV. Conclusions and Future Work

In this work, the performance of A2G communications for low-height small-sized UAVs was evaluated by using a measurement-based channel model. The measurement campaign was conducted in a suburban environment, considering both LoS and OLoS scenarios. The performance metrics considered included the end-to-end delay, the packet success rate, and the throughput, which were used to further determine whether terrestrial commercial BS can support critical communications for UAV applications.

From the results, it can be seen that the measurement scenario can greatly influence the communication performance. Architectural elements close to the flight route can severely decrease the communications performance even when the visibility between the BS and the UAV is permanently ensured. These kinds of obstructions can lead to sudden changes on the end-to-end delay, success rate of the transmitted packets, and throughput, whereas the changes in these performance metrics are smooth and dominated by the BS-UAV distance for scenarios without obstructions.

As a general result, it can be seen that all the performance metrics are highly correlated with the SINR at the receiver, being the SINR determined by both the BS-UAV distance and the effect of the objects in the propagation environment. When the SINR decreases, the number of retransmissions required per packet starts to increase, and the end-to-end delay increases accordingly. More required transmission attempts per packet also lead to lower values of packet success rate and hence, to a lower throughput. In particular, when the SINR decays to values close to 0 dB, most of the packets are dropped, and the throughput becomes 0 Mbps.

Based on the obtained results, we have shown that the QoS requirements for critical communications proposed by 3GPP (in terms of end-to-end latency, reliability, and throughput) are fulfilled for all the cases in which the packet success rate is not severely decreased, which in practice happens when the SINR is higher than 0 dB. This proves that the SINR can be used as a condensed performance metric for evaluating the viability of critical communications for UAV applications, and for the design of safe flight routes for critical applications, which should consider the influence of both the BS-UAV distance and the architectural elements in the propagation environment. Moreover, the goal should not only be ensuring the fulfillment of the minimum performance requirements, but to increase the performance to the highest level achievable. In order to do this, schemes on dynamic optimization of the modulation and coding scheme (MCS) based on different performance figures of merit (e.g., throughput, delay or reliability) constitute one of our current research topics.

Acknowledgment

This work was supported by the National Natural Science Foundation of China (NSFC) under Grant 61971313; as well as by the Xunta de Galicia (by grant ED431C 2020/15, and grant ED431G 2019/01 to support the Centro de Investigacin de Galicia "CITIC"), the Agencia Estatal de Investigacin of Spain (by grants RED2018-102668-T and PID2019-104958RB-C42), and ERDF funds of the EU (FEDER Galicia 2014-2020 & AEI/FEDER Programs, UE). The efforts from our colleagues at the Sino-German Center of Intelligent Systems, Tongji University, are also gratefully acknowledged.

References

[1] Y. Zeng, R. Zhang, and T. J. Lim, "Wireless communications with unmanned aerial vehicles: opportunities and challenges," *IEEE Communications Magazine*, vol. 54, no. 5, pp. 36–42, 2016.

[2] D. W. Matolak and R. Sun, "Air-ground channel characterization for unmanned aircraft systems-part I: Methods, measurements, and models for over-water settings," *IEEE Trans. Veh. Technol.*, vol. 66, no. 1, pp. 26–44, 2017.

[3] 3GPP, "Technical specification group radio access network: Study on enhanced LTE support for aerial vehicles," 3GPP, Tech. Rep. 3GPP TR 36.777 V15.0.0, December 2017.

[4] C. She, C. Liu, T. Q. S. Quek, C. Yang, and Y. Li, "Uav-assisted uplink transmission for ultra-reliable and low-latency communications," in *2018 IEEE International Conference on Communications Workshops (ICC Workshops)*, 2018, pp. 1–6.

[5] K. Chen, Y. Wang, Z. Fei, and X. Wang, "Power limited ultra-reliable and low-latency communication in uav-enabled iot networks," in *2020 IEEE Wireless Communications and Networking Conference (WCNC)*, 2020, pp. 1–6.

[6] M. Horani and M. O. Hasna, "Latency analysis of uav based communication networks," in *2018 International Conference on Information and Communication Technology Convergence (ICTC)*, 2018, pp. 385–390.
[7] Z. Huang, J. Rodríguez-Piñeiro, T. Domínguez-Bolaño, X. Yin, D. Matolak, and J. Lee, "Performance of 5G terrestrial network deployments for serving UAV communications," in *14th European Conference on Antennas and Propagation (EuCAP 2020)*, Copenhagen, Denmark, March 2020, pp. 1–5.
[8] H. Zhu, J. Rodríguez-Piñeiro, Z. Huang, T. Domínguez-Bolaño, X. Cai, X. Yin, J. Lee, and D. Matolak, "On the end-to-end latency of cellular-connected UAV communications," in *15th European Conference on Antennas and Propagation (EuCAP 2021)*, Düsseldorf, Germany, March 2021, pp. 1–5.
[9] H. Zimmermann, "OSI reference model - the ISO model of architecture for open systems interconnection," *IEEE Transactions on Communications*, vol. 28, no. 4, pp. 425–432, 1980.
[10] J. Rodríguez-Piñeiro, T. Domínguez-Bolaño, X. Cai, Z. Huang, and X. Yin, "Air-to-ground channel characterization for low-height UAVs in realistic network deployments," *IEEE Transactions on Antennas and Propagation*, vol. 69, no. 2, pp. 992–1006, February 2021.
[11] T. Domínguez-Bolaño, J. Rodríguez-Piñeiro, J. A. García-Naya, and L. Castedo, "The GTEC 5G link-level simulator," in *1st International Workshop on Link- and System Level Simulations (IWSLS2 2016)*, Vienna, Austria, July 2016, pp. 1–6.
[12] "GTEC Testbed Project," https://bitbucket.org/tomas_bolano/gtec_testbed_public.git [retrieved: July, 2021].
[13] B. H. Fleury, M. Tschudin, R. Heddergott, D. Dahlhaus, and K. I. Pedersen, "Channel parameter estimation in mobile radio environments using the SAGE algorithm," *IEEE J. Sel. Areas Commun.*, vol. 17, no. 3, pp. 434–450, 1999.
[14] J. Rodríguez-Piñeiro, Z. Huang, X. Cai, T. Domínguez-Bolaño, and X. Yin, "Geometry-based MPC tracking and modeling algorithm for time-varying UAV channels," *IEEE Transactions on Wireless Communications*, vol. 20, no. 4, pp. 2700–2715, April 2021.
[15] Z. Huang, J. Rodríguez-Piñeiro, T. Domínguez-Bolaño, X. Cai, and X. Yin, "Empirical dynamic modeling for low-altitude UAV propagation channels," *IEEE Transactions on Wireless Communications*, vol. Early Access, March 2021.
[16] S. Sesia, I. Toufik, and M. Baker, *LTE-the UMTS long term evolution: from theory to practice*. John Wiley & Sons, 2011.
[17] J. Rodríguez-Piñeiro, M. Lerch, J. A. García-Naya, S. Caban, M. Rupp, and L. Castedo, "Emulating extreme velocities of mobile LTE receivers in the downlink," *EURASIP Journal on Wireless Communications and Networking*, vol. 2015, no. 106, April 2015.
[18] 3GPP, "Multiplexing and channel coding," 3GPP, Tech. Rep. 3GPP TS 36.212 V8.0.0, 2007.
[19] L. Yang and Z. Liao, "A hybrid automatic repeat request (HARQ) with turbo codes in OFDM system," in *2010 Intl. Conference on Computational Intelligence and Software Engineering*, 2010, pp. 1–4.

Communications for Massive UAV Scenarios

Uwe-Carsten Fiebig
Institute of Communications and Navigation
German Aerospace Research (DLR)
Wessling, Germany
e-mail: uwe.fiebig@dlr.de

Abstract— **In this article, we look 20 to 30 years ahead and provide some thoughts about communication technologies for future massive Unmanned Aerial Vehicle (UAV) scenarios in the Very Low Level (VLL) airspace. We use the term "massive" to stress that the number of UAVs will be in the order of the number of cars as of today: we treat scenarios where the number of UAVs is about 1 UAV per person. We expect UAVs to fly autonomously. Onboard sensors, communication and software will be key elements to ensure a safe operation. We address fundamental questions and provide thoughts on communication solutions.**

Keywords-component; UAV communications; drone-to-drone communications; massive UAV scenarios.

I. Introduction

In a near future, autonomously operating small to mid-sized Unmanned Aerial Vehicles (UAVs) enable prompt parcel delivery to every household and fast delivery of goods to shops, companies, restaurants, hospitals and the like. The Very Low Level (VLL) airspace will accommodate millions of UAVs. We may see scenarios which have been described so far only in science fiction novels. However, we are progressively getting closer to such a world: since many years already, UAVs support commercial, military and private purposes, and their number is dramatically growing.

In this article, we take a closer look on appropriate communication technologies for massive UAV scenarios. These scenarios are described in Section II and are very different from those of controlled airspaces: the density of UAVs will be considerably higher than today's density of aircraft in crowded regions. In Section III, we discuss fundamental aspects in terms of communications load and the number of simultaneously received messages. We sketch first results on the communication performance in Section IV.

II. The Mass Market UAV Scenario

We consider scenarios with 1 UAV per person. This figure reflects our vision that the number of UAVs will be similar to the number of road motor vehicles as of today. The motorization rate in major European countries and in the United States is in the order of 60 to 70 % [1], respect. 80% [2], including automobiles, trucks, vans, buses, commercial vehicles and freight motor road vehicles.

Eventually, we look on a selected region and consider a UAV scenario in a larger city with 1.5 million inhabitants and dense traffic situations. Such a city can be Munich, Germany, and Philadelphia, Pennsylvania, United States. These cities have about 1.5 million inhabitants [3][4] and an area of about 310 and 350 km^2 [3][4], respectively. Thus, both cities have a similar number of inhabitants per km^2. And both cities have about the same number of road motor vehicles [3][5], i.e., about 700,000.

We follow our analogy of today's car usage pattern and the fact that the layout of cities does not dramatically change during the next decades. In our analysis, we assume that UAVs have a maximum speed of 15 m/s, that the average length of their flight paths is 7 km, and that 10 % of all UAVs are airborne during a UAV rush hour. Thus, we get an average flight duration of 8 minutes. For a UAV rush hour 150,000 UAVs are airborne over an area of about 300 km^2 resulting in a density of 500 UAVs per km^2; we also obtain about 0.75 million flights in the UAV rush hour.

From these numbers, it becomes obvious that traffic control of massive UAV scenarios cannot be handled in the same way as traffic control for today's IFR (Instrument Flight Rules) flights: due to the tremendous number of airborne UAVs a manual and semi-automated way of control is not feasible. Therefore, only fully automated traffic control systems are an option which in turn require robust and highly reliable Communication, Navigation and Surveillance (CNS) technologies. We also need very robust collision avoidance techniques which rely on the robustness and suitability of CNS technologies. In this contribution, we present a de-centralized communication concept for collision avoidance.

III. Communication Load

We estimate the communication load for a city like Munich or Philadelphia. Thus, following our vision of 1 UAV per person, we get 1.5 million UAVs for such a city. Assuming that 10 % of all UAVs are airborne simultaneously during a UAV rush hour, we will have 150,000 UAVs in the air.

In order to get an estimate for the data volumes to be handled we refer to car-to-car communications technologies where cars broadcast periodically messages at 1 Hz (normal operation) to 10 Hz (in emergency situations). We believe that these rates can be transferred to UAV communications. A data packet shall encompass 500 bit (optionally 5000 bit) and contains the current position and orientation of the UAV, its future way points, its destination, information about its size, volume, freight type, priority mode and flight characteristics. Each UAV shall broadcast such a data packet with 1 Hz. Thus, the overall bit rate, i.e., the bit rate simultaneously transmitted by 150,000 UAVs is obtained as 75 Mbit/s.

We see that the overall bit rate is relatively small. A single LTE-Advanced Pro base station provides a total bit rate of up to 1000 Mbit/s and 500 Mbit/s for down- and uplink, respectively. Thus, the overall amount of data (and even ten times more in case of data packets of 5000 bit) is manageable even with today's technologies. The decisive question is whether a de-centralized or a centralized communication architecture shall be applied.

In this article, we promote direct communications between drones as in other traffic control systems: TCAS, the Traffic Collision Avoidance System for air traffic; AIS, the Automatic Identification System for maritime users; RCAS, a new Railway Collision Avoidance System acting as additional safety system; and ITS G5, a car-to-car communications standard. Traffic participants periodically broadcast data to surrounding aircraft, ships or vehicles, communicate directly with each other and use neither a central communications entity nor a centralized communication infrastructure. Beaconing, the periodic or quasi-periodic broadcast of information, is an established transmission mode.

An important issue to look at is the question up to which range the transmitted data shall be correctly received. We derive the communication range from two parameters: (1) UAVs will travel with a velocity of up to 15 m/s; (2) a potential collision course shall be detectable at least 33 seconds prior to the time instant at which this collision would occur when no action is taken. From a collision avoidance perspective, the worst case happens when both UAVs are heading directly towards each other resulting in the highest relative velocity and, hence, in the shortest amount of time to detect and solve this situation; this worst case requires a communication range of

$$R_{com} = 2 \cdot 15\mathrm{m/s} \cdot 33s \approx 1000m\ . \qquad (1)$$

Assuming all UAVs are equally distributed, the number of UAVs within the communication range is obtained as

$$N_{UAV} = R_{com}^2 \cdot \pi \cdot 500\mathrm{km}^{-2} \approx 1600\ . \qquad (2)$$

The result reveals that each UAV must be able to correctly receive data from 1600 neighboring UAVs every second. Since the transmission rate is 500 bit/s, each UAV has to process a total of 0.8 Mbit every second. In view of these figures, we do not expect that it will be a problem for future UAV communication systems to receive, decode, and read 1600 data packets per second carrying a total of 0.8 Mbit of data. Also, managing the communication load for larger cell sizes or larger data packets should not be a problem: e.g., doubling the cell radius results in 6300 UAVs per cell and, in turn, in 6300 data packets carrying a total of 3.2 Mbit.

We are also confident that it won't be a problem to check 1600, respectively 6300 flight trajectories for potential collision courses every second and to suggest alternative routes if needed. Note that it is not required to repeat checking for potential collisions as long as trajectories remain unchanged. Thus, trajectories from only those UAVs have to be checked which either enter the communication range or have changed their trajectories.

IV. First Results

At the workshop, the author will provide first results on the performance of slotted ALOHA [6] when applied to a massive UAV scenario with UAV densities of 100 to 500 UAV/km^2. He will present a relation between communication failures (i.e., non-received messages) and the expected number of UAV collisions and will apply it to two different scenarios: one where all UAVs choose a direct flight path between departure and destination locations and one where UAVs fly on a grid-like pattern. All UAVs fly above rooftops and have line-of-sight conditions. In our first assessment, we consider neither multipath propagation although it may degrade the communication performance nor take-off and landing maneuvers although they are crucial due to shadowing situations. The communication system may operate at C-band.

The analysis will follow a framework which has been presented in [7] and is based on the missed detection probability that not a single beacon message is received correctly at a UAV while approaching another one on a collision course. Both UAVs have at least 30 opportunities (during 33s) to detect beacon messages of the other UAV before the collision happens, and a collision is unavoidable of none of the two UAVs correctly receives at least one data packet at least 3s prior to the potential collision.

The first investigations reveal that an ALOHA-type beaconing system with 1 MHz bandwidth and 1 Hz beaconing rate can support UAV densities up to 150 UAV/km^2 when UAVs fly direct paths and more than 500 UAV/km^2 when UAVs fly along a predefined grid while guaranteeing less than 1 accident per year for a city like Munich. With larger packets the bandwidth increases linearly. Note that self-organized Time Division Multiple Access (TDMA) or Location-Based TDMA may allow even higher UAV densities.

Acknowledgment

The author thanks Lukas Schalk from DLR for numerous fruitful discussions on this subject.

References

[1] European Automobile Manufacturers Association. https://www.acea.auto/files/ACEA_Report_Vehicles_in_use-Europe_2019-1.pdf

[2] Bureau of Transportation Statistics of the U.S. Department of Transportation (DOT). https://www.bts.gov/content/number-us-aircraft-vehicles-vessels-and-other-conveyances

[3] City of Munich. https://www.muenchen.de/

[4] U.S. Census Bureau of the U.S. Department of Commerce. https://www.census.gov/quickfacts/fact/table/philadelphiacity pennsylvania,US/PST045219

[5] Pennsylvania Department of Transportation. http://www.dot.state.pa.us/public/dvspubsforms/BMV/Registr ation%20Reports/Reportofregistration2019.pdf

[6] N. Abramson, "The ALOHA System - Another Alternative for Computer Communications" in Proc. 1970 Fall Joint Computer Conference, 1970, pp. 281–285.

[7] L. M. Schalk, "Techniques for improving the cooperative Traffic Conflict Detection among Drones." In Proc. of IEEE 89th Vehicular Technology Conf. (VTC Spring) 2019, Kuala Lumpur, Malaysia, doi: 10.1109/VTCSpring.2019.8746350

A High-Accuracy DOA-Based Localization Method: UAV Virtual Multiantenna Array

Jianqiao Cheng
Brussels School of Engineering
Université libre de Bruxelles (ULB)
Brussels, Belgium
Jianqiao.Cheng@ulb.be

Ke Guan
State Key Lab of Rail Traffic Control and Safety
Beijing Jiaotong University (BJTU)
Beijing, China
kguan@bjtu.edu.cn

François Quitin
Brussels School of Engineering
Université libre de Bruxelles (ULB)
Brussels, Belgium
fquitin@ulb.be

***Abstract*—Reliable location-aware services and corresponding localization techniques are essential in Unmanned Aerial Vehicle (UAV) communications. In this paper, localization technology based on Direction of Arrival estimation is proved to be promising for UAV channels due to limited angular spread in the air. Then, a method is proposed to estimate the direction of a ground radio-frequency transmitter by using a UAV equipped with a single antenna, which is critical when considering the form factor and computational capabilities of a UAV. By considering the received signal at several points along its trajectory, the receiver implicitly creates a virtual multi-antenna array, which can be used to estimate the direction of the transmitter. The first difficulty is estimating the relative positions of the UAV. The other main challenge is the Local Oscillator frequency offset between the transmitter and the UAV receiver, which adds an additional cumulative phase offset to the received signal at each antenna of the virtual array.**

***Index Terms*—Direction Finding, DoA Estimation, Localization, Multi-antenna System, Radiogoniometry**

I. Introduction

Estimation of the location of passive Radio Frequency (RF) sources (e.g., emitting radio, etc.) has been a subject of research for decades and plays a significant role in many applications, including radar and sonar processing, search and rescue missions, and wireless sensor networks [1]. Measurements used for passive localization can be classified into four categories: Time Of Arrival (TOA), Time Difference Of Arrival (TDOA), Direction Of Arrival (DOA), and Received Signal Strength (RSS) [2]. Also, in most cases, a basic assumption for passive localization is that the Line-Of-Sight (LOS) visibility exists between a transmitter and receiver, as the transmitter location estimates can be significantly biased due to multipath transmission and shadow fading [3]. While this assumption is rigid to guarantee in the ground communication channels (e.g., a dense urban environment) due to rich obstacles, the LOS path is easy to establish in the Air-To-Ground (ATG) channels, as scatters are limited in high altitudes [4]. In other words, the accuracy of localization services can be significantly improved by utilizing measurements from the sky, and Unmanned Aerial Vehicles (UAVs) are a promising platform to serve as an aerial localization node.

The investment in UAVs has surged in recent years due to their low cost, ease of on-demand deployment, and excellent mobility. UAVs are widely used in various applications, including target reconnaissance, image acquisition, surveillance, and wireless communication [5]. Furthermore, as an essential part of the future Low Altitude Platform (LAP) communication system, UAV has tremendous amounts of excellent characteristics, such as the high probability of a LOS path, unencumbered by rough terrain and fewer reflections from obstacles on the ground [6]. Current studies are focusing on the UAV serves as a mobile terminal (e.g., base stations and relays), and the UAV serves as new aerial users that access the cellular network from the sky [7]. Alongside the enormous connectivity potential, reliable location-aware services are also essential in UAV-based communications. Therefore, localize ground users with UAVs is becoming an important topic and has drawn significant attention. For example, UAVs have been used to localize WiFi devices and GPS jammers [8].

Despite the high potential, performing localization with UAVs also has some drawbacks: UAVs also have limited payloads and flight times due to hardware and battery limits. Therefore, some localization methods are not suitable in UAV-based scenarios. For example, the TOA-based and TDOA-based localization systems usually require precise and consistent time synchronization, which is complex in UAV scenarios. Likewise, DOA estimation uses phase interferometry, i.e., the phase differences among the bearing measurements w.r.t. multiantenna array elements [9]. However, since UAVs are usually small, the consequent constraints on the size of the multiantenna array will lead to poor spatial resolution [2]. Ranging localization with RSS methods is attractive due to their intrinsic simplicity. However, its accuracy is usually not satisfactory. Therefore, a simple, cost-effective localization method using a minimum number of UAVs, without heavy hardware implementation and complex synchronization, is precious for the development of aerial RF localization.

In this work, we investigate the feasibility of DOA estimation with a UAV equipped with a single antenna only [10]. The unknown signal source to be located is referred to as the transmitter. The UAV is flying and carried with a single patch antenna (mounted facing downward), referred to as the receiver. While the UAV hovers overhead at a certain altitude, the receiver antenna receives the incoming signal consistently along the UAV's trajectory, as shown in Figure 1. Bearing measurements are taken at fixed time intervals during the flight and are then processed to extract the phase difference at these observation points. Therefore, we implicitly create a *virtual Multiantenna Array* (VMA) in 3D space. Combining these bearing measurements with UAV's position, an estimate of the source's DOA (including azimuth angle and elevation angle) is obtained. The receiver antenna at each observation point can be considered a virtual antenna element in VMA. Like conventional multiantenna arrays, the element spacing should be smaller than the half wavelength of the carrier frequency to avoid aliasing effects.

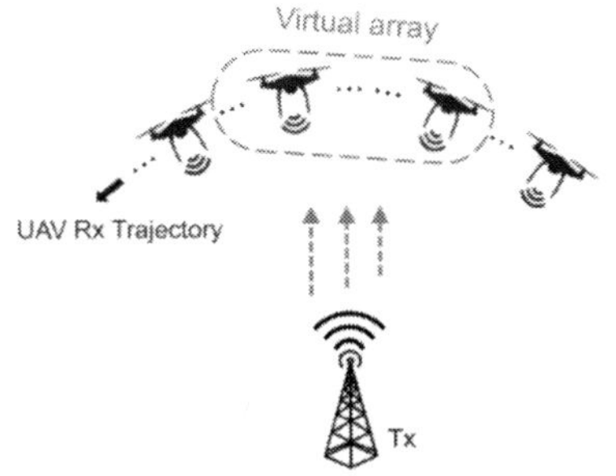

Fig. 1. UAV virtual array concept. Single UAV receiver equipped with one single antenna, moves and create a virtual array.

The difficulties of such a UAV-based VMA method are threefold: 1) The aerial channel between UAV stations and ground users differs significantly from conventional terrestrial channels, and the effect of aerial channel properties (e.g., angular spread) on DOA localization needs to be investigated. 2) The relative coordinates of UAV array elements are essential when calculating the array response vector that necessary for DOA estimation. 3) The concept of VMA is based on a consumption that the phase difference is only caused by the UAV movement. However, this is not the case in practice. As the Local Oscillator (LO) in transmitter and receiver has different frequency stability due to manufacturing tolerances and temperature variations [2], a LO offset usually appears and caused cumulative phase drifts for the received signal over time. Common RF devices usually equip with LOs that containing significant LO offset. For this reason, we provide two methods to compensate for the effect of LO offset, and their performance is tested in simulations.

In summary, the significance of our work lies in proving the feasibility of the VMA method with cheap, portable hardware that is already available in modern smartphones. Also, a UAV-based scenario provides a suitable, favorable propagation condition for VMA to show localization ability. Furthermore, by exploiting the potential of UAV's excellent mobility, our VMA system does not increase energy consumption or require multiantenna arrays. The results from simulations and experiments show that the VMA significantly outperforms the conventional localization algorithms in UAV-based scenarios in terms of localization accuracy and system simplicity.

Contributions: The main contributions of this paper are as follows.

- We proposed a technology to localize ground RF transmitters by creating a virtual multiantenna array with a single UAV platform. The proposed system is easy to implement for remote electronics.
- The spatial property of the ATG channel is studied with the ray-tracing method from a localization perspective. Our simulation results show that angular spreads at the UAV are minimal, which is beneficial for DOA-based localization due to limited power dispersion.
- The proposed system is implemented with simulations, and simulation results prove the feasibility of the VMA method.

The remainder of the paper is organized as follows. Section II provides a detailed spatial channel characteristics analysis of the ATG channel from a localization perspective. Section III proceeds with the design and system model of the VMA model. Two algorithms are provided to eliminate the bias introduced by LO offset. Section IV concludes this paper and presents our future work.

II. Spatial Property of UAV Channel

The estimation of the bearing angle is usually estimated based on antenna measurements with conventional array processing algorithms (e.g., Multiple Signal Classification (MUSIC), Beamforming). Nearly all of these algorithms assume that the source signal arrives at UAV with a discrete, distinct angle. This assumption leads to a signal subspace of low rank, and the low-rank property is exploited to find the impinging direction.

However, in actual spatial channels (e.g., a macro-cell), several replicas of the signal will be incident on UAV with multiple angles due to multipath propagation. More specifically, the signal that incident on UAV array may spatially be distributed (i.e., with an angular spread around a mean DOA) and no longer propagate along with a plane wave due to local scatters surrounding the ground transmitter. The angular spread usually denotes the standard deviation of DOAs from multipath, also indicates the power dispersion in the angular domain. Generally speaking, a large angular spread value will directly degrade the antenna array correlation, which gives rise to the inaccuracy of the DOA estimation; For small angular spread, it follows from the consistency that the mean DOA will only deviate slightly from the true DOA. These mismatches between the mean DOA and true DOA in the ground channel is well investigated in [11]. However, very limited research has thoroughly investigated similar spatial properties in UAV channels from a localization perspective to the best of our knowledge.

To ensure the effectiveness of DOA measurements in UAV-based localization, we investigate the spatial characteristics of the ATG channel with Ray-Tracing simulations. Given the purpose of localization, i.e., the UAV-based platform locates ground users according to their emitted signal, we consider the ground users serve as Mobile Terminals (MTs, emulating a transmitter), the UAV serves as an aerial receiver (Rx), to locate ground MTs according to their emitted signal. Moreover, When the carrier frequency does not change (which is our case), the angular spreads in the uplink and downlink are equivalent due to the channel reciprocity. Therefore, although the signal travels from MT to UAV, the channel can still be referred to as the ATG channel.

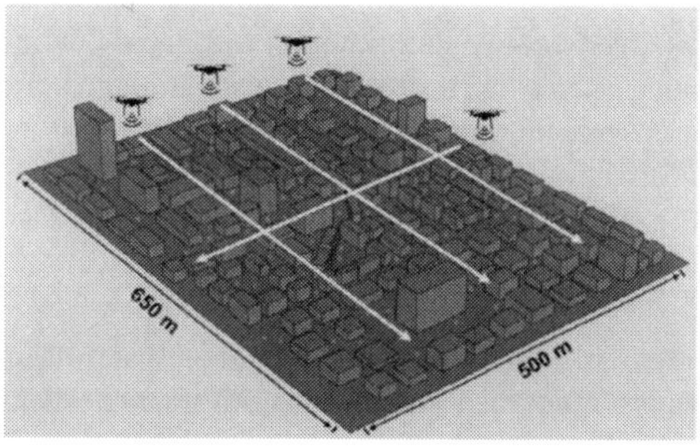

(a) Ray-tracing simulation scenarios

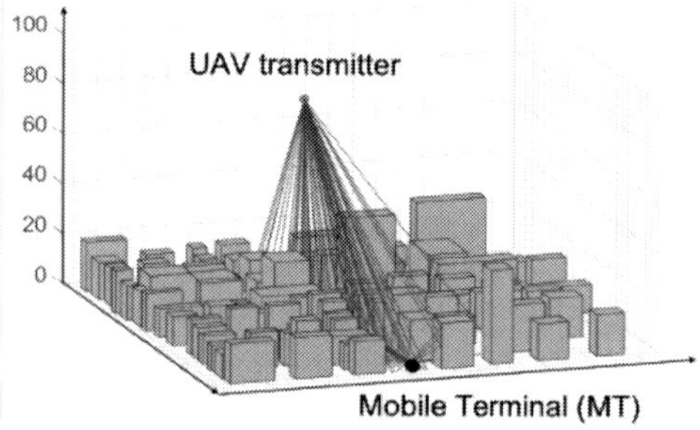

(b) One example snapshot from ray-tracing simulations

Fig. 2. The Ray-tracing simulations. (a) The scenario contains 4 linear UAV trajectories, and 250 MTs randomly distributed on the ground. (b) An example from the RT simulation results. The solid red line represents the line-of-sight path, the blue lines represent all the multipath components, including reflected rays, scattered rays and diffracted rays.

Ray-tracing is a powerful map-based hybrid channel modeling approach to describe multipath effects for a given environment model and deployment configuration [12]. Our simulations are carried out by using CloudRT, the 3D ray-tracing software developed by Beijing Jiaotong University. In this work, we modeled a typical 3D urban city, with 137 buildings under different heights going from 5 m to 70 m. The total dimensions of the modeled terrain are 650 m by 500 m. The area has 250 ground MTs distributed uniformly over the whole map, and the MT height is set to 2 m above ground. The UAV is equipped with a downwards-facing patch antenna, and MTs are equipped with vertically-oriented dipole antennas. It is worth mentioning that the tilts of MTs antenna are randomly distributed but deviate no more than $\pm$ 45 $^{\circ}$ from the vertical direction. Both the UAV antenna and the MT antenna are vertically polarized with 0 dBi gain, and the transmission power is set to 0 dBm. The simulation is conducted by fixing the MT while changing the position of the UAV along four linear trajectories. Each trajectory has a length of 450 m and contains 50 UAV positions, with a resolution of 9 m, as shown in Figure 2(a). Considering that Long-Term Evolution (LTE) is a reliable technology to support the required link performance of UAV networks [5], we set the carrier frequency at 2.6 GHz, corresponding to the LTE carrier frequencies. Moreover, the UAV altitude in simulations is conducted at 100 m.

The CloudRT software allows to simulate the direct ray between transmitters and receivers, first- and second-order reflections, diffracted rays along building edges, and diffuse scatterings on rough surfaces, as depicted in Figure 2(b). During the simulation, rays are collected, and then a Channel Impulse Response (CIR) is calculated by the software, including received power strength, phase, propagation time, angle of arrival, and angle of departure (for both azimuth and elevation). Also, the direct path between the UAV and MTs can be obstructed by obstacles; thus, we have a collection of the LOS and the Non-Line-Of-Sight (NLOS) cases. For the UAV altitude to be set to 100 m, we collected $250 \times 50 \times 4$ snapshots in total, containing 28626 LOS cases and 21374 NLOS cases. For each snapshot, the different Multipath Components (MPC) between the UAV and MT were recorded. These were used to determine the Azimuth-Of-Arrival (AOA) spread and the Elevation-Of-Arrival (EOA) spread. The Probability Density Function (PDF) of the angular spreads in the LOS scenario and the NLOS scenario are plotted in Figure 3, where the PDF function is used to specify the probability of an angular spread falling within a particular range of values.

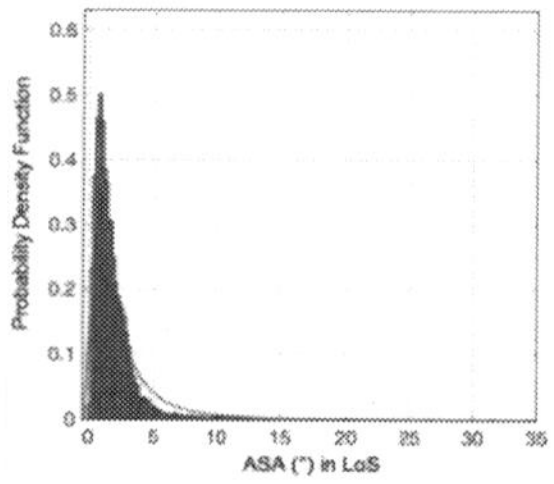

(a) Distribution of ASA in LOS

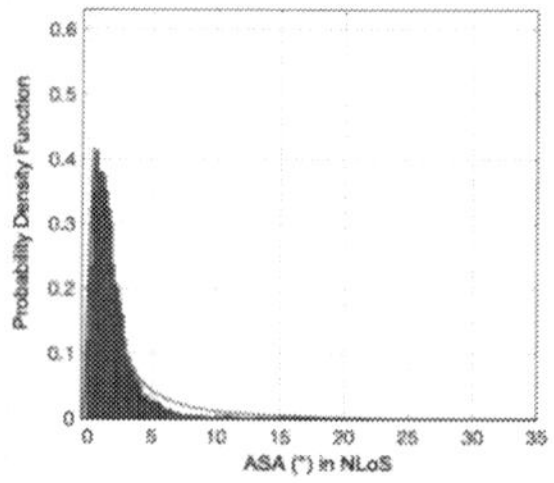

(b) Distribution of ASA in NLOS

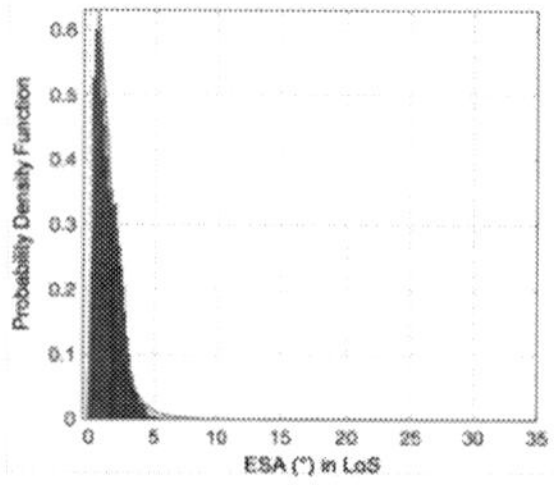

(c) Distribution of ESA in LOS

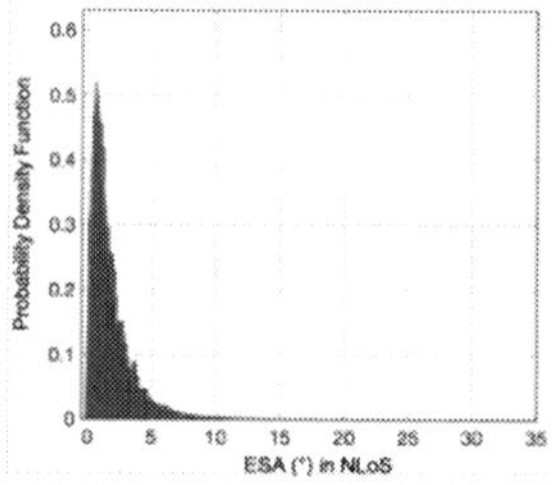

(d) Distribution of ESA in NLOS

Fig. 3. Distributions of ASA/ESA in LOS scenarios and NLOS scenarios. The superimposed red curves are lognormal distributions used to model the PDF.

To better characterize the distribution of angular spreads at the UAV, the lognormal distribution is chosen to be the most appropriate function to fit the ASA and the ESA. For example, in LOS scenarios, the PDF of the ASA can be mathematically expressed by:

$$f_{ASA}(x) = \frac{1}{\sqrt{2\pi}x\sigma_{ASA}} exp\left[\frac{-(\ln x - \mu_{ASA})^2}{2\sigma_{ASA}^2}\right] \quad (1)$$

where μ_{ASA} and σ_{ASA} are the mean and Standard Deviation (STD) of the fitting PDF, respectively. The fitting of ESA is similar by replacing parameters μ_{ASA}, σ_{ASA} with μ_{ESA}, σ_{ESA}. The value of μ and σ for ASA/ESA spreads in both LOS and NLOS scenarios are provided in Table I.

TABLE I
LOGNORMAL MODELING PARAMETERS

Parameters	ASA		ESA	
	LOS	NLOS	LOS	NLOS
μ	0.42	0.52	0.15	0.24
σ	1.01	1.29	0.68	0.91

By comparing the PDF distribution and the established statistical model, the spatial multipath propagation characteristics can be observed as follows.

- The first observation from Figure 3 is that the ESA and ASA are distributed over a narrow range less than 10° (with an average angular spread around 2.5°), for both LOS and NLOS scenarios. These magnitudes are much smaller than the ESA and ASA in conventional 3D cellular channels, e.g., average ASA around 9° and average ESA around 15° in [13]. Such observations indicate that the spatial dispersion of received power at the UAV side is very limited, and all the multipath components arrived at the UAV with similar incident angles. Therefore, the power-weight mean AOA/EOA is a good representation of the real bearing to the ground MT.
- In Figure 3, the histograms for both ASA and ESA are steeper in the LOS scenarios than the NLOS scenarios. The μ and σ in LOS are also smaller than NLOS. Therefore, the angular spread in NLOS scenarios tends to be slightly larger than in the LOS scenarios. This phenomenon is expected and can be explained by the fundamental of angular spread: When scattered MPCs make a considerable contribution to the total received power, the angular spread will be large; When the LOS path is dominant among the received power, the angular spread will be small. In NLOS scenarios where the LOS path has been blocked by obstacles, the direct signal will be attenuated; Thus, MPCs will make more significant contributions in the total received power, caused a bigger angular spread in both azimuth and elevation domain.

The analysis above leads to the following conclusion. In urban environments, the angular spread at the UAV is minimal, which means the power dispersion at the UAV is very limited. Therefore, the DOA-based estimation has a great potential in UAV-based cellular networks to localize ground targets since the estimated DOA should be close to the true DOA.

III. UAV VIRTUAL MULTIANTENNA ARRAY SYSTEM MODEL

A. *UAV-based Virtual Array System*

The system model of the virtual antenna array is following. We consider that a single transmitter broadcasts an RF signal periodically while the UAV-carried receiver is moving. The periodically transmitted RF signal in our system is in the form of digital data packets. Both the transmitter and the receiver know the preamble of the packets. Those preambles are defined by existing communication standards, e.g., the Primary Synchronization Signal (PSS) broadcast by the base stations in LTE standard [9].

As for the DOA localization, the unknown location of the stationary transmitter in three-dimensional Cartesian coordinates is represented by $s = [x, y, z]^T$ (the superscript ^{T} denotes the matrix transpose operator). The knowledge of UAV's location is represented by $s_i = [x_i, y_i, z_i]^T$ for $i = 1, \ldots, N$. Here, i denotes the ith virtual array element along UAV's trajectory, and N represents the total number of these points. Generally, we can determine the location of s as long as we estimated the DOA, as seen from the UAV. The DOA, including the AOA φ and the EOA θ, is calculated by analyzing the phase difference in received packets. As the signal arrives at s_i from the far-field, the DOA at each observation point is considered the same.

Let us denote $s[m]$ the baseband representation of the transmitted packet preamble (for $m = 1, ..., M$) and $r[n, m]$ the m-th baseband sample of the n-th received packet, which can be represented as:

$$r[n, m] = h[n, m] * s[m] \cdot e^{j(\phi_0 + 2\pi f_0 (t_n + mT_s))} + \omega[n, m] \quad (2)$$

where $h[n, m]$ is the CIR, which provides temporal and spatial information and power of multipath components. The term ϕ_0 is the phase of the first received packet (which contains the phase offset and accumulated frequency offset at time t_0 between the transmitter and receiver front-ends), f_0 is the LO frequency offset between transmitter and receiver, t_n is the elapsed time between the initial packet and the n-th packet. The term T_s indicates the receiver sample time and $\omega[n, m]$ is an independent and identically distributed Gaussian noise with distribution $\omega[n, m] \sim \mathcal{CN}(0, \sigma^2)$. We assume that f_0 is constant during the observation interval at each interception position, which means the movement of receiver can not exceed a certain time limit, e.g. a few seconds. The term ϕ_0 is considered constant between multiple received packets [9].

In the following (unless otherwise stated), we will consider a narrowband LOS channel. The narrowband channel $h[n]$ when the receiver receives the n-th packet can be written as:

$$h[n] = \alpha \cdot e^{j\vec{\beta}(\varphi, \theta) \cdot \vec{r}[n]} \quad (3)$$

where α is amplitude of the channel, $\vec{\beta}(\varphi, \theta)$ is the wave vector, $\vec{r}[n]$ is the n-th virtual array coordinate when receiving the n-th packet relative to initial coordinate, which requires knowledge of the location of the UAV to within a small fraction of the carrier wavelength. While the UAV flying at a fixed altitude (as will be considered in the following sections), the term $\vec{\beta}(\varphi,\theta)\cdot\vec{r}[n]$ can be developed as

$$\vec{\beta}(\varphi,\theta)\cdot\vec{r}[n]=\frac{2\pi}{\lambda}(x[n]\,sin(\varphi)cos(\theta)+ y[n]\,cos(\varphi)sin(\theta)+z[n]\,cos(\theta)) \tag{4}$$

where $x[n]$, $y[n]$, $z[n]$ represent the displacement of the receiver along the x-, y- and z- axis when receiving the n-th packet.

Combining equations (2) and (3), the full signal model can be written as:

$$r[n,m]=\alpha\cdot s[m]\cdot e^{j(\phi_0+2\pi f_0(t_n+mT_s)+\vec{\beta}(\varphi,\theta)\cdot\vec{r}[n])}+\omega[n,m] \tag{5}$$

The main difference between (5) and the received signal with conventional multi-antenna systems is twofold:

1) the frequency offset f_0 does not appear in conventional multi-antenna systems, since the signal is received on all antenna elements simultaneously;
2) the coordinates $\vec{r}[n]$ are perfectly known in a conventional multi-antenna system, since the array form factor is known by design.

In principle, the DOA estimation in the virtual array is only feasible after the LO phase offset caused by f_0 is eliminated, and the relative array element positions $\vec{r}[n]$ is known. The algorithms and techniques to deal with these two challenges are provided in the next sections.

B. Estimating the relative UAV Coordinates

While UAV is flying in the sky, its coordinates have to be known with an accuracy of a fraction of a wavelength. Current UAV-embedded GPS sensors usually far short from this requirement in higher frequency, but new generations of GNSS receivers in the near future may allow knowing the position of the UAV with such precision, especially since UAVs benefit from excellent satellite visibility. To address this challenge with off-the-shelf hardware, we add a 3D inertial measurement unit (IMU) on the UAV-mounted receiver, containing a combination of accelerometers, gyroscopes, magnetometers to measure angular velocity and linear acceleration with respect to the UAV's body coordinate frame. The relative position and orientation are characterized by the IMU readings through so-called dead-reckoning integration algorithms, with an Extended Kalman Filter (EKF) or an Unscented Kalman Filter (UKF) [9].

Due to the integration of biases in the IMU processing, the navigation solution obtained from IMU measurements will drift from the real trajectory, and the error of the navigation solution will increase over time. However, for the Wide-Sense Stationary Uncorrelated Scattering (WSSUS) assumption to hold [2], the time over which the UAV forms the virtual array would be short so that the navigation error incurred by the IMU is also limited. For typical UAV or vehicle speeds, the required movement duration is up to a few seconds.

C. Local Oscillator Frequency Offset Compensation

To estimate and compensate the LO frequency offset in (5), we proposed two methods, based on our previous research in [9], [10]. The first method is the Stop-and-Start (SaS) approach, where the UAV first stands still before starting to move. During standstill, only the LO frequency offset causes the phase in (5) to change with time and can therefore be easily estimated. This estimated value f_0 is then used during the movement of the UAV to compensate the LO frequency offset, where each received subsequent packet can be expressed as follows:

$$r'[n,m]=r[n,m]\,e^{-j2\pi f_0\cdot(t_n+mT_s)} \tag{6}$$

The compensated signal $r'[n,m]$ contains the phase interferometry and can be used directly in conventional DOA estimation techniques. Although the SaS approach is straightforward and easy to implement. This method suffers from two disadvantages. The most obvious disadvantage is that the SaS approach restricts the movement of the UAV, as the UAV first needs to stand still before moving. The second disadvantage is that the LO frequency offset should not change too much between the moment that the UAV stands still to the moment that the receiver moves, which might not always be verified in practice (especially for low-quality LOs).

The other method is called the joint estimation approach, which has more advantages in practical applications for providing higher usage flexibility and no need to stop the UAV before the movement. In this method, we apply the MUSIC algorithm with an adapted signal model by including the LO phase offset into the steering vector of the virtual array. Let us rewrite (5) by stacking the N received packets in a column vector:

$$r[m]=a(f_0,\varphi,\theta)\,X[m]+\omega[m] \tag{7}$$

with the array steering vector lies in a three-dimensional space over f_0, φ and θ and defined as:

$$a(f_0,\varphi,\theta)=\begin{bmatrix} e^{j(2\pi f_0 t_1+\vec{\beta}\cdot\vec{r}[1])} \\ e^{j(2\pi f_0 t_1+\vec{\beta}\cdot\vec{r}[2])} \\ \vdots \\ e^{j(2\pi f_0 t_1+\vec{\beta}\cdot\vec{r}[N])} \end{bmatrix} \tag{8}$$

and $X[m]$ is constant for all virtual antennas, defined as

$$X[m]=\alpha_0\cdot s[m]\cdot e^{j(\phi_0+2\pi f_0 mT_s)} \tag{9}$$

By developing the eigen-decomposition of the covariance matrix of $r[m]$, we can then estimate the nominal DOA and frequency offset $\left(\hat{f}_0,\hat{\varphi},\hat{\theta}\right)$ via a 3D-MUSIC search, and the corresponding MUSIC spectrum will exhibit the largest peak at the estimated DOA due to the orthogonality of the signal subspace and noise subspace [9].

D. Implementing VMA with Simulations

We have simulated the proposed virtual array system by using MATLAB software. We illustrate the DOA estimation results under each of the two LO frequency offset compensation techniques in the next steps. The azimuth φ for each path in (4) is set to a random angle between 0° and 180° and the elevation θ is set to a random angle between 0° and 90°. The LO drift is simulated using the LO model described in [14].

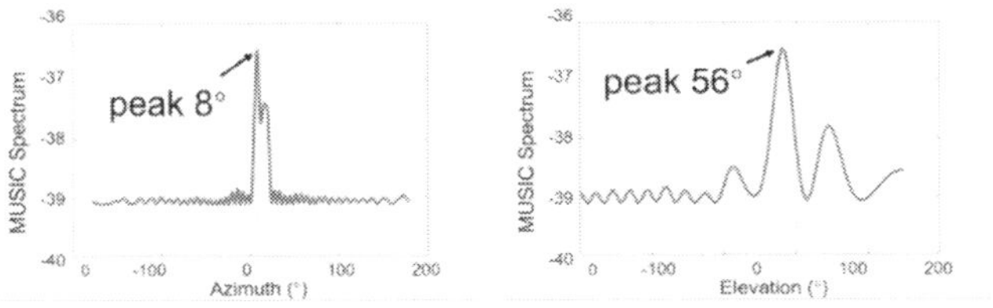

(a) Azimuth estimation for SaS (b) Elevation estimation for SaS

Fig. 4. Simulation results of the SaS estimation approach based on 2D MUSIC search (versus φ and θ, where f_0 is estimated in prior).

Figure 4 shows an example of the MUSIC spectrum of the SaS method after frequency offset compensation, which is used to estimate the azimuth and elevation angle simultaneously. In this snapshot, a clear peak is observed at azimuth 8° and elevation 56°, which is very close to the true DOA (12° for azimuth and 52° for elevation).

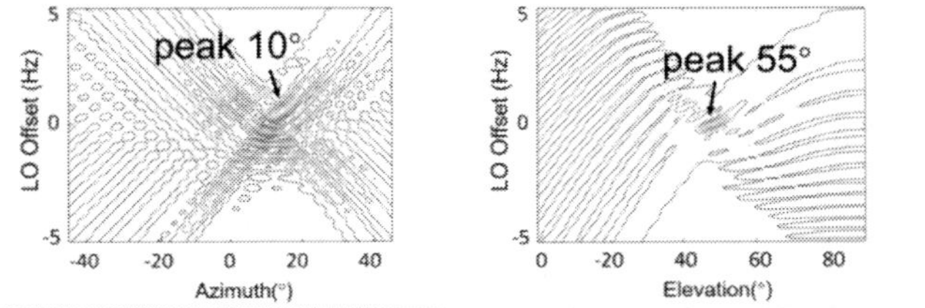

(a) Joint estimation for Azimuth (b) Joint estimation for Elevation

Fig. 5. Simulation results of the joint-estimation approach based on 3D MUSIC search (versus f_0, φ, and θ).

Figure 5 presents an example of the joint-estimation method for the same snapshot in Figure 4. In this case, only the received packets during the UAV movement were used for processing. The peak of the spectrum indicates the estimated LO frequency offset f_0, and also the estimated DOA (azimuth and elevation) corresponding to the peak. A clear peak can be identified at 10° for azimuth and 55° for elevation, close to the true DOA of 12° for azimuth and 52° for elevation as well.

IV. Conclusion and Future Work

In this paper, the DoA-based localization is proved to be a suitable technology for UAVs to locate ground targets due to limited angular spreads for aerial nodes. A promising method is proposed to estimate the DOA of a ground RF transmitter with a UAV equipped with a single antenna. This method actively exploits the UAV movement, which can effectively be controlled and leveraged to obtain DOA estimations. By considering received packets along a planned trajectory, the UAV receiver creates a virtual multi-antenna array that can use conventional DOA estimation algorithms. In addition, we propose two alternative methods to compensate for the local oscillator frequency offset between ground RF transmitters and UAV receivers. The feasibility of our UAV virtual array method is verified with simulations. Our future work will focus on evaluating and improving the proposed method's robustness and implementing the VMA system with UAV platforms and software-defined radios. The whole DoA estimation system will be tested in outdoor scenarios to investigate the effect of 1) the UAV movement states (height, trajectory length); 2) the hardware configurations (LO qualities, LO offset compensation methods); 3) the channel conditions (LOS visibility, SNR, multipath power).

References

[1] B. Ilya and T. Joseph, "Target detection and localization using mimo radars and sonars," *IEEE Transactions on Signal Processing*, vol. 54, no. 10, pp. 3873–3883, 2006.

[2] J. Cheng, K. Guan, and F. Quitin, "Direction of arrival estimation with virtual antenna array: Observability analysis, local oscillator frequency offset compensation, and experimental results," *IEEE Transactions on Instrumentation and Measurement*, pp. 1–1, 2021.

[3] J. Rodríguez-Piñeiro, T. Domínguez-Bolaño, X. Cai, Z. Huang, and X. Yin, "Air-to-ground channel characterization for low-height uavs in realistic network deployments," *IEEE Transactions on Antennas and Propagation*, vol. 69, no. 2, pp. 992–1006, 2021.

[4] X. Cai, T. Izydorczyk, J. Rodríguez-Piñeiro, I. Kovács, J. Wigard, F. Tavares, and P. Mogensen, "Empirical low-altitude air-to-ground spatial channel characterization for cellular networks connectivity," *IEEE Journal on Selected Areas in Communications*, 2021.

[5] Z. Yong, Z. Rui, and L. Joon, "Wireless communications with unmanned aerial vehicles: Opportunities and challenges," *IEEE Communications Magazine*, vol. 54, no. 5, pp. 36–42, 2016.

[6] X. Cai, J. Rodríguez-Piñeiro, X. Yin, N. Wang, Ai B, Frølund P, and Y. Pérez, "An empirical air-to-ground channel model based on passive measurements in lte," *IEEE Transactions on Vehicular Technology*, vol. 68, no. 2, pp. 1140–1154, 2018.

[7] X. Cai, I. Kovács, J. Wigard, and P. Mogensen, "A centralized and scalable uplink powercontrol algorithm in low sinr scenarios," 2020.

[8] P. Adrien, D. Louis, L. Sherman, and E. Per, "Antenna characterization for uav based gps jammer localization," in *Proceedings of the 28th International Technical Meeting of The Satellite Division of the Institute of Navigation (ION GNSS+ 2015)*, 2015, pp. 1684–1695.

[9] F. Quitin, P. De Doncker, F. Horlin, and TW. Peng, "Virtual multiantenna array for estimating the direction of a transmitter: System, bounds, and experimental results," *IEEE Transactions on Vehicular Technology*, vol. 67, no. 2, pp. 1510–1520, 2017.

[10] J. Cheng, K. Guan, and F. Quitin, "Virtual multiantenna array for estimating the doa of a transmitter in uav-assisted networks," in *2020 IEEE 31st Annual International Symposium on Personal, Indoor and Mobile Radio Communications*. IEEE, pp. 1–6.

[11] Y. Jin and B. Friedlander, "Detection of distributed sources using sensor arrays," *IEEE transactions on signal processing*, vol. 52, no. 6, pp. 1537–1548, 2004.

[12] D. He, B. Ai, K. Guan, L. Wang, Z. Zhong, and T. Kurner, "The design and applications of high-performance ray-tracing simulation platform for 5g and beyond wireless communications: A tutorial," *IEEE Communications Surveys Tutorials*, vol. 21, no. 1, pp. 10–27, 2019.

[13] R. Zhang, X. Lu, J. Zhao, L. Cai, and J. Wang, "Measurement and modeling of angular spreads of three-dimensional urban street radio channels," *IEEE Transactions on Vehicular Technology*, vol. 66, no. 5, pp. 3555–3570, 2016.

[14] Z. Cristina and T. Patricia, "The clock model and its relationship with the allan and related variances," *IEEE transactions on ultrasonics, ferroelectrics, and frequency control*, vol. 52, no. 2, pp. 289–296, 2005.

Characterizing the Small-Scale Fading for Low Altitude UAV Channels

Xuesong Cai†‡, Jian Song†, José Rodríguez-Piñeiro*, Preben E. Mogensen†♮, and Fredrik Tufvesson‡
†Department of Electronic Systems, Aalborg University, Aalborg, Denmark, {xuc, jians, pm}@es.aau.dk
*College of Electronics and Information Engineering, Tongji University, Shanghai, China, j.rpineiro@tongji.edu.cn
♮Nokia, Aalborg, Denmark.
‡Department of Electrical and Information Technology, Lund University, Lund, Sweden,
{xuesong.cai, fredrik.tufvesson}@eit.lth.se

Abstract—**In this contribution, a recently conducted measurement campaign in a suburban scenario for the Unmanned Aerial Vehicle (UAV) Air-to-Ground (A2G) radio channel is introduced. The downlink signals in an in-service Long Term Evolution (LTE) network were collected and utilized to extract the Channel Impulse Responses (CIRs). A high-resolution parameter estimation algorithm derived based on the Space-Alternating Generalized Expectation-maximization (SAGE) principle is applied to estimate the delays, Doppler frequencies and complex amplitudes of MultiPath Components (MPCs) from the CIRs. Based on the MPC estimation results, fast fading characteristics of the A2G channels are investigated. It is found that the Rician distribution models the fast fading the best compared to Nakagami, Lognormal and Rayleigh distributions. Rician K-factors are also calculated for the A2G channels.**

Keywords- UAV; air-to-ground; LTE; multipath components; fast fading.

I. Introduction

Unmanned Aerial Vehicles (UAVs) have recently attracted a surge of research interest. They can be exploited as aerial Base Stations (BS) [1] and/or aerial user equipments [2] to enable various applications such as sensing, delivery, etc. [3]. There has been a certain amount of works conducted to understand the Air-to-Ground (A2G) channels, e.g., in [2], [4]–[10] and references therein. Channel characteristics including path loss, delay dispersions, Doppler spread, etc. were investigated. It is worth noting that the first comprehensive measurement-based angular characterization of the A2G channels was carried out in [4]. Although some previous works characterized the small-scale fading, i.e., fast fading, using the Rician K factor, it is not known whether the Rician distribution is really suitable for the A2G channels. In this contribution, we conduct measurement-based analysis, to see which distribution is the most suitable for modeling the fast fading. The rest of this paper is structured as follows. The measurement equipment, scenario and raw data processing are described in Section II. Section III elaborates the investigation on the fast fading behavior. Finally, conclusive remarks are drawn in Section IV.

II. Measurement Equipment, Scenario, and Raw Data Processing

The measurement equipment, scenario, CIR extraction and MPC parameter estimation are briefly introduced in this section. Detailed information can also be found in [6].

A. Transmitter and receiver

In the measurement campaign, a commercial Frequency Division Duplexing Long Term Evolution (FDD-LTE) base station was exploited as the transmitter with its real-time downlink signals collected by the receiver. The receiver system mainly consisted of the following components: a UAV, a Universal-Software-defined Radio-Peripheral (USRP) device of type B210 [11], an Oven-Controlled Crystal Oscillator (OCXO), a cube Lenovo computer, an omnidirectional antenna and three lithium batteries. The OCXO provided a stable local oscillator for the USRP. The cube computer controlled the USRP via the GNU radio software and stored the received data. These components were loaded on the UAV fixed tightly as illustrated in in Figure 1(a).

B. Measurement scenario

The measurement was performed in the suburban scenario as illustrated in Figure 1(c). There were several tall buildings and many metal containers with lower heights. The LTE base station was located in front of and almost in the Line-of-Sight (LoS) of the UAV. The carrier frequency of the LTE downlink signals was 1.8 GHz, and the bandwidth was 13.5 MHz. The UAV flied vertically from the ground to the height of 50 m in about 35 seconds as indicated in Figure 1(b). The signals were acquired by using the USRP with a sample rate of 30.72 MHz. Due to the hardware data steaming limitations, the data were stored in fragments each lasting 15 seconds.

C. Raw data processing

The CIRs were extracted from the Cell Specific Signals (CRSs) as elaborated in [2], [12]. Briefly, synchronization and physical cell detection were first done. With the transmitted CRSs known according to [13], the channel transfer functions can be calculated, and so the CIRs. The signal model of a CIR in the SAGE algorithm [14] is formulated as

$$h(t,\tau) = \sum_{\ell=1}^{L} \alpha_\ell(t)\delta(\tau - \tau_\ell(t)) \exp\left\{ j2\pi \int_0^t \nu_\ell(t)dt \right\}, \quad (1)$$

where L, $\alpha_\ell(t)$, $\tau_\ell(t)$, and $\nu_\ell(t)$ denote the number of paths, complex amplitudes, delays and Doppler frequencies, respectively, and $\delta(\cdot)$ is the Dirac delta function. Four consecutive CIRs were considered as one snapshot. The SAGE algorithm was applied with $L = 18$ that was found proper to fully extract the dominant MPCs in each snapshot.

Figure 1. The measurement equipments and scenario. a) All the components used in the experiments. b) The UAV was flying from the ground to the air. c) The surroundings of the scenario.

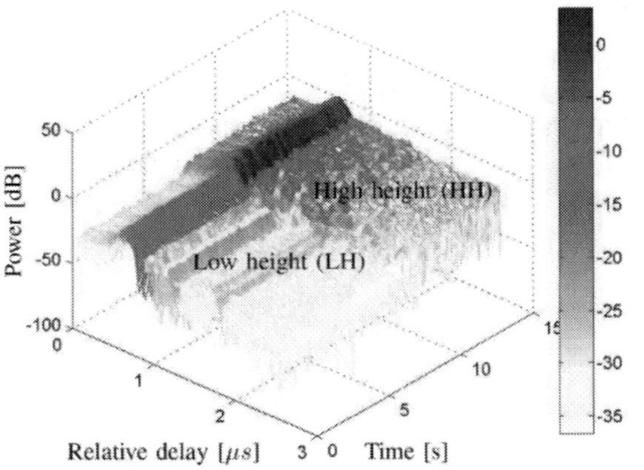

Figure 2. An example concatenated PDPs lasting 15 seconds [6].

III. Small-scale fading

As illustrated in Figure 2, we first show concatenated power-delay-profiles (PDPs) lasting 15 s that correspond to the UAV flying from the ground to the air. It can be observed that the channels before and after 7.5 seconds are different. We use Low Height (LH) and High Height (HH) to distinguish them. Our conjecture [6] for the difference is that when the height was low, the UAV could only receive the LoS signals and the signals reflected from buildings with high heights or side walls of containers. However, when the UAV flied high above the containers and buildings, signals reflected from the roofs started impinging into the UAV, and the signal power also increased. The SAGE estimation results are also illustrated in Figure 3 for the example channel shown in Figure 2.

Based on the SAGE estimation results, the channel fading

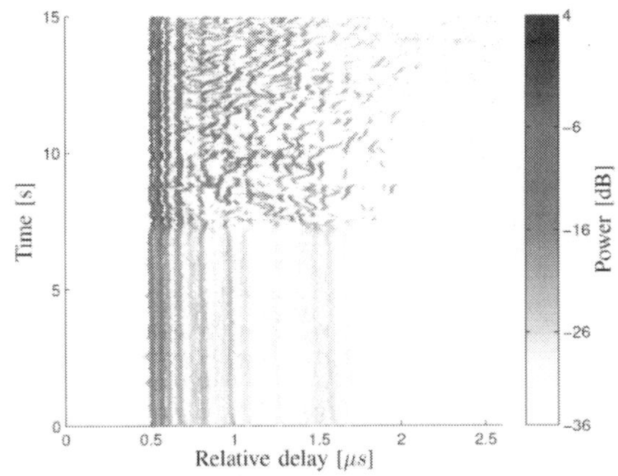

Figure 3. The SAGE estimation results for the channels as illustrated in Figure 2 [6].

amplitude is calculated as

$$G = \sum_{\ell=1}^{L} \alpha_\ell. \tag{2}$$

To fully understand the small-scale fading behaviors, Akaike's Information Criteria (AIC) is applied to select the best fitting model for the fading amplitudes in both cases, among all the J ($J = 4$) candidate distributions: Rician, Nakagami, Log-normal and Rayleigh. AIC is a measure of the relative fitting goodness of a statistical model, and is widely used in the wireless communications [15], [16]. Akaike weights derived from AICs which satisfy $\sum_{i=1}^{J} \omega_j = 1$ are applied to select the best distribution with the largest Akaike weight. We choose 80 SAGE snapshots to obtain reliable Akaike weights. Note that $N/U \geq 40$ should be satisfied to obtain reliable Akaike weights, where N is the sample number, U is the number of free model parameter(s). Readers are referred to [16] for elaborated discussions about AIC. The distance that the UAV moves in 80 SAGE snapshots is about 4 times the half wavelength, which is in the small-scale level. Figs. 4(a) and 4(b) illustrate the AIC weights for the four candidate distributions in the LH and HH cases respectively. It can be observed that in both cases, the Rician distribution best fits the small-scale fading, the goodness of Nakagami and Log-normal distributions is similar, and the Rayleigh distribution is not suitable for modelling the fading behaviors. Furthermore, the best fitting rate of Rician distribution in the HH case (70.9%) is lower than that of the LH case (74.3%). This is consistent with the fact that the HH channel measured in this specific scenario herein includes more non-negligible MPCs.

Since the Rician distribution has the best goodness of fit in both cases and is commonly used to model the propagation channel with a dominant path, the Rician K-factor is investigated by using the moment-based method, specified in [17],

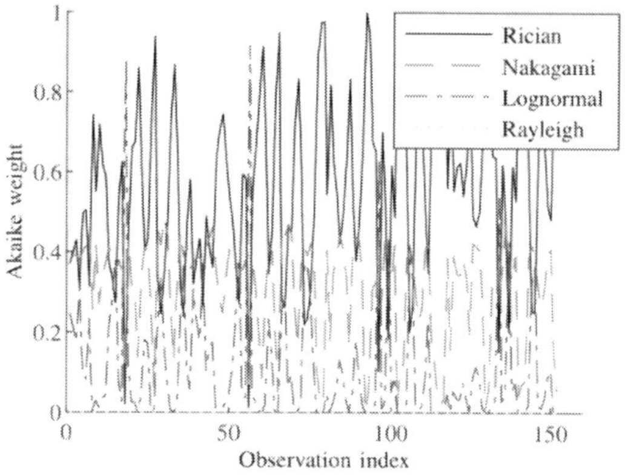

(a)

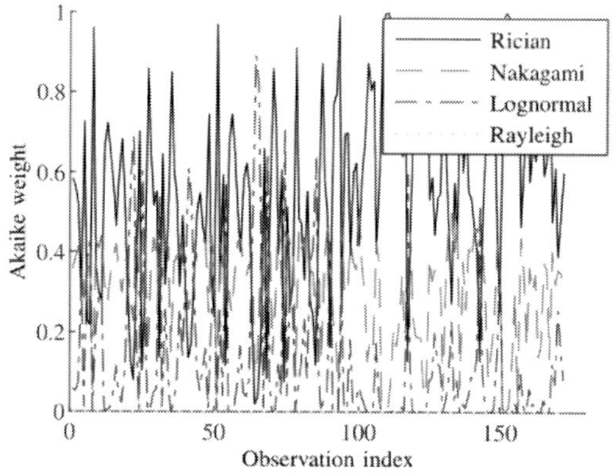

(b)

Figure 4. Akaike weights for the four candidates in the LH case and the HH case. a) LH case. Rician 74.3% best, Nakagami 19.2% best, Lognormal 6.5% best, and Rayleigh 0% best. b) HH case. Rician 70.9% best, Nakagami 15.7% best, Lognormal 13.4% best, and Rayleigh 0% best.

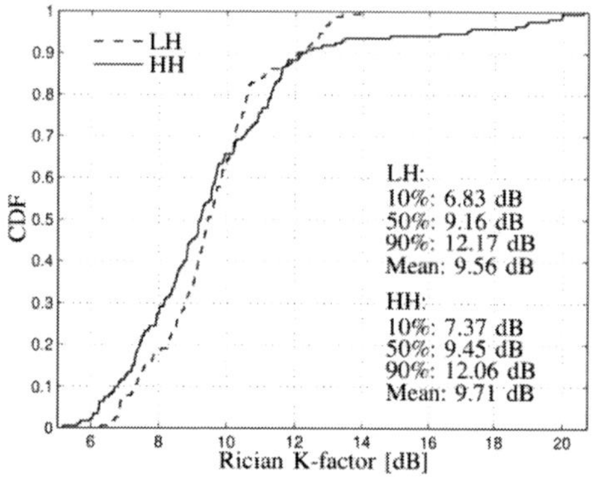

Figure 5. CDFs for Rician K-factors in the LH case and the HH case.

as

$$K = \frac{\sqrt{1 - \frac{\mathrm{Var}[G^2]}{(\mathrm{E}[G^2])^2}}}{1 - \sqrt{1 - \frac{\mathrm{Var}[G^2]}{(\mathrm{E}[G^2])^2}}}, \tag{3}$$

where $\mathrm{Var}(\cdot)$ and $\mathrm{E}(\cdot)$ represent the variance and the expectation of the argument, respectively. Figure 5 illustrates the CDFs for the K-factors in the LH and HH cases respectively. It can be observed that the HH K-factor is smaller than the LH K-factor under the 65% level. This is consistent with the fact that the more MPCs with non-negligible powers in the HH case can sometimes result in more severe fading compared to the LH case. However, the maximum HH K-factor is larger than that of the LH case. This is also understandable since the blockage to the LoS path is lower.

IV. Conclusions

The low altitude UAV radio channel in a suburban scenario was investigated. Based on the downlink data received from a commercial LTE base station, high resolution estimation results of multipath components were obtained using the SAGE algorithm. Based on the SAGE estimation results, fast fading behaviors were analyzed. Among Rician, Nagakami, Lognormal and Rayleigh distributions, it has been found that the Rician distribution can best model the fast fading of the UAV channel with a best-fitting rate of more than 70%. Moreover, large Ricean K-factors, with average values of 10 dB and maximum ones of 20 dB, were found. In addition, it is interesting to find that in this special suburban scenario, the UAV channel became less Los-dominant (probably due to the reflections at the roofs of buildings and metallic containers), which is different from the common belief that the A2G channel at a higher hight should be more LoS-dominant.

Acknowledgement

The authors wish to express their thanks to Prof. Cesar Briso at the Technical University of Madrid for his help in conducting the measurement. The work of José Rodríguez-Piñeiro is supported in part by the National Natural Science Foundation of China (NSFC) under Grant 61971313, and in part by the Sino-German Center of Intelligent Systems, Tongji University, Shanghai, China.

References

[1] N. Babu, C. B. Papadias, and P. Popovski, "Energy-efficient 3-D deployment of aerial access points in a UAV communication system," *IEEE Communications Letters*, vol. 24, no. 12, pp. 2883–2887, 2020.

[2] X. Cai *et al.*, "An empirical air-to-ground channel model based on passive measurements in LTE," *IEEE Transactions on Vehicular Technology*, vol. 68, no. 2, pp. 1140–1154, 2019.

[3] S. Hayat, E. Yanmaz, and R. Muzaffar, "Survey on unmanned aerial vehicle networks for civil applications: A communications viewpoint," *IEEE Communications Surveys Tutorials*, vol. 18, no. 4, pp. 2624–2661, 2016.

[4] X. Cai *et al.*, "Empirical low-altitude air-to-ground spatial channel characterization for cellular networks connectivity," *IEEE Journal on Selected Areas in Communications*, pp. 1–1, 2021.

[5] ——, "Interference modeling for low-height air-to-ground channels in live LTE networks," *IEEE Antennas and Wireless Propagation Letters*, vol. 18, no. 10, pp. 2011–2015, 2019.

[6] ——, "Low altitude UAV propagation channel modelling," in *11th European Conference on Antennas and Propagation (EUCAP)*, 2017, pp. 1443–1447.

[7] C. Yan, L. Fu, J. Zhang, and J. Wang, "A comprehensive survey on UAV communication channel modeling," *IEEE Access*, vol. 7, pp. 107 769–107 792, 2019.

[8] J. Rodríguez-Piñeiro, Z. Huang, X. Cai, T. Domínguez-Bolaño, and X. Yin, "Geometry-based mpc tracking and modeling algorithm for time-varying UAV channels," *IEEE Transactions on Wireless Communications*, vol. 20, no. 4, pp. 2700–2715, 2021.

[9] J. Rodríguez-Piñeiro, T. Domínguez-Bolaño, X. Cai, Z. Huang, and X. Yin, "Air-to-ground channel characterization for low-height UAVs in realistic network deployments," *IEEE Transactions on Antennas and Propagation*, vol. 69, no. 2, pp. 992–1006, 2021.

[10] Z. Huang, J. Rodríguez-Piñeiro, T. Domínguez-Bolaño, X. Cai, and X. Yin, "Empirical dynamic modeling for low-altitude UAV propagation channels," *IEEE Transactions on Wireless Communications*, pp. 1–1, 2021.

[11] "USRP B210 Datasheet," Tech. Rep. [Online]. Available: https://www.ettus.com/product/details/UB210-KIT, 2021.

[12] X. Ye, X. Cai, Y. Shen, X. Yin, and X. Cheng, "A geometry-based path loss model for high-speed-train environments in LTE-A networks," in *2016 International Conference on Computing, Networking and Communications (ICNC)*, Feb 2016, pp. 1–6.

[13] *Technical Specification Group Radio Access Network; Evolved Universal Terrestrial Radio Access (E-UTRA); Physical channels and modulation*, 3rd Generation Partnership Project 3GPP TS 36.211 V13.2.0 (2016-07) Std.

[14] B. Fleury, M. Tschudin, R. Heddergott, D. Dahlhaus, and K. Ingeman Pedersen, "Channel parameter estimation in mobile radio environments using the SAGE algorithm," *IEEE Journal on Selected Areas in Communications*, vol. 17, no. 3, pp. 434–450, 1999.

[15] R. He *et al.*, "Short-term fading behavior in high-speed railway cutting scenario: Measurements, analysis, and statistical models," *IEEE Transactions on Antennas and Propagation*, vol. 61, no. 4, pp. 2209–2222, April 2013.

[16] U. G. Schuster and H. Bolcskei, "Ultrawideband channel modeling on the basis of information-theoretic criteria," *IEEE Transactions on Wireless Communications*, vol. 6, no. 7, pp. 2464–2475, July 2007.

[17] L. J. Greenstein, D. G. Michelson, and V. Erceg, "Moment-method estimation of the Ricean K-factor," *IEEE Communications Letters*, vol. 3, no. 6, pp. 175–176, June 1999.

Bounded Path-Loss Model for UAV-to-UAV Communications

Jian Song*, Xuesong Cai*†, Lam-Thanh Tu‡, and Preben E. Mogensen*
*Department of Electronic Systems, Aalborg University, 9220 Aalborg, Denmark
†Department of Electrical and Information Technology, Lund University, 22100 Lund, Sweden
‡Institute XLIM, University of Poitiers, 86000 Poitiers, France
Email: {jians,xuc,pm}@es.aau.dk, lam.thanh.tu@univ-poitiers.fr

***Abstract*—In this paper, we focus on ultra-dense network modeling where both the Base Stations (BSs) and Mobile Terminals (MTs) are UAVs. In this case, two communication nodes can be very close to each other. However, existing cellular network analyses typically use the standard unbounded path loss model where received power decays like r^{β} over a distance r. This standard model is a good approximation for the path-loss in wireless communications over large values of r but is not valid for small values of r due to the singularity at 0. This model is often used along with a random uniform node distribution, even though in a group of uniformly distributed nodes some may be arbitrarily close to one another, thus, it will lose accuracy and may be not applicable for UAV-to-UAV communications. To tackle this problem, by using mathematical tool behind stochastic geometry, we propose tractable analytical frameworks of coverage and rate based on the novel unbounded path-loss model with a constant distance factor r_0 for analyzing the UAV-to-UAV communications.**

***Index Terms*—Cellular Networks, UAV, Stochastic Geometry, Bounded Path-Loss Model**

I. Introduction

Unmanned Aerial Vehicles (UAVs) have received significant attention in wireless research as they can not only be exploited as aerial BSs, but also functioned as a new type of MTs. In most of the available literatures, the path-loss models for UAVs are devised and formulated via experimental measurement [1], [2], which may not yield a tractable analytical approach for system-level analysis. Due to the simplicity and mathematical tractability, the unbounded path-loss model $L(r) = r^{\beta}$ has been widely applied to characterize channel power gain caused by large scale fading in wireless networks [3], especially when transmission distance is large in the rural areas. However, as the network density becomes larger in the fifth generation (5G) and wireless networks, it becomes more likely that the transmission distance is small. Despite its simplicity, unbounded path-loss model fails to accurately characterize channel power gain in this case. In particular, when $r \in (0, 1)$, applying unbounded path-loss model would artificially force the received signal power to be greater than the transmitted signal power, which is physically impossible.

Therefore, a more realistic model, namely, bounded pathloss model, has been adopted to model the channel power gain caused by pathloss, especially for dense urban scenarios. Widely applied bounded path-loss models include $(1 + r)^{\beta}$, $1 + r^{\beta}$ and $\max\{1, r^{\beta}\}$. In literature, the impact of bounded path-loss model on wireless network performance has been extensively investigated, e.g., [4]. However, all the previous investigated models are based on the fixed distance factor, i.e., 1m, which is not suitable for modeling and analyzing UAV networks. The generalization to a generic bounded distance is never analyzed in the previous studies for ultra-dense UAV networks.

Motivated by these considerations, in the present paper, we propose the novel bounded path-loss model with a generic distance factor, r_0 as an approximated formulation for a measured path-loss model [5]. To evaluate the performance, tractable analytical frameworks of coverage probability and average rate are obtained with aid of the mathematical tool behind stochastic geometry. Specifically, a closed-form expression of coverage probability is derived, which could provide the potential insights for the system-level analysis and optimization.

II. System Model

Consider a bi-dimensional downlink ultra-dense cellular networks with aerial BSs and MTs, i.e., drones or UAVs. The BSs are modeled as points of a homogeneous Poisson point process (PPP), denoted by Ψ_{BS}, of density λ_{BS}. The MTs are densely distributed as another independent homogeneous PPP, denoted by Ψ_{MT}, of density λ_{MT}. Each BS is assumed to emit a constant transmit power P. Without any loss of generality, the analytical frameworks are developed for the typical MT, denoted by MT_0, that is located at the origin. The BS serving MT_0 is denoted by BS_0. The subscripts 0, i and n identify the intended link, a generic interfering link, and a generic BS-to-MT (UAV-to-UAV) link. The set of interfering BSs is denoted by $\Psi_{\mathrm{BS},i}$.

For each BS-to-MT link, path-loss and fast-fading are considered. Shadowing is not explicitly taken into account because its net effect lies in modifying the density of the BSs [6]. All BS-to-MT links are assumed to be mutually independent and identically distributed (i.i.d.).

1) Path-Loss: Consider a generic BS-to-MT link of length r_n, the path-loss is $L(r_n) = k(r_0 + r_n)^{\beta}$, where k and $\beta > 2$ are the path-loss constant and the path-loss slope (exponent).

2) Fast-Fading: Consider a generic BS-to-MT link. The power gain due to small-scale fading is assumed to follow an exponential distribution with mean Ω. Without loss of generality, $\Omega = 1$ is assumed. The power gain of a generic BS-to-MT link is denoted by h.

3) Cell Association Criterion: A cell association criterion based on the highest average received power is assumed. Let $\mathrm{BS}_n \in \Psi$ denote a generic BS of the network. The serving BS, BS_0, is obtained as follows:

$$\mathrm{BS}_0 = \arg \max_{\mathrm{BS}_n \in \Psi} \{1/L(r_n)\} \tag{1}$$

$$\mathrm{P}_{\mathrm{cov}} = \vartheta\left(\frac{1}{k}\right)^{\frac{1}{\beta}} \frac{\eta}{4\Upsilon_2^2} \left\{2\Upsilon_2\left(\sqrt{-\Upsilon_2} + \sqrt{\Upsilon_2}\varepsilon(\xi)\right) r_0 + \left(\frac{1}{k}\right)^{\frac{1}{\beta}} \left[\Upsilon_1\sqrt{-\Upsilon_2} - 2\exp\left((L_{r_0})^{\frac{1}{\beta}}\Upsilon_1 + (L_{r_0})^{\frac{2}{\beta}}\Upsilon_2\right)\left(\Upsilon_2 - \Upsilon_1\sqrt{\Upsilon_2}\mathcal{F}(\xi)\right)\right]\right\} \tag{5}$$

As for the intended link, $L_0 = \min_{r_n \in \Psi}\{L(r_n)\}$ holds.

III. Coverage Probability and Rate

In this section, we present the analytical frameworks of coverage probability and average rate of a typical MT, which are defined by [6]:

$$\mathrm{P}_{\mathrm{cov}} = \Pr\{\mathrm{SIR} \geqslant \gamma_{\mathrm{th}}\} \tag{2}$$

$$R = \mathrm{E}\{\ln(1+\mathrm{SIR})\} = \int_0^{\infty} \frac{\mathrm{P}_{\mathrm{cov}}(t)}{t+1} dt \tag{3}$$

where SIR denotes the signal-to-interference ratio and γ_{th} is the reliability threshold for the successful decoding of information data. SIR is formulated by:

$$\mathrm{SIR} = \frac{P(h_0/L_0)}{P \sum\limits_{i \in \Psi_{\mathrm{BS},i}} (h_i/L_i)\mathbf{1}(L_i > L_0)} \tag{4}$$

The analytical framework of coverage probability can be derived into a closed-form, which is given by (5), and the short-hands in (5) are defined in Table I, where $\mathrm{erfi}(\cdot)$ is the imaginary error function and $\mathcal{F}(\cdot)$ is the Dawson function. The general mathematical proof of stochastic geometry background follows the steps in [6].

TABLE I: AUXILIARY FUNCTIONS.

Function definition
$\vartheta = 2\pi\lambda_{\mathrm{BS}}\exp\{-\pi\lambda_{\mathrm{BS}} r_0^2\}$, $\eta = \exp\left(-\frac{\Upsilon_1^2}{4\Upsilon_2}\right)\sqrt{\pi}$
$\xi = \frac{\Upsilon_1 + 2\left(k r_0^{\beta}\right)^{\frac{1}{\beta}}\Upsilon_2}{2\sqrt{\Upsilon_2}}$, $\varepsilon(\xi) = \mathrm{erfi}(\xi)$, $L_{r_0} = k r_0^{\beta}$
$\Upsilon_1 = 2\pi\lambda r_0\left(\frac{1}{k}\right)^{\frac{1}{\beta}} {}_2F_1\left(-\frac{1}{\beta}, 1, 1-\frac{1}{\beta}, -\gamma_{\mathrm{th}}\right)$
$\Upsilon_2 = -\pi\lambda\left(\frac{1}{k}\right)^{\frac{2}{\beta}} {}_2F_1\left(-\frac{2}{\beta}, 1, 1-\frac{2}{\beta}, -\gamma_{\mathrm{th}}\right)$

IV. Numerical and Simulation Results

In this section, we illustrate the numerical results of proposed analytical framework based on the bounded path-loss model with a generic distance r_0.

In Fig. 1, we evaluate the performance of coverage probability and average rate as a function of density of BSs for different values of r_0 based on (2), (3) and closed-form formulation in (5). Note that the density of BSs is represented by the cell radius R_{cell}, and $\lambda_{\mathrm{BS}} = 1/\pi R_{\mathrm{cell}}^2$. In addition, Monte-Carlo simulation results are provided to validate the accuracy of proposed analytical frameworks.

It is worth noting that the performance trends of both coverage and rate for the unbounded path-loss model are independent with cell radius or density of BSs. Nevertheless, with the bounded path-loss model, the trends of rate would be monotonically increasing when cell radius increases. In addition, it is indicated that lower r_0 value could enhance the system performance for ultra-dense scenario, and vice versa.

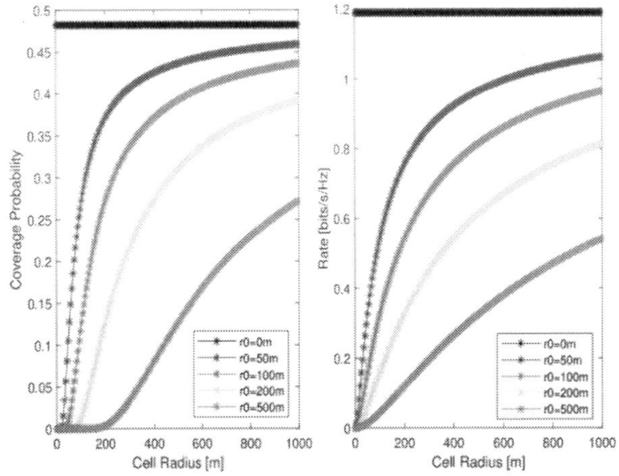

Fig. 1: Coverage probability & rate versus density of BSs. Markers: Monte-Carlo simulations. Solid lines: Analytical frameworks.

V. Conclusion

In this paper, we have introduced new analytical frameworks of coverage probability and average rate under the application of the bounded path-loss model with r_0. The proposed mathematical approach is in a good agreement with Monte-Carlo simulations. Through the performance comparisons of the conventional unbounded path-loss model, it is verified that the bounded path-loss model could provide different performance trends as a function of BSs density, which delivers potential insights and design guidelines for UAV network deployment.

References

[1] X. Cai, T. Izydorczyk, J. Rodríguez-Piñeiro, I. Z. Kovács, J. Wigard, F. M. L. Tavares, and P. E. Mogensen, "Empirical low-altitude air-toground spatial channel characterization for cellular networks connectivity", *IEEE Journal on Selected Areas in Communications.*, 2021.

[2] X. Cai, J. Rodríguez-Piñeiro, X. Yin, N. Wang, B. Ai, G. F. Pedersen, and A. P. Yuste, "An empirical air-to-ground channel model based on passive measurements in LTE", *IEEE Transactions on Vehicular Technology.*, vol. 68, no. 2, pp. 1140-1154, Nov. 2019.

[3] J. G. Andrews, F. Baccelli, and R. K. Ganti, " Tractable Approach to Coverage and Rate in Cellular Networks", *IEEE Transactions on Communications.*, vol. 59, no. 11, pp. 3122–3134, Nov. 2012.

[4] H. Inaltekin, M. Chiang, H. V. Poor, and S. B. Wicker "On unbounded path-loss models: effects of singularity on wireless network performance", *IEEE J. Sel. Areas Commun.*, vol. 27, no. 7, pp. 1078-1092, Sep. 2009.

[5] R. Amorim, P. Mogensen, T. Sorensen, I. Z. Kovács, and J. Wigard, "Pathloss measurements and modeling for UAVs connected to cellular networks", *2017 IEEE 85th Vehicular Technology Conference (VTC Spring)*, 2017.

[6] M. D. Renzo, W. Lu, and P. Guan, "The Intensity Matching Approach: A Tractable Stochastic Geometry Approximation to System-Level Analysis of Cellular Networks", *IEEE Transactions on Wireless Communications*, vol. 15, no. 9, pp. 5963-5983, Sep. 2016.

Comparison of Techno-Economic Solutions for 5G Networks and beyond

1st Christos Bouras
Computer Engineering & Informatics Dept.
University of Patras
Patras, Greece
bouras@cti.gr

2nd Fotios Kaisoudis
Computer Engineering & Informatics Dept.
University of Patras
Patras, Greece
kaisoudis@ceid.upatras.gr

3rd Anastasia Kollia
Computer Engineering & Informatics Dept.
University of Patras
Patras, Greece
akollia@ceid.upatras.gr

***Abstract*—5G envisions a society that is constantly interconnected with a large number of devices, anywhere and anytime. The developed technologies play an important role, allowing low latency, a large data traffic, and improved quality of services. 5G encourages providers and investors to develop innovative services that meet consumer demands. However, the viability of a new service is being investigated from an economic perspective. This paper analyzes 5G technologies and evaluates them from a techno-economic point of view and pricing models. In particular, the main factors used to estimate the cost are CAPEX and OPEX, which compare the viability of the investment. 5G is proved to be a profitable investment due to its low cost and the increase in the average data consumption of each consumer. Finally, reusing existing sites is less costly in developing a dense macro-cell network.**

***Index Terms*—5G, models, IoT, CAPEX, OPEX.**

I. Introduction

5G will play a vital role in the transmission of mobile data to provide higher capabilities to individual mobile radio cells. On the other hand, mobile data are not used appropriately by users due to reckless usage and increased demand. Due to this increment in data traffic, mobile providers are fighting to normalize the massive demand with high-speed and multi-site data links providing a faster and wide-ranging wireless network.

The 5G technology is based on Orthogonal Frequency Division Multiplexing (OFDM) using various technologies such as Multi-user Multiple-Input Multiple-Output (mu-MIMO), Distributed Antenna Systems (DAS), Femtocells, Network Function Virtualization & Software Defined Network (NFV & SDN), Cognitive Radio (CR), Millimetre Wave (mmWave). Also, 5G enables support for almost infinite innovations and uses. It is undoubtedly the network of the future supporting more new services, besides digital communication and wireless Internet. 5G is a communication standard and not just a wireless standard. Since the digital relationship between humans and machines is evolving rapidly, robust infrastructure and appropriate networks are required. Increasing data volume requires faster data transfer. Therefore, the 5G network needs to face the enormous and complex range of requirements.

The current mobile standard is known as Long Term Evolution (LTE). The present technology satisfies almost all the requirements of the subscribers for various applications.However, the advent of 5G does not mean that LTE has come to an end, but rather it will be an upgrade that will expand the existing network resulting in the simultaneous operation of both technologies that will lead to higher capacities and internet speeds. In addition to the billions of people already using mobile internet, more than 100 billion connected devices will connect and the 5G network is a solution to the demands of digitalization.

The development of 5G mobile broadband technology will have a significant impact on the future economy according to several techno-economic studies. Adapting to the IoT means that remarkable changes will occur in the current communication networks. According to [1], crucial factors that will radically affect the dimensioning of the network must be considered and are the coverage, range, capacity, and data rate. Furthermore, it is important to indicate the cost and energy consumption of the base stations that will be used for the needs of the network coverage, for example, an urban or rural area [2]. Also, according to [2], which refers to an analysis made between macro and femtocell, it appears that Operator Mobile Network (OMNs) need to formulate the appropriate strategies to adapt to future business developments. Finally, it is important to mention the CAPEX and OPEX costs associated with BS strategy carried out in urban areas where traffic demand is high [3].

The remaining part of this paper is structured as follows: in Section II, the characteristics of 5G technologies are presented. Section III refers to compare & contrast the aforementioned technologies. Section IV refers to cost analysis and needs for upgrading to 5G network. In Section V, conclusions are summarized and future research is proposed.

II. Synopsis of 5G Technologies

In this section will analyze the features of technologies such as mu-MIMO, DAS, Femtocells, NFV & SDN, Cognitive Radio, mmWave.

A. mu-MIMO

MIMO technology utilizes limited resources to meet user demand, but due to the insufficient number of antennas at the MIMO system base station, system performance problems are caused. It constitutes the fundamental technologies of the future 5G, MIMO technology must meet the requirements of wireless companies, improve the effectiveness of the spectrum, the capability of the system communication, the reliability of the connections, and the data rate. If the number of antennas is equal to 4, 8, or 16, then the technology is called MIMO. In case there is a enormous number of antennas in each transceiver, for example, 128, 256, or more, then it is called mu-MIMO or Massive MIMO [1]. Figure 1 describes the concept of mu-MIMO architecture.

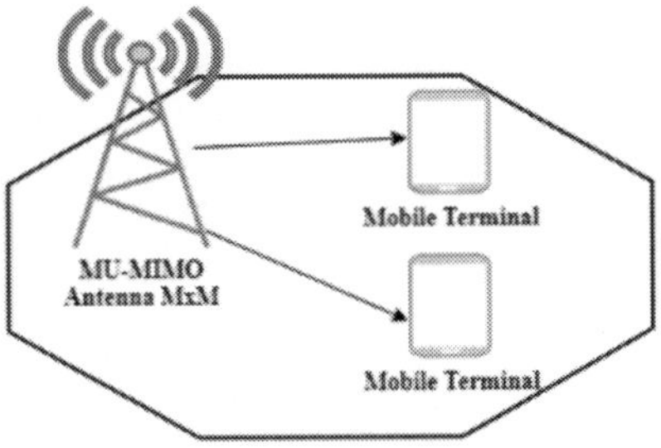

Fig. 1: mu-MIMO architecture scheme.

B. DAS

The Distributed Antenna System (DAS) contains several antennas that are considered as nodes and are connected to a transmission medium, for example, optical fiber. As mentioned in [1], at least two antennas must be per floor of a building, so that they adequately cover the floor of an apartment complex or a non-densely populated building. Also, the DAS includes two basic structures. The first basic structure is a base station (BS) and a distributed system (DS - Distributed System). The second basic structure is several antennas representing the DS along with many transceivers that facilitate the transmission.

C. Femtocells

Femtocells are known as Femto Access Point (FAP) or Home NodeBs (HNBs) and the transmission of base stations consumption is around 100 mW, which is installed indoors. Femtocells use the licensed range and provide services like voice and data to mobile subscribers. Subscribers using femtocell technology enjoy high-quality voice dialing and peak data rates because of improved Radio Frequency (RF) coverage. Furthermore, mobile providers benefit from the low cost of infrastructure development, considering coverage improvements and capacity upgrades. Also, to expand coverage, femtocells minimize the movement of a macrocell network and significantly increase network capacity by using the same range many times over smaller pieces. That helps to achieve higher efficiency, as fewer subscribers share valuable resources macrocell [4]. Figure 2 describes the concept of Femtocell architecture.

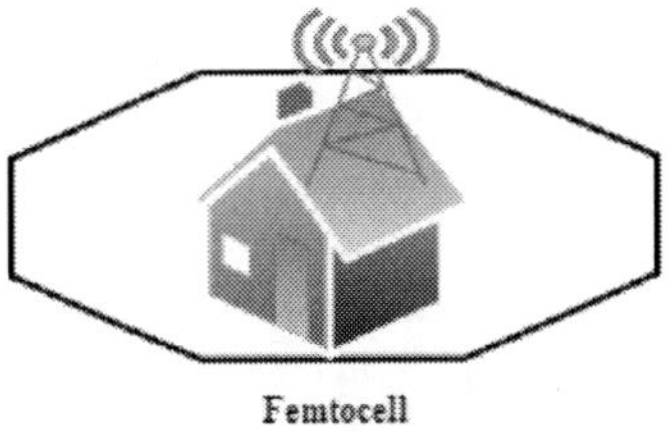

Fig. 2: Femtocell architecture scheme.

D. NFV & SDN

Network and telecommunications applications that use NFV technology currently operate exclusively from specific platforms on NFV cloud infrastructures. The devices that the user uses increase, because of the requirements of the users increased. That results in limitations such as expensive equipment and complex control protocols. At the same time, it has an impact on the innovation of new services, the creation of new architectures and technologies in general. Networking is defined by SDN and NFV, which are critical tools for the future of the IoT [5].

Utilizing both SDN and NFV technologies for dynamic Virtual Mobile Network (VMN) development is fundamental. SDN and NFV technologies are being developed with the goal of control, reliability, scalability, cost-effectiveness, and flexibility for VMN [5], [6] development. Also, these technologies allow VMN to flexibly control the virtual core of their mobile network by considering traffic load, Radio Access Network (RAN), and Evolved Packet Core (EPC). Figure 3 describes the concept of SDN architecture.

E. Cognitive Radio

Cognitive Radio Networks (CRNs) make greater use of the spectrum because they exploit the points of a spectrum

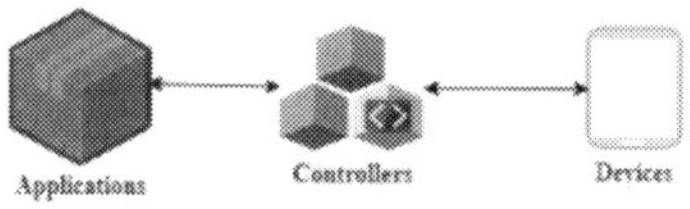

Fig. 3: SDN architecture scheme.

that are used less or not at all. Unauthorized users are given access by the spectrum if their interference is negligible. The operation of CRN is based on the Cognitive Radio Devices (CRD), which can automatically adjust some parameters such as bandwidth, waveform, and transmission power depending on the environment, avoiding bottlenecks, exploiting parts of the spectrum. The Cognitive Process (CP) is known to contribute to gathering relevant information, machine learning, reasoning, and decision making. There are regulated radio platforms such as Software Defined Radio (SDR) software to execute the decisions of the CP [7].

It is necessary to clarify the difference between the terms cognitive communication system based on SDR and CR software. SDR consists of a group of radio frequencies, in which most of the intermediate radio frequencies are converted to digital format, to be compared with the classic radio technology, providing greater flexibility in radio operation. On the other hand, CR is related to the control that contributes to the SDR to determine the mode of operation as well as the necessary parameters that will be applied in the specific networking mode [7].

Cognitive communication devices (CRD) are designed to respond to complex wireless environments which are [7]: Multi-band, Multi-channel, Multi-mode, Multi-standard and Multi-service.CRDs and CRNs are characterized as complex and designed to operate in these situations. The functions used for management are four and are [7]: spectrum detection, spectrum management spectrum sharing and spectrum mobility. Figure 4 describes the concept of CR architecture.

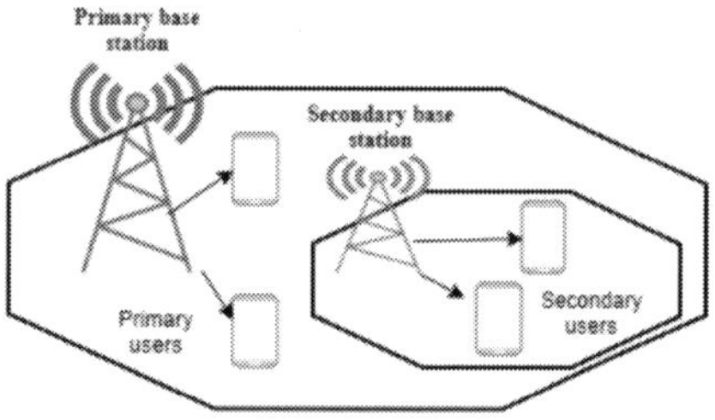

Fig. 4: Cognitive Radio architecture scheme.

F. mmWave

MmWave cellular systems operate in the 30-300 GHz band and are candidates for 5G cellular systems supporting high speeds. An innovative technology consisting of millimeter-wave (mmWave) communications and providing two advantages [8]: 1) proper management of unlicensed additional spectrum bands and 2) huge bandwidth up to 1GHz to provide high data rates for demanding subscribers.

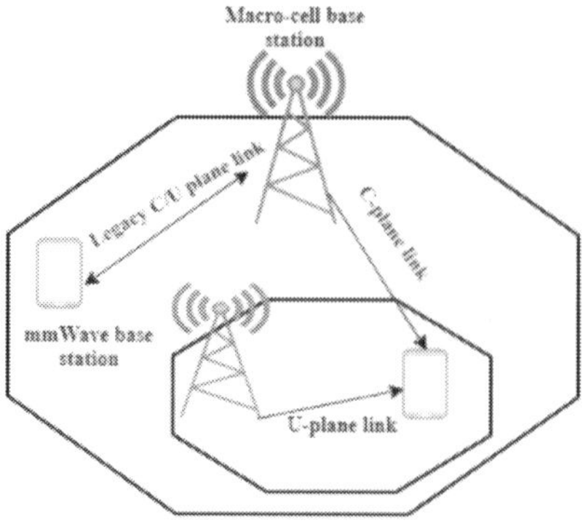

Fig. 5: mmWave C-/U- plane architecture scheme.

However, the use of mmWave presents some propagation barriers, which are [8]: loss of travel due to a high carrier frequency, reduced dispersion, which helps to reduce the available diversity, increased blockage, atmospheric absorption and rain, and noise power due to the use of the high bandwidth.

To address the prior issues, mmWave can be combined with other technologies such as Massive MIMO, SDN and femtocells, which help to achieve an optimal system [8]. Such as: massive MIMO and Beamforming, Ultra-Dense Networks (microcell development), a cellular architecture that supports heterogeneous layers and integrates the SDN standard and the functional split between the user layer (U-level) and the control layer (level-C), and a geographical database, that will include information related to the environment of each geographical area to increase the efficiency of cell functions, which will support the ability to store and process information related to previous cell discoveries. Figure 5 describes the concept of mmWave architecture.

III. Compare & Contrast

In this section, a comparative analysis of the technologies will be performed based on the characteristics explained below, (see Table I [9]):

Adoption: Each technology has its degree of adoption. Low means that its adoption rate is not widespread enough. High means that its adoption rate is quite widespread. Future means that it will be presented in the future.

Appeared: The first introduction of each technology according to research studies.

Bandwidth: Some of the previous technologies need more bandwidth to increase their efficiency, while others directly reallocate the existing bandwidth. Table I presents the technologies, which are characterized as reallocate, in need, and virtual.

Capacity: Each technology offers the appropriate capacity.

TABLE I: Comparison of 5G Technologies.

Factors	5G Technologies					
	mu-MIMO	DAS	Femtocells	NFV & SDN	CR	mmWave
Adoption	High	High	High	Low	Future	Future
Appeared	2018	1987	2010	2012 / 2011	1999	2017
Bandwidth	Need	Need	Reallocate	Virtual / Reallocate	Reallocate	Reallocate
Capacity	✓		✓	✓	✓	✓
Coverage	✓	✓	✓	✓	✓	
Cost	High CAPEX High OPEX	Low CAPEX Low OPEX	Low CAPEX Low OPEX	Low CAPEX Low OPEX	Low CAPEX Low OPEX	High CAPEX High OPEX
Efficiency	✓	✓	✓	✓	✓	✓
Heterogeneous	✓		✓	✓	✓	
Interference	✓	✓		✓ NFV only		✓
Power Consumption	✓	✓		✓	✓	✓
Scalability	✓		✓	✓	✓	✓
Standardization	IEEE	IEEE	IEEE	Many / OpenFlow	IEEE	IEEE

Coverage: Each technology must meet the needs of the network, either by redistributing or by purchasing more resources.

Cost: The development of each technology has a specific valuation. The cost-valuation for each technology is characterized by CAPEX and OPEX. CAPEX is the capital expenditure relating to the initial purchase or investment in new equipment, a service, or a product. OPEX is the operating costs relating to the costs of maintenance, operation, and energy consumption e.tc.

Efficiency: The continuous development of technologies offers increased efficiency and better resource management in a network.

Heterogeneous: Heterogeneity exists between some technologies, for example, they can corporate together.

Interference: In some technologies, interferences are resulting in signal distortion.

Power Consumption: Each technology consumes electricity according to its requirements for functionality.

Scalability: Scalability is an vital feature for many technologies and means whether it is possible to expand a network by adding the right resources.

Standardization: The standardization of technologies means a description of the core functions they perform. According to Table I, some technologies are standardized, while others are not.

IV. Cost analysis and needs for upgrading to 5G network

A. *Prediction and assumptions of cost analysis in Shanghai.*

It is a fact that OMNs are considering ways in which migrating to a 5G network will be profitable or not. First, in [2], a high-level model is examined, which describes the factors on which it depends whether it is worth investing in 5G networks. The factors that contribute to the completion of the investment are the forecast of the number of users, the churn rate, the pricing model, and the cost forecast. Regarding the prediction of the number of users, a Bass forecasting model has been chosen, which explains well the market forecasting system for the types of products or services. It is achieved according to the formula [10]:

$$N(t) = M * \frac{1 - e^{-(t-t_0)(p+q)}}{1 + \frac{q}{p} * e^{-(t-t_0)(p+q)}} \quad (1)$$

where M is the Market Capacity, $p > 0$ is the innovation factor and symbolizes the probability of starting a service and is related to the initial size of the adopters, $q \geq 0$ is the imitation coefficient which refers to the size of the potential future subscribers or adopters' imitators. N(t) is the number of subscribers at time t and t_0 the initial time. From formula (1) and setting the appropriate coefficients p=0.009, q=0.42 and M=50000000 [2]. It appears that the number of adopters or subscribers until 2021 will remain low and then will increase exponentially until 2025, as shown in Figure 6.

The churn rate or transfer rate from provider to provider is used to calculate lost and new revenue. Also, the transfer rate from provider to the provider must be of the order of [4%, 10%] where the four represents the best case and ten the worst case [2], so it is concluded that when a user leaves not only the future revenue is lost, but also the resources acquired for the needs of the investment are spent.

About the pricing model, a volume-based pricing strategy is currently being used, which is not efficient for the 5G mobile network [11]. That is why a hybrid pricing strategy has been developed that is a combination of volume-based and value-based and aims at profitability. The volume-based pricing strategy includes parameters such as location, usage time, and content. The value-based pricing strategy includes parameters such as time, speed, and data. In addition, a prerequisite for OMNs is to find the optimal service price which has been approached in two perspectives and is transparency and PED.

OMNs collect information related to the cost of their services to properly assess subscriber behavior. Therefore, to minimize risk and uncertainty, two economic concepts are proposed, which help to predict the sales of volume-based data and to determine their prices. The first concept is Price Elasticity of Volume $E_V(P)$ and proportional to the price elasticity of demand and is defined as the percentage change in actual volume V per percentage change in unit price P. So, the following formula applies [2]:

$$E_V(P) = \lim_{P'-P \to 0} \frac{\frac{V'-V}{\frac{1}{2}(V+V')}}{\frac{P'-P}{\frac{1}{2}(P+P')}} = \frac{P \cdot \Delta V}{V \cdot \Delta P} \Rightarrow \frac{\Delta V}{P} = E_V(P) \cdot \frac{\Delta P}{P} \tag{2}$$

The second concept is Volume Elasticity of Revenue $E_R(V)$: defined as the percentage change in revenue R (charge) per percentage change in actual volume V. So, the following formula applies [2]:

$$E_R(V) = \lim_{V'-V \to 0} \frac{\frac{R'-R}{\frac{1}{2}(R+R')}}{\frac{V'-V}{\frac{1}{2}(V+V')}} = \frac{V \cdot \Delta R}{R \cdot \Delta V} \Rightarrow \frac{\Delta R}{R} = E_R(V) \cdot \frac{\Delta V}{V} \tag{3}$$

The two formulas (2) and (3) apply the following [2]: 1) for the subscriber, if $E_V(P) < 1$ means that the increase in volume demand contributes to the reduction of service prices, otherwise there is an increase in service prices. 2) For the provider, if $E_R(V) > 1$ means that that the increase in volume demand affects the increase in profits. In addition to the above, the following applies to PED:1) When the $|PED| < 1$ means that it is inelastic, specifically changes in price have little impact on the volume of service required. 2) When $|PED| > 1$ the means that it is elastic, specifically changes in price have a crucial impact. 3) When PED = 1 subscriber and the provider are benefitted.

Based on the results reported [2], the hybrid pricing model uses subscriber contents (usage time, content, location) and according to formulas (2) and (3) it is concluded that if the price of services decreases then the demand for subscribers increase and vice versa. Therefore, the ideal solution is when the PED is equal to one where both the user and the provider are benefitted. Finally, another conclusion that emerges is the effect of value and volume on profit at 5G, specifically 5G technologies are more beneficial than 4G, due to low cost and increased average data consumption.

Then, two scenarios have been developed for cost forecasting and estimation [2]: The first scenario concerns the creation of new Radio Access Technology (RAT) technology by replacing the previous BS equipment. The second scenario concerns the addition of new carriers and equipment to the existing RAT to reuse the previous BS equipment in conjunction with the latest equipment and a software upgrade.

Based on the results from [2], which relate to the predicted CAPEX and OPEX values, the scenario two is more efficient due to lower CAPEX, but for OPEX the two scenarios do not show a significant difference.

It is known that the demand for network traffic is proportional to the population density since the volume of data per subscriber does not depend on the growth scenario. According to [12], the estimamtion of the traffic demand for 1 km^2 in Shanghai shows that the level of demand corresponding to the average user data rates is 2.59 Mbps, which was obtained during the eight working hours. However, the formula (2) shows that it needs an output of 20 Gbps / km^2 [2].

A key issue is the modeling of indoor network investments using various scenarios to achieve the rate of 20 Gbps per 1 km^2. The main features to consider are cost, coverage, and capacity for each BS category. However, for all of these scenarios there are penetration losses due to a specific wall barrier, so to address this issue two possible solutions have been proposed: creating a denser 2.6 GHz network or developing a network using 10 MHz and 0.8 GHz bands within the zone in order to maximize internal coverage [2] [13].

Based on the results reported in [2], it appears that developing many new sites is costly as opposed to reusing existing sites, which are less expensive even if the sites are equipped with a new RAT. Also, the 5G mmW Pico Base Station (PBS) strategy provides the lowest cost but is limited in terms of network coverage, which results in that if the network is expanded, it will have a high overall CAPEX [14]. In addition, a more efficient strategy with low base station density is to use the LTE-A RAT carrier aggregation. Also, the option to develop new carrier aggregation sites is a more cost-effective solution than new site development scenarios, and the development of Femto Base Station (FBS) and Wi-Fi IEEE 802.11ac becomes more cost-effective when FBS deployment can support a large number of users. Finally, the above concludes that the main disadvantage of the 5G network is that the limited coverage resulting from the use of small cells such as femtocells, picocells developed with 5G mmW and Wi-Fi, and the lack of capacity limited by macro-cell sites and one solution is to combine Macro Base Station (MaBS), femtocells, 5G mmW PBS or Wi-Fi to achieve the right balance between cost, capacity, and coverage.

B. Prediction and assumptions of cost analysis in three cities.

The study carried out in Indonesia to upgrade the network to 5G includes the following cities Jakarta, Surabaya, and Medan. As mentioned above, using the Bass model which predicts the number of users of a market and applying the appropriate rates in formula (1), based on the data taken from [2], [3] where p=0.0267, q=0.3356 and M is 15000000 for Jakarta, 3500000 for Surabaya and 2500000 for Medan. The

TABLE II: Needs in BS and in Bandwidth per km^2 for each city.

Cities	BS Strategy						CAPEX (k$)	OPEX (k$)
	MaBS (4G LTE-A)		MetBS (5G mmW)		PBS (5G mmW)			
	Number	Band (MHz)	Number	Band (MHz)	Number	Band (MHz)		
Jakarta	35	40	6	400	6	400	4352.4	1094.4
Surabaya	16	40	3	400	3	400	1996.2	502.2
Medan	14	40	3	400	3	400	1756.2	442.2

accruing forecast results are shown in Figure 6, where the forecast number of subscribers is being increased by 2025 for all cities.

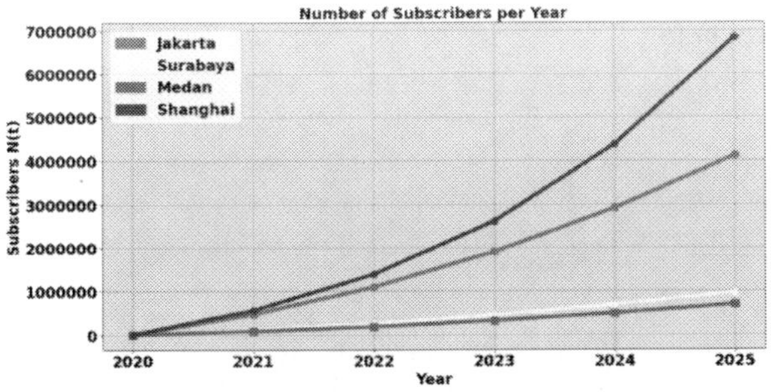

Fig. 6: Forecast of subscribers for six years for four cities [2], [3].

Besides, the different strategies used for the development of the 5G network are MaBS, Metro Base Station (MetBS), and PBS. The design of the network was carried out by dividing areas into three categories of network requirements based on the total demand, in high, medium, and low. According to [3], the results are summarized in Table II and relate to the needs of each city in BS, bandwidth, and used for the evaluation of CAPEX and OPEX. Therefore, Jakarta is the dominant city concerning the rest in terms of network needs and investments related to the development of 5G networks.

V. Conclusions & Future Work

Today there is a relatively large number of 5G IoT technologies. But to use a communication technology must be considered whether it is cost-effective and whether it is a solution to be implemented by providers. In this paper, the characteristics of 5G technologies are introduced and a comparison between them in numerous terms was studied. A forecast model for the development of a 5G mobile network in Shanghai was also studied, which includes the estimation of subscriber numbers, the churn rate, a hybrid pricing model, the estimation of traffic demand, the capacity, the CAPEX cost for the FBS, WiFi IEEE 802.11ac and the macro site's strategy with carrier aggregation and wall losses compensation. Finally, a high-demand model for the development of a 5G mobile network in the cities of Jakarta, Surabaya, and Medan was studied, in which the number of subscribers, the total CAPEX and OPEX costs for the BS strategies MaBS, MetBS, and PBS were estimated.

For future study, based on the above, further research is needed on energy consumption and the impact it will have on the profit and the further improvement of the 5G network. Also, there is a need for research for improving the heterogeneity, scalability, efficiency, and cost of 5G cellular technologies.

References

[1] C. Bouras, S. Kokkalis, A. Kollia, and A. Papazois, "Techno-economic analysis of mimo das in 5g," in *2018 11th IFIP Wireless and Mobile Networking Conference (WMNC)*, pp. 1–8, 2018.

[2] G. Smail and J. Weijia, "Techno-economic analysis and prediction for the deployment of 5g mobile network," in *2017 20th Conference on Innovations in Clouds, Internet and Networks (ICIN)*, pp. 9–16, March 2017.

[3] A. A. Kusuma and M. Suryanegara, "Upgrading mobile network to 5g: The technoeconomic analysis of main cities in indonesia," in *2019 16th International Conference on Quality in Research (QIR): International Symposium on Electrical and Computer Engineering*, pp. 1–6, 2019.

[4] C. Patel, M. Yavuz, and S. Nanda, "Femtocells [industry perspectives]," *IEEE Wireless Communications*, vol. 17, no. 5, pp. 6–7, 2010.

[5] D. Sinh, L. Le, L. Tung, and B. Lin, "The challenges of applying sdn/nfv for 5g & iot," in *14th IEEE-VTS Asia Pacific Wirel. Commun. Symp.(APWCS), Incheon, Korea*, 2017.

[6] C. Bouras, A. Kollia, and A. Papazois, "Sdn & nfv in 5g: Advancements and challenges," in *2017 20th Conference on innovations in clouds, internet and networks (ICIN)*, pp. 107–111, IEEE, 2017.

[7] A. Popescu, Y. Yao, M. Fiedler, and A. Popescu, "Communication mechanisms for cognitive radio networks," in *2013 IEEE International Conference on Pervasive Computing and Communications Workshops (PERCOM Workshops)*, pp. 429–434, IEEE, 2013.

[8] I. Filippini, V. Sciancalepore, F. Devoti, and A. Capone, "Fast cell discovery in mm-wave 5g networks with context information," *IEEE Transactions on Mobile Computing*, vol. 17, no. 7, pp. 1538–1552, 2017.

[9] C. Bouras, P. Fotakopoulou, and A. Kollia, "5g networks: Advancement and challenges," in *The Fifteenth International Conference on Wireless and Mobile Communications (ICWMC 2019)*, pp. 33–38, 2019.

[10] S. Sundqvist, L. Frank, and K. Puumalainen, "The effects of country characteristics, cultural similarity and adoption timing on the diffusion of wireless communications," *Journal of business research*, vol. 58, no. 1, pp. 107–110, 2005.

[11] N. et. al., "Rethinking flat rate pricing for broadband services," *White Paper, Cisco Internet Business Solutions Group*, 2012.

[12] T. et. al., "Is backhaul becoming a bottleneck for green wireless access networks?," in *2014 IEEE international conference on communications (ICC)*, pp. 4029–4035, IEEE, 2014.

[13] J. Markendahl and Ö. Mäkitalo, "A comparative study of deployment options, capacity and cost structure for macrocellular and femtocell networks," in *2010 IEEE 21st International Symposium on Personal, Indoor and Mobile Radio Communications Workshops*, pp. 145–150, IEEE, 2010.

[14] F. Khan and Z. Pi, "mmwave mobile broadband (mmb): Unleashing the 3–300ghz spectrum," in *34th IEEE Sarnoff Symposium*, pp. 1–6, IEEE, 2011.

Keep it Flat (KiF): Resource Management in Integrated Cloud-Fog Networks

Neam M. Farroukh
Computer Science Department
American University of Beirut
Beirut, Lebanon
Email: nmf14@mail.aub.edu

Mohamed Nassar
Computer Science Department
American University of Beirut
Beirut, Lebanon
Email: mn115@aub.edu.lb

Shady Elbassuoni
Computer Science Department
American University of Beirut
Beirut, Lebanon
Email: se58@aub.edu.lb

Haidar Safa
Computer Science Department
American University of Beirut
Beirut, Lebanon
Email: hs33@aub.edu.lb

***Abstract*—Fog computing extends the cloud services and brings them to the edge of the network. By taking advantage of edge devices that have sufficient resources (i.e., storage, compute, and bandwidth), the cloud becomes closer to the edge. The fog has been proved as a promising solution for avoiding unbearable latency and network capacity saturation with the proliferation of Internet of Things (IoT) end-devices. Lately, researchers have investigated the impact of cloud-fog cooperation on the performance of the network in terms of latency, network capacity and security. While the cloud can handle heavy-weight delay-tolerant tasks, the fog becomes in charge of all light-weight delay-sensitive tasks. In such integrated networks, resource management becomes a key challenge that must be addressed effectively. In this paper, we design and study two different resource management strategies at the fog layer: a flat one versus a clustered one. Both strategies are formalized as optimization problems and constrained by minimum resource allocation requirements, as well as Quality of Service (QoS) and privacy requirements. The comparison of the two strategies shows the superiority of the flat approach in terms of overall performance and fog delay, while the clustered approach results in lower number of overall tasks being rejected.**

***Keywords*—fog computing; resource management; security; latency; optimization.**

I. INTRODUCTION

Computing in general is an on-demand utility model where users opt to benefit from services without worrying about where these services are hosted or how they will be delivered. Cloud computing is a well established technology defined as a tool that provides ready-to-consume resources like CPU, I/O, and memory based on the users' demands. Lately, the number of smart end-devices, renowned as the Internet of Things (IoT), has been proliferating at a tremendous scale. Consequently, such a number of devices is going to produce trillion gigabytes of data [1]. Imagine this huge amount of data being sent to a centralized and far located cloud. This will cause network saturation and severe degradation in users' experience. Thus, cloud computing will lose its luster for latency-sensitive applications that require resources just in the vicinity.

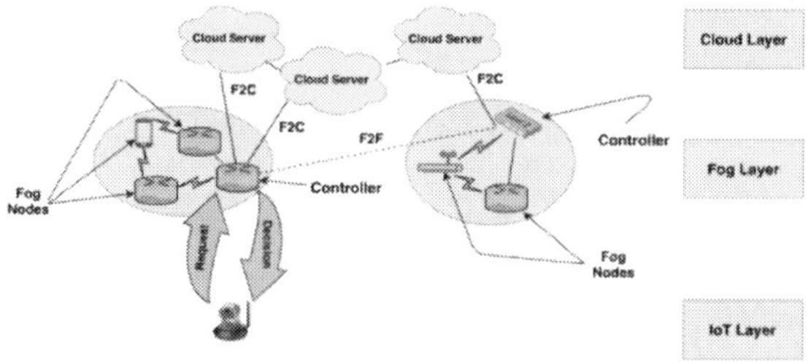

Figure 1. Network Architecture.

To address this issue and to meet the delay and mobility requirements of various IoT applications, it is necessary to have an intermediate control layer that resides between the end-devices and the far located cloud. This shifting from the core to the edge of the network is termed as edge computing. Subsequently, Cisco proposed Fog Computing (FC) in 2012 [2]. According to Cisco, the fog is just another cloud layer that is closer to the IoT devices. The fog extends the assets of the original cloud as storage, computing and networking services to the edge of the network by taking advantage of devices, e.g., access points, routers, that are rich in resources and located near end-devices. The aim of the fog is to provide lower latency and better user experience.

Resource management in fog computing is still considered as a key challenge due to the limited computational resources of edge devices and their heterogeneity. It is essential to address this challenge in a way that optimizes the fog resources while satisfying the QoS and privacy requirements of the IoT applications and their computational tasks. Therefore, the research question that we address in this paper is the following: *Given a backend cloud with "infinite" resources and considerable latency, a pool of fog nodes with different characteristics and arriving IoT tasks with different requirements, what is the best distributed and hierarchical strategy to support scheduling and assignment decisions?*

The rest of the paper is organized as follows: In Section II, we present background information. In Section III, we review related work. Section IV discusses the system model. The scheduling strategies are detailed in Section V. Simulation and experimental results are tailored in Section VI. Finally, Section VII concludes the paper and sheds the light on future work.

II. Background

Cloud computing replaced traditional hosting by enabling customers to rent compute resources like applications, storage and virtual machines through Internet. Similar to any other utility like water and electricity, users do not need to worry about managing and maintaining the utility infrastructure [3]. Cloud computing follows the Pay-as-You-Go usage model, which facilitates the scaling and customization of computing resources. The edge is any computing and network resources that reside between the end-users and the cloud data centers. The aim behind fog computing is to perform all the processing and computing at the proximity of data resources and thus to minimize the latency. An IoT device is any device that is able to transmit and receive data, and has an attached sensor or actuator. IoT devices are becoming part of every aspect of our lives since they give more control on routine work and personal tasks. For that, IoT applications have been deployed in various areas such as smart homes, smart cities, transportation, and healthcare. Examples of IoT applications are door locks, smart heating, coagulation testing in medicine and smart traffic signals.

III. Related Work

A task scheduling algorithm in the fog layer based on priority levels is proposed in [4]. The fog nodes in the fog layer can communicate with each other for efficient resource allocation and load balancing. The tasks are first processed in the fog layer based on their priority levels. Only when all the micro datacenters in the fog layer are saturated that tasks are propagated to the cloud layer. A more real-time oriented resource management approach is proposed in [5]. Factors, such as fluctuating relinquish probability of the customer, service type, service price, and variance of the relinquish probability are taken into account. In the proposed architecture, the fog node is capable of predicting the consumption of resources for a particular customer. The Distributed Earliest deadline First (DEF) algorithm was proposed in the context of symbiotic fog computing [6]. The presented model accounts for dynamic resources that arrive into the system for an interval of time and lend a fraction of their computing capacities against financial incentives. The assignment design is seen as a recommendation system. Given a task's requirements, multiple nodes can be recommended based on task similarity, node similarity and node previous performance on a similar task. A Fog Resource Selection algorithm (FResS) is proposed in [7]. The proposed model collects and maintains a repository of performance data in the form of execution logs, and uses the data to train a neural network model. When a new task arrives, the neural network model predicts the amount of required resources and uses it for task placement and estimating the execution time. The load balancing problem under the constraint of achieving the minimum latency in Fog networks is also addressed in [8]. A reinforcement Q-learning based decision-making process is proposed to find the optimal offloading decision with the assumption of unknown reward and transition functions. The proposed process allows fog nodes to offload an optimal number of tasks to the cloud. The lack of approaches for the leasing and releasing of resources in fog computing is also highlighted in [9]. A conceptual framework and an optimization problem for fog resource provisioning are presented. The optimization problem has the goal to provide delay-sensitive utilization of available fog nodes. The resource provisioning plan is generated by an orchestration node. We follow a similar approach in this paper. Our work is different from previous related work for two reasons: (1) we focus on the orchestration topology and differentiate between a flat one versus a clustered one, (2) we add abstract variables representing security and privacy to our model.

IV. System Model

Our model (Figure 1) is derived from [10]: the cloud manages the fog and handles the heavy-weight delay-tolerant IoT tasks, while the fog is responsible for handling the light-weight delay-sensitive IoT tasks. Each fog cluster is assigned a number of IoT devices that are directly connected to it. In the flat scenario, an IoT device can reach to any of the other fog clusters for requesting a task. In the clustered scenario, the task issued from an IoT device is directed to the controller of the cluster it is connected to. Fog controllers communicate to migrate a task from a cluster to another. Inter-cluster communication should be harnessed to achieve load balancing and efficient task distribution. Moreover, fog controllers communicate with the cloud to avoid fog saturation and offload tasks that are deemed heavy weight or delay-tolerant.

Each fog node f_j is represented as a profile vector $\{CPU_j, Memory_j, PM_j\}$ corresponding to its available CPU type and available Instructions Per Second (IPS), memory, and privacy, at time t, respectively. We omit t to simplify the notation. The privacy measure is a trust value representing the security and privacy strength of a fog node. Many approaches can be used to build such a trust model, [11] in particular. Each task T_i arriving at the fog layer is represented by a profile vector $\{CPU_i, Memory_i, SL_i, IC_i, Bytes_i, MAD_i, SC_i\}$. The entries in the vector correspond to the minimum required CPU type and available IPS, the minimum required memory, the minimum security level, the task instruction count, the task data size in bytes, the maximum allowed delay, and the scheduling class (priority level), respectively. The scheduling class is one if

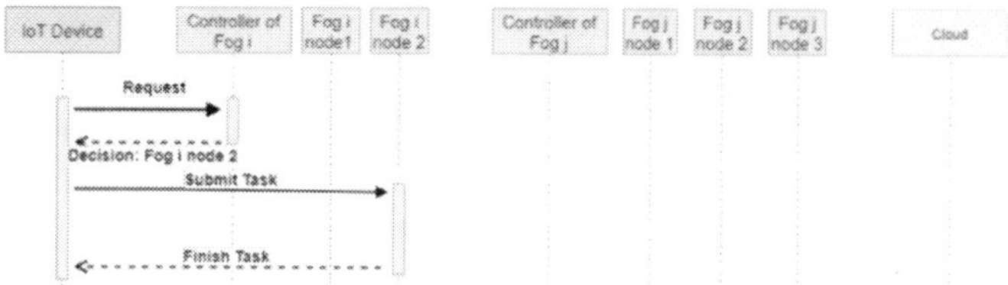

(a) Choosing a Local Fog Node.

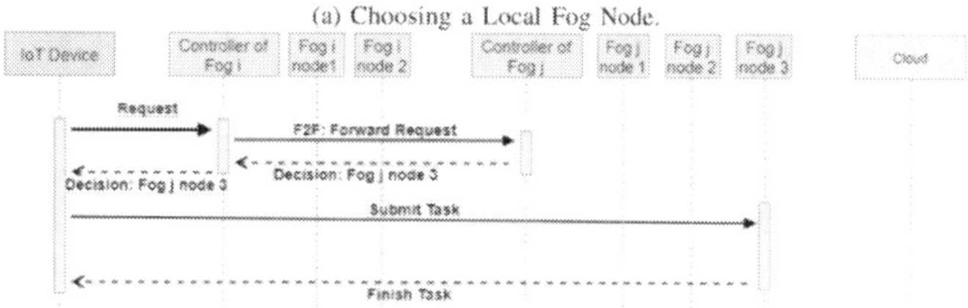

(b) Choosing a Local Node in another Fog.

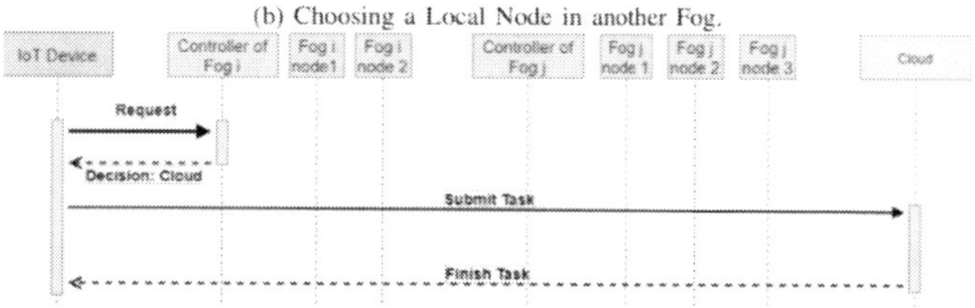

(c) Offloading Task to Cloud.

Figure 2. Three Possible Scenarios for an IoT task.

the task is delay tolerant and zero otherwise. The maximum allowed delay attribute determines the latency requirement of the task. Thus, a fog node can be assigned a task if the total time it takes to process the task along with the total transmission, routing and propagation delays do not exceed the maximum allowed delay attribute of the task. We represent the link between any two network devices, source s and destination d, by the profile vector $\{BW_{s,d}, PD_{s,d}\}$ corresponding to the upload bandwidth and propagation delay, respectively.

Each fog controller is logically connected to a set of IoT devices. The IoT device is homed with one or more fog controllers. Upon receiving a request from an IoT device, the controller's job is to take a decision on the best way to handle this task. The controller replies to the IoT source with the decision and additional information that helps proceeding with the task. As shown in Figure 2, three scenarios are possible:

(a) the controller predicts that the task can be accomplished by a local node and responds with the IP address of this node,
(b) the controller has a busy cluster, estimates that some extra delay is tolerable and forwards the task to a neighbor cluster's controller. Note that this can be done in an iterative way by forwarding the task and relaying the response to the client, or in a recursive way by directly responding with the IP address of the next fog controller.
(c) the controller decides that the task is delay-tolerant and not computationally affordable at the fog layer at this moment, the task can be offloaded to the cloud. The controller replies with IP address of the cloud service.

In case where the constraints cannot be fulfilled by any of these three scenarios, the task is rejected and the IoT device has to try at another time, or try another controller in the case of multi-homing.

V. The Task Allocation Strategies

Our formulation uses Integer Linear Programming (ILP) since our decision variables are discrete (0 or 1). ILP problems are NP-complete, however, efficient solvers can be used to deal with our formulations. For instance, we have used the *pywraplp* linear solver module from OR-Tools [12].

A. Flat-Based Fog Node Selection

In this variation, the controller has the full knowledge of the fog layer. It can build this knowledge by receiving periodic updates from the other controllers. The updates contain timely information about the available fog nodes and their capabilities. The controller has to keep measurements of the Round Trip Times (RTTs) for all the nodes. We define X_i^j as the decision variable for our optimization problem. $X_i^j = 1$ means that Task T_i is assigned to fog node f_j and 0 otherwise. In case where the output of the optimization is all-zeros decision variables, none of the reachable fog nodes is suitable for executing the task. If the scheduling class of the task is one, the decision will be to offload the task to the cloud, otherwise the task will be rejected. The Spare Time (ST_i^j) is the difference between the maximum allowed delay and the predicted total delay for node f_j (TD_i^j) as in (1) and (2).

$$ST_i^j = MAD_i - TD_i^j \tag{1}$$

$$ST_i^j \geq 0 \tag{2}$$

We denote P_i^j the difference between the minimum required privacy/security level for task T_i and the privacy measure PM_j of the fog node f_j as in (3) and (4).

$$P_i^j = SL_i - PM_j \tag{3}$$

$$P_i^j \geq 0 \tag{4}$$

Assuming that a fog controller receives a batch of tasks $i = 1, 2, .., N$ and has a set of reachable nodes $j = 1, 2, ..., M$, the controller has to solve for a sequence of objective functions. Each function finds an integer vector assignment X_i that maximizes the weighted average of the spare time and the privacy difference as controlled by a variable α. The sequence of objective functions is depicted in (5) and is subject to constraints (6), (7), (8), (9), and (10).

$$\begin{aligned} \text{maximize} \quad & \sum_{j=1}^{M} (\alpha ST_i^j + (1-\alpha) P_i^j) * X_i^j \\ & \forall i \in \{1, \dots, N\} \end{aligned} \tag{5}$$

Each task can be assigned to exactly one fog node. This constraint is formalized in (6). To guarantee (2) and (4), we add the constraints in (7) and (8).

$$\begin{array}{lll} \sum_{j=1}^{M} X_i^j \leq 1 & & \forall i \\ X_i^j \in \mathbb{Z} & \forall j & \forall i \\ X_i^j \geq 0 & \forall j & \forall i \end{array} \tag{6}$$

$$\sum_{j=1}^{M}(ST_i^j * X_i^j) \geq 0 \quad \forall i \tag{7}$$

$$\sum_{j=1}^{M}(P_i^j * X_i^j) \geq 0 \quad \forall i \tag{8}$$

Moreover, we need to meet the resources requirements of CPU and memory of the task by comparing it to the dynamic remaining (available) CPU and memory at the node as in (9) and (10).

$$\sum_{j=1}^{M}(\text{CPU}_j^R - \text{CPU}_i) * X_i^j \geq 0 \quad \forall i \tag{9}$$

$$\sum_{j=1}^{M}(\text{Mem}_j^R - \text{Mem}_i) * X_i^j \geq 0 \quad \forall i \tag{10}$$

B. Clustered-Based Fog Node Selection

A second variation is to go along the clustered topology. We allow the controller to select the best cluster instead of directly searching for the best node. For this purpose, we represent each fog cluster k by a profile vector: $\{AvgCPU_k, AvgMem_k, AvgPM_k\}$. This vector specifies the cluster's average available CPU, average available memory, and average privacy measure, respectively. These values are computed based on the profile vectors of the fog nodes belonging to each cluster. Each fog controller periodically receives timely cluster profiles from the other controllers. The profile can also be retrieved in a pull manner. This method reduces the size of the optimization problem as we are currently looking for the best cluster rather than the best fog node. We define Y_i^k as the decision variable for the cluster C_k and task T_i. $Y_i^k = 1$ means that cluster C_k is selected for task T_i, and the request will be forwarded to its fog controller. If C_k happens to be the controller's cluster, a local fog node is selected. If the output of the optimization is the all-zeros vector, the decision is solely based on the task scheduling class. If it is delay tolerant, we offload it to the cloud, otherwise, we reject it.

The Spare Time (ST_i^k) is the difference between the maximum allowed delay and the predicted total delay for a node f_j in cluster C_k in average, as in (11) and (12).

$$ST_i^k = MAD_i - TD_i^k \tag{11}$$

$$ST_i^k \geq 0 \tag{12}$$

We denote P_i^k the difference between the minimum required privacy/security level for task T_i and the average privacy measure of the cluster C_k, as in (13) and (14).

$$P_i^k = SL_i - AvgPM_k \tag{13}$$

$$P_i^k \geq 0 \tag{14}$$

The sequence of objective functions is defined in (15) and is subject to constraints (16), (17), (18), (19), and (20).

$$\text{maximize} \quad \sum_{j=1}^{M}(\alpha ST_i^k + (1-\alpha)P_i^k) * X_i^k \quad \forall i \in \{1, \dots, N\} \tag{15}$$

α is a hyper-parameter used to control the weights of privacy versus QoS. Each task can be assigned to exactly one cluster node as in (16). To guarantee (12) and (14), we add the constraints in (17) and (18), respectively.

$$\begin{array}{lll} \sum_{k=1}^{K} Y_i^k \leq 1 & & \forall i \\ Y_i^k \in \mathbb{Z} & \forall k & \forall i \\ Y_i^k \geq 0 & \forall k & \forall i \end{array} \tag{16}$$

$$\sum_{k=1}^{K}(ST_i^k * Y_i^k) \geq 0 \quad \forall i \tag{17}$$

$$\sum_{k=1}^{K}(P_i^k * Y_i^k) \geq 0 \quad \forall i \tag{18}$$

The selected cluster also needs to meet the resources requirements of CPU and memory of the task by comparing them to the dynamic available average CPU and average memory at the cluster, as in (19) and (20).

$$\sum_{k=1}^{K}(\text{AvgCPU}_k^R - \text{CPU}_i) * Y_i^k \geq 0 \quad \forall i \tag{19}$$

$$\sum_{k=1}^{K}(\text{AvgMem}_k^R - \text{Mem}_i) * Y_i^k \geq 0 \quad \forall i \tag{20}$$

C. Delay Calculation

The Total Delay (TD) is an important optimisation factor since it represents the QoS contribution to the decision taken by the controller. The total (or end-to-end delay) for a given task is the time difference between the moment when the task has been issued and the moment marking the end of the task execution. The controller has to estimate the round trip time between the IoT device and each of the fog nodes in the selection pool. We describe the delay calculation for the flat versus clustered scenarios:

Flat. The delay for task T_i is the sum of the delay at the controller C_j and the delay at the selected fog node f_j:

$$TD_i^j = d_{C_j} + d_{f_j} \tag{21}$$

Clustered. The delay for task T_i is the sum of the delay at the controller C_j, the delay at the chosen cluster's controller C_k and the delay at the selected fog node $f_{k'}$:

$$TD_i^j = d_{C_j} + d_{C_k} + d_{f_{k'}} \tag{22}$$

Other delay calculations are also possible. For instance, a task can be forwarded from a cluster to another more than one time. The task can be offloaded to the cloud, or rejected. We do not consider the delay calculation for these cases in our work. Note that we overloaded the notation of a cluster C_k to denote the controller at this cluster. We only consider the iterative scenarios.

The delay at a controller C_k or at fog node j is calculated as the sum of four terms:

$$d = d_{\text{transmission}} + d_{\text{propagation}} + d_{\text{processing}} + d_{\text{queuing}} \tag{23}$$

Note that some of these terms are also composed as a sum of multiple delays of the same nature. For example, $d_{\text{transmission}}$ involves the round trip transmission. $d_{\text{propagation}}$ involves the round trip propagation as well. The profile vectors $\{BW_{s,d}, PD_{s,d}\}$ $\forall s$ $\forall d$ are used in these calculations.

VI. Simulation and Experimental Results

To implement and analyze our proposed variations, we used the Yet Another Fog Simulator (YAFS) [13]. Preliminary simulations showed that a value of $\alpha = 0.9$ achieves a good balance in between privacy and QoS. Four types of topology were created, each containing 5, 10, 15, and 20 clusters, respectively. Each fog cluster consists of a number of fog nodes, having a single controller and a number of IoT devices directly connected to it. Each cluster in every type of topology has a small number of fog nodes, since as mentioned in [10], small scale fogs would result in better performance metrics. In the simulation, the number of fog nodes belonging to a cluster ranges between 4 and 8. Each fog cluster has a range between 3 to 5 IoT devices directly connected to it. To set the characteristics of the fog nodes, we used values from real servers. As for the privacy measure attribute, we sampled values from a uniform distribution. We assumed that each cluster has a range of privacy measures. The privacy measure for any fog node belonging to the cluster is within this specified range. For example, assume having fog cluster k with privacy measure range between 0.3 and 0.5. Each value in the range represents a trust value. The trust value can be obtained in reality based on a security and privacy assessment tool as described in [11]. The CPU and IPS parameters of the cloud are set higher than any value being set to the fog nodes. This is due to the fact that the cloud has higher processing capabilities than any fog node. As for the connections, the bandwidth between an IoT device and a fog node could be either 54 Mbits/s as in wireless 802.11g networks or 100 Mbits/s as in fast Ethernet. The bandwidth between the controllers, which act as routers for IoT devices, and the cloud is set to 10 Gbits/s. While the bandwidth between fog controllers is set to 100 Mbits/s. We adopted these values from the topology created in [14]. We created five sets each containing 100 different types of tasks. For every set of tasks and each type of topology (which differs by the number of clusters available), four experiments were performed. In each experiment, different simulation times were set to increase the number of tasks being generated.

The results were evaluated based on the average fog delay which is the delay of tasks being executed in the fog layer, the average total delay, the number of tasks being rejected, and the number of tasks being offloaded to the cloud. We present the results for when a low and a high number of tasks are generated based on simulator time (138 tasks and 816 tasks on average). Our goal is to evaluate the behavior of both variations when the number of tasks being generated in the network increases. The results for both approaches are shown in Figure 3. The results of the flat based approach show that the number of tasks being rejected and offloaded to the cloud and the average fog and total delay decreases as the number of fog clusters in the network increases from 5 to 20. This decrease is due to the higher probability of task to node assignment with the increase in the number of fog nodes that the generated IoT tasks can be assigned to in the network. As for the results of the clustered based approach, it shows that the average fog delay and number of tasks being rejected and offloaded to the cloud decreases as the number of clusters available in the network increases. The average total delay starts to decrease as the number of clusters increases to reach 15 then increases as this number reaches 20. This can be justified by the increase in the number of clusters that the controller has to examine when selecting a suitable fog node for assignment. Comparing results of both variations in Figure 3 shows that the flat based variation is more applicable when having a large scale fog topology consisting of 20 or more clusters. This can be justified by the fact that this variation gives lower values for the fog and total delays as desired and decreases the number of tasks being propagated to higher layers (cloud). On the other hand, when having an average scale topology of around 15 clusters, both variations behave the same and thus both are applicable.

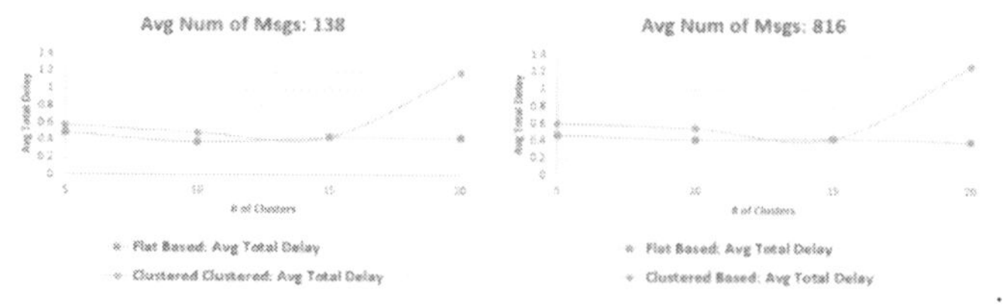

(a) Average Total Delay.

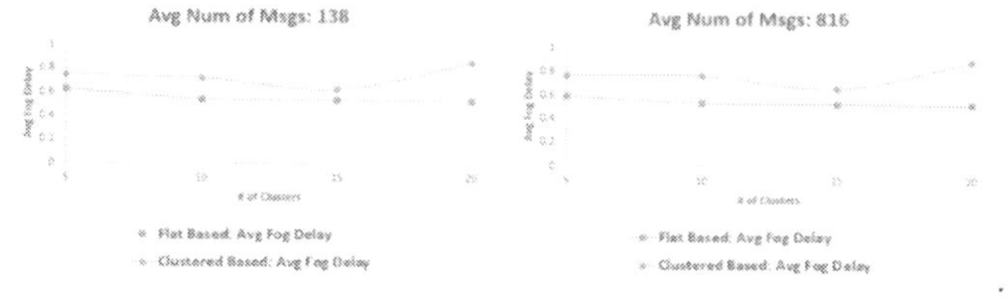

(b) Average Fog Delay.

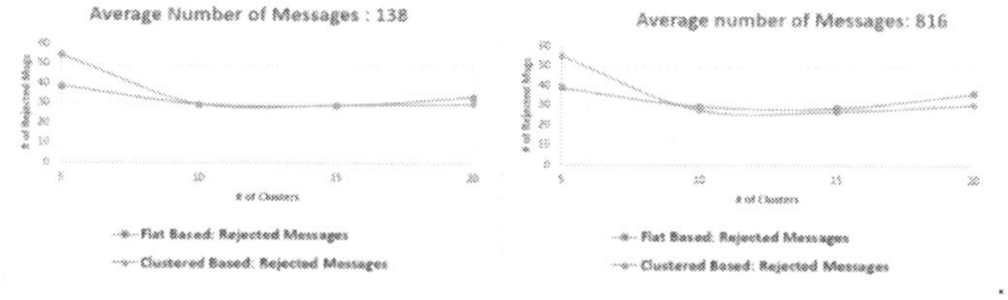

(c) Rejected Tasks.

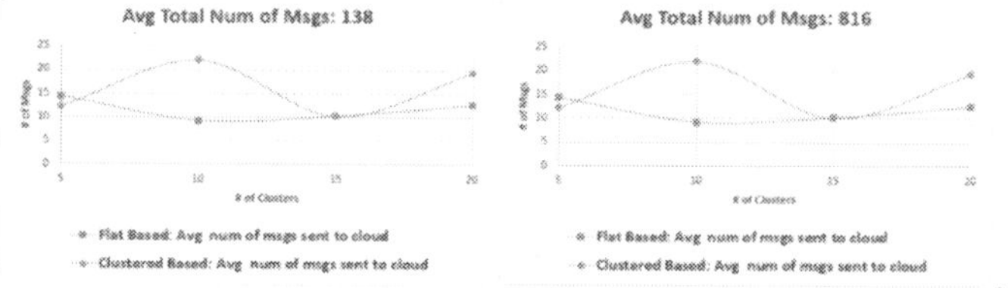

(d) Offloaded Tasks to Cloud.

Figure 3. Flat Based vs. Clustered Based.

Figure 4 and Figure 5 show the impact of including and excluding the privacy and security factors from the formalized optimization problem. The figures show that a security aware variation leads to a higher probability of task rejection and task propagation to higher layers. For repeatability, we provide the

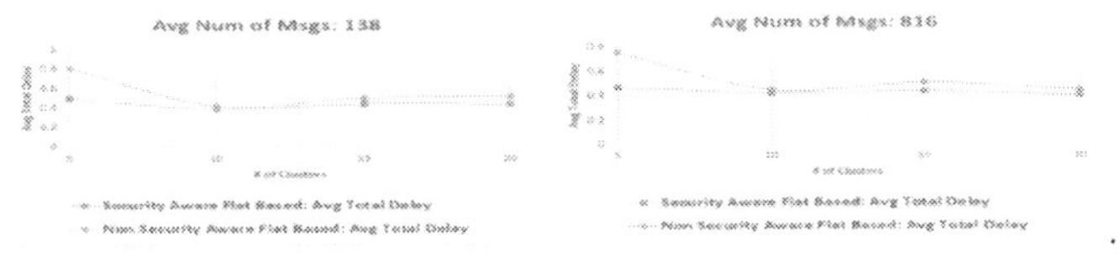

(a) Average Total Delay.

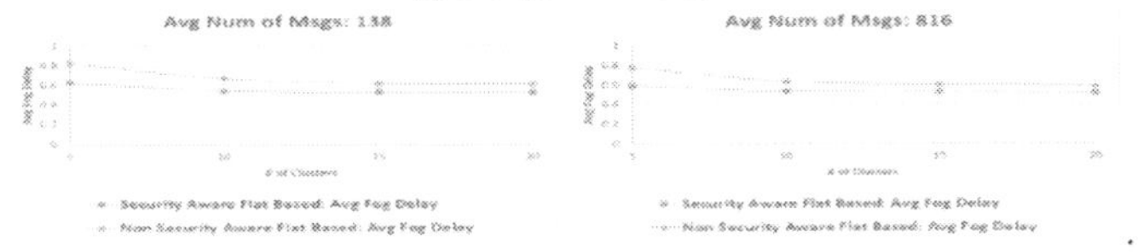

(b) Average Fog Delay.

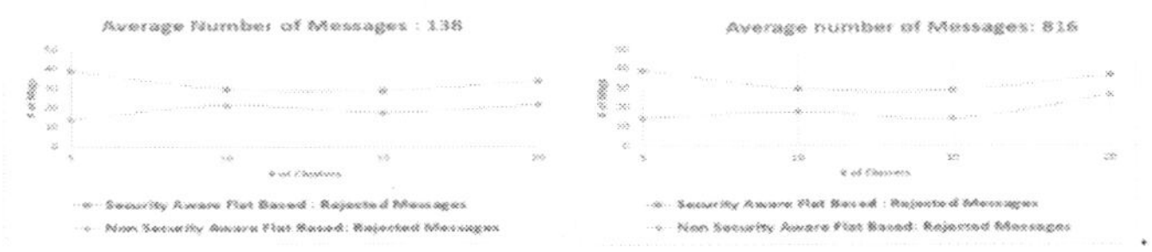

(c) Rejected Tasks.

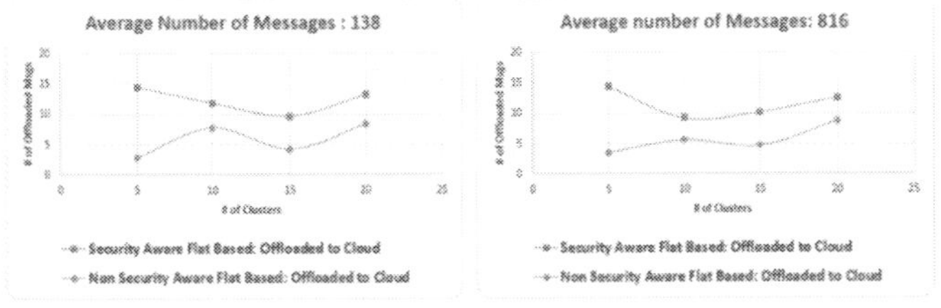

(d) Offloaded Tasks to Cloud.

Figure 4. Flat Based Fog Selection: Security Aware vs. Non Security Aware.

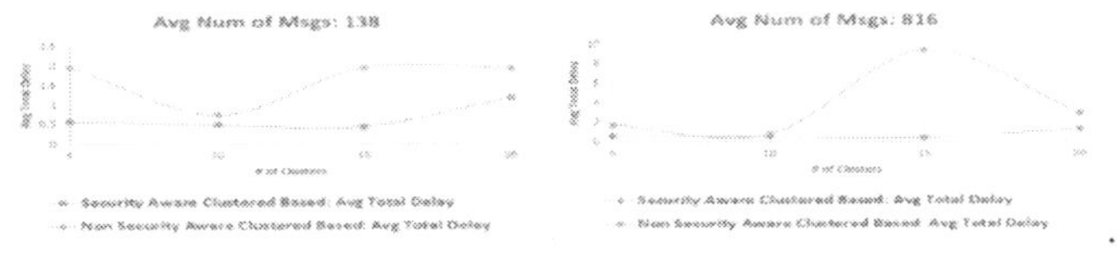

(a) Average Total Delay.

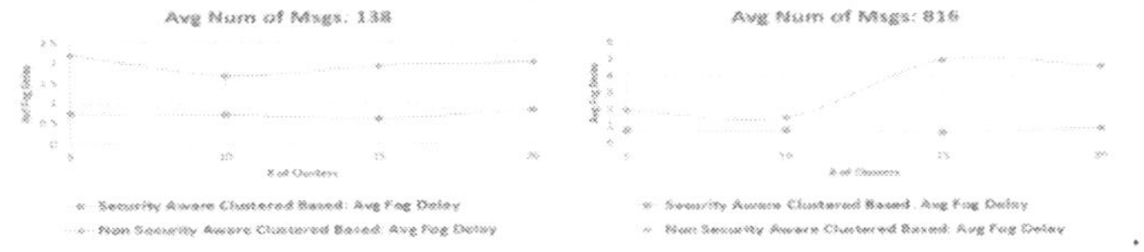

(b) Average Fog Delay.

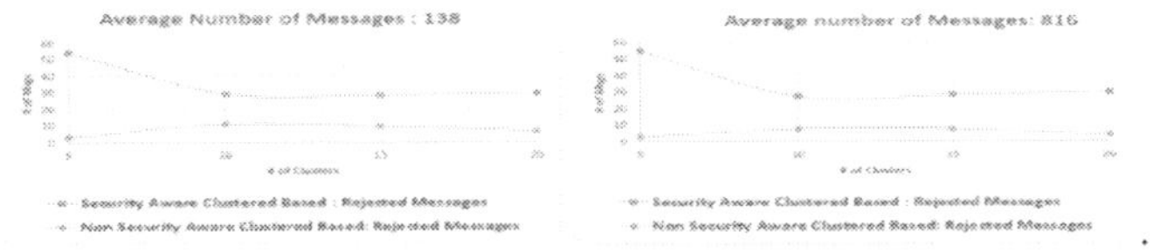

(c) Rejected Tasks.

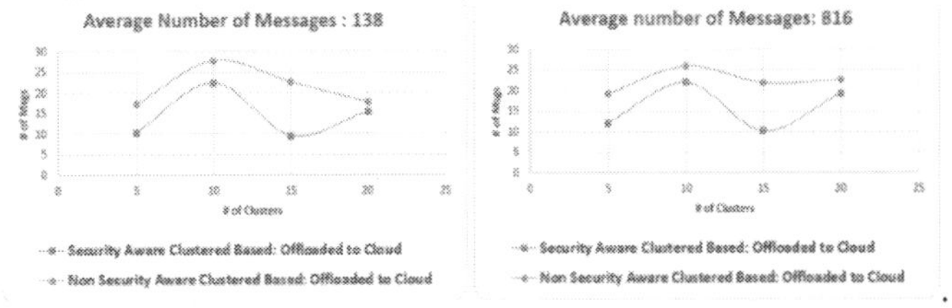

(d) Offloaded Tasks to Cloud.

Figure 5. Clustered Based Fog Selection: Security Aware vs. Non Security Aware.

source code of all experiments at [15].

VII. Conclusion and Future Work

In this paper, we proposed, designed and studied two run-time resource allocation strategies, flat-based fog node selection and clustered-based fog node selection.

The results showed that the flat-based strategy permits better performance, especially when the number of clusters in the fog increases. We attribute this result to the potential number of layers of indirection required for demanding IoT tasks. The flat approach promotes a "take it or leave it" behaviour.

In future work, we intend to provide more insights on solving the optimisation problems and the scalability of the solving method for large-scale settings. We want to report measurements on using different solvers, their solving time and accuracy. We will also consider the comparison between solving the optimization problems in batch mode and in direct (one-by-one) mode. We will also consider refining our model to include inter-cluster communication and the exchange of updates. We would like to assess our approaches based on real-world data, and explore whether using reinforcement learning can lead to better recommendations for task allocation in the fog.

Acknowledgements

This work was partially supported by a grant from the university research board of the American University of Beirut (URB-AUB-2020/2021).

References

[1] B. Varghese, N. Wang, D. S. Nikolopoulos, and R. Buyya, "Feasibility of fog computing," *arXiv preprint arXiv:1701.05451*, 2017.

[2] S. Yi, C. Li, and Q. Li, "A survey of fog computing: concepts, applications and issues," in *Proceedings of the 2015 workshop on mobile big data*. ACM, 2015, pp. 37–42.

[3] Y. Jadeja and K. Modi, "Cloud computing-concepts, architecture and challenges," in *2012 International Conference on Computing, Electronics and Electrical Technologies (ICCEET)*. IEEE, 2012, pp. 877–880.

[4] T. Choudhari, M. Moh, and T.-S. Moh, "Prioritized task scheduling in fog computing," in *Proceedings of the ACMSE 2018 Conference*, 2018, pp. 1–8.

[5] M. Aazam and E.-N. Huh, "Dynamic resource provisioning through fog micro datacenter," in *2015 IEEE international conference on pervasive computing and communication workshops (PerCom workshops)*. IEEE, 2015, pp. 105–110.

[6] V. Kochar and A. Sarkar, "Real time resource allocation on a dynamic two level symbiotic fog architecture," in *2016 Sixth International Symposium on Embedded Computing and System Design (ISED)*. IEEE, 2016, pp. 49–55.

[7] N. Mostafa, I. Al Ridhawi, and M. Aloqaily, "Fog resource selection using historical executions," in *2018 Third International Conference on Fog and Mobile Edge Computing (FMEC)*. IEEE, 2018, pp. 272–276.

[8] J.-y. Baek, G. Kaddoum, S. Garg, K. Kaur, and V. Gravel, "Managing fog networks using reinforcement learning based load balancing algorithm," in *2019 IEEE Wireless Communications and Networking Conference (WCNC)*. IEEE, 2019, pp. 1–7.

[9] O. Skarlat, S. Schulte, M. Borkowski, and P. Leitner, "Resource provisioning for iot services in the fog," in *2016 IEEE 9th international conference on service-oriented computing and applications (SOCA)*. IEEE, 2016, pp. 32–39.

[10] L. Peng, A. R. Dhaini, and P.-H. Ho, "Toward integrated cloud–fog networks for efficient iot provisioning: Key challenges and solutions," *Future Generation Computer Systems*, vol. 88, pp. 606–613, 2018.

[11] R. Shaikh and M. Sasikumar, "Trust model for measuring security strength of cloud computing service," *Procedia Computer Science*, vol. 45, pp. 380–389, 2015.

[12] L. Perron and V. Furnon, "Or-tools," Google, https://developers.google.com/optimization/ [accessed July 2021].

[13] I. Lera, C. Guerrero, and C. Juiz, "Yafs: A simulator for iot scenarios in fog computing," *arXiv preprint arXiv:1902.01091*, 2019.

[14] A. Yousefpour, G. Ishigaki, and J. P. Jue, "Fog computing: Towards minimizing delay in the internet of things," in *2017 IEEE international conference on edge computing (EDGE)*. IEEE, 2017, pp. 17–24.

[15] N. Farroukh, "KiF Github Repository," https://github.com/NeamFarroukh/Keep-it-Flat-KiF-Resource-Management-in-Integrated-Cloud-Fog-Networks.

Dynamic and Opportunistic Millimeter-Wave Spectrum Access in 5G New Radio Multi-Operator Cognitive Radio Networks

Rony Kumer Saha
Radio and Spectrum Laboratory
KDDI Research, Inc.
2-1-15 Ohara, Fujimino-shi, Saitama, Japan
email: ro-saha@kddi-research.jp

Abstract—**In this paper, we present a Dynamic and Opportunistic Spectrum Access (DOSA) technique that allows access to the static and equal licensed 28 GHz millimeter-wave (mmWave) spectrum of each Fifth-Generation (5G) New Radio (NR) Mobile Network Operator (MNO) to every other MNOs in a country to serve their respective in-building Small Cells (SCs) subject to avoiding Co-Channel Interference (CCI). We derive the system-level Average Capacity (CA), Spectral Efficiency (SE), and Energy Efficiency (EE) performance metrics for an arbitrary number of NR MNOs. With extensive simulation results and analyses for four MNOs, we show that the proposed DOSA can provide CA and SE 2.5 times and improve EE by about 60% as compared to that of the traditional Static and Equal Spectrum Access (SESA) technique. Moreover, DOSA can achieve both SE and EE requirements expected for the Sixth-Generation (6G) mobile networks by reusing the countrywide mmWave spectrum for 46.87% fewer buildings of SCs than that required by SESA.**

Keywords—5G; 28 GHz; in-building; small cell; millimeter-wave; multi-operator; new radio; dynamic spectrum access.

I. INTRODUCTION

Traditionally, the mobile radio spectrum specified for a country is allocated statically in an equal amount to each of its Mobile Network Operator (MNO) regardless of the inequality in the number of subscribers of one MNO from another. This uniform distribution of spectrum causes one MNO to allocate more spectrum than necessary, whereas the other MNO suffers from the lack of a sufficient amount of spectrum, resulting in low spectrum utilization. Due to this reason, such Static and Equal Spectrum Allocation (SESA) is no longer considered effective. Recently, Cognitive Radio (CR) has been considered an effective technology to address this issue. In CR, the spectrum is given access to the secondary User Equipment (UE) with the primary UE to use unused spectra of the primary UE opportunistically, resulting in improving spectrum utilization.

Several research studies have addressed the spectrum allocation problem in CR systems. For example, to address constraints with SESA, an underlay CR access technique in Saha [1] and an interweave shared-use model in Saha [2] have been presented to share the unused millimeter-wave (mmWave) spectrum of one MNO to another. However, both studies are limited by the assumption of a specific number of MNOs in a country. In this paper, we address this constraint by relaxing this assumption and present a Dynamic and Opportunistic Spectrum Access (DOSA) technique for an arbitrary number of MNOs to share the 28 GHz spectrum opportunistically with in-building Small Cells (SCs) of each Fifth-Generation (5G) New Radio (NR) MNO with that of other MNOs in a country.

The paper is organized as follows. In Section II, the system model, including the system architecture and the proposed DOSA technique, is presented. We formulate the problem in Section III. Section IV covers the performance results of the proposed technique where the Spectral Efficiency (SE) and Energy Efficiency (EE) performances are compared with that of the prospective Sixth-Generation (6G) mobile systems. We conclude the paper in Section V.

II. SYSTEM MODEL

A. *System Architecture*

A system architecture consisting of an arbitrary O number of 5G NR MNOs in a country is considered. Each MNO comprises three Base Stations (BSs), including Macrocell BSs (MBSs), Picocell BSs (PBSs), and Small Cell BSs (SBSs). An SBS of each MNO is located in each apartment of any building, and each SBS can serve one Small Cell UE (SUE) at a time. SBSs operate in the 28 GHz, whereas MBSs and PBSs operate in the 2 GHz, bands. Assuming similar architecture of all MNOs, Figure 1 shows the system architecture of MNO 1.

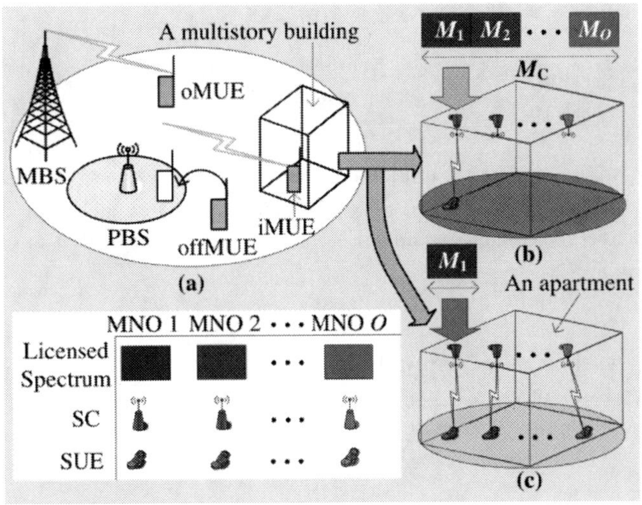

Figure 1. (a) System architecture of MNO 1 and SBSs of MNO 1 with the shared mmWave spectrum of other O-1 MNOs (b) maximum (c) none. oMUE, offMUE, and iMUE denote, respectively, outdoor, offloaded, and indoor macrocell UEs.

B. *Proposed DOSA Technique*

The proposed DOSA technique can be stated as follows. *Static allocation of an equal amount of mmWave spectrum to a*

5G NR MNO x in the primary level can be reallocated in the secondary level to SBSs of another MNO y in a building l as long as no UE of x exists within l to avoid Co-Channel Interference (CCI) between SBSs of x and y.

Let $\boldsymbol{O}$ denote a set of 5G NR MNOs in a country such that $o \in \{1, 2, ..., O\}$. Let each MNO is allocated to an equal amount of 28 GHz spectrum, denoted as M in Resource Blocks (RBs) where an RB=180 kHz. To analyze the performance, we consider that the occurrence (i.e., either presence or absence) of an SUE of each MNO within an apartment is equally likely over an observation period of $|\boldsymbol{T}| = Q$ such that any combination of the occurrence of SUEs of all MNOs happens with a probability of $Q/2^{O-1}$. The reallocated spectrum to an SUE of MNO o can be expressed as a set of $\{0, M, ..., (n \times M)\}$ with each component scaled by a Binomial coefficient $\mathbf{C}(n,k)$ of row $n = O-1$ of the left-justified Pascal's triangle [3] corresponding to $n \geq k \geq 0$. For example, the minimum reallocated spectrum of 0 and the maximum reallocated spectrum of $n \times M$ occur for an SUE of o, respectively, for no absence (Figure 1(c)) and no presence (Figure 1(b)) of SUEs of MNOs $\boldsymbol{O}\backslash o$ in an apartment of a building.

III. PROBLEM FORMULATION

Let M_{C} denote the countrywide mmWave spectrum for all 5G NR MNOs. Let P_{MC}, P_{PC}, and P_{SC} denote the transmission power of an MBS, a PBS, and an SBS, respectively for each MNO o. Let each MNO has the same number of MBSs S_{M}, PBSs S_{P}, and SBSs S_{F} per building. By Shannon's formula, a link throughput at RB i in TTI t in bps per Hz is given by [4],

$$\sigma_{t,i}(\rho_{t,i}) = \begin{cases} 0, & \rho_{t,i} < -10\,\mathrm{dB} \\ \beta \log_2\left(1 + 10^{(\rho_{t,i}(\mathrm{dB})/10)}\right), & -10\,\mathrm{dB} \leq \rho_{t,i} \leq 22\,\mathrm{dB} \\ 4.4, & \rho_{t,i} > 22\,\mathrm{dB} \end{cases} \quad (1)$$

where β denotes implementation loss factor. Let M_o^{MC} in RBs denote the spectrum of an MBS of MNO o such that the average capacity of an MBS can be given as follows.

$$\sigma_o^{\mathrm{MC}} = \sum_{t \in \boldsymbol{T}} \sum_{i=1}^{M_o^{\mathrm{MC}}} \sigma_{o,t,i}(\rho_{o,t,i}) \quad (2)$$

where σ and ρ are responses of MNO o over M_o^{MC} RBs in $t \in \boldsymbol{T}$. For DOSA, the capacity of SBS s of MNO o is given by [5],

$$\sigma_{\mathrm{DOSA},o,s} = \sum_{t \in \boldsymbol{T}} \sum_{i=1}^{M} \sigma_{t,i,o}(\rho_{t,i,o}) + \sum_{k=1}^{O-1} \mathbf{C}(O-1,k) \left(\sum_{t=1}^{(Q/2^{O-1})} \sum_{i=1}^{kM} \sigma_{k,t,i,o}(\rho_{k,t,i,o}) \right) \quad (3)$$

Assume that each building has similar indoor characteristics, so that by linear approximation, the countrywide average capacity, SE, and EE of MNOs O for L buildings of SBSs are given, respectively, by,

$$\sigma_{\mathrm{DOSA},O} = \sum_{o=1}^{O} \left(\sigma_o^{\mathrm{MC}} + L \sum_{s=1}^{S_{\mathrm{F}}} \sigma_{\mathrm{DOSA},o,s} \right) \quad (4)$$

$$\gamma_{\mathrm{DOSA},O} = \frac{\sigma_{\mathrm{DOSA},O}}{\left(\left(M_{\mathrm{C}} + \sum_{o=1}^{O} M_o^{\mathrm{MC}} \right) \times Q \right)} \quad (5)$$

$$\varepsilon_{\mathrm{DOSA},O} = \frac{O \times (L S_{\mathrm{F}} P_{\mathrm{SC}} + S_{\mathrm{P}} P_{\mathrm{PC}} + S_{\mathrm{M}} P_{\mathrm{MC}})}{\left(\frac{\sigma_{\mathrm{DOSA},O}}{Q} \right)} \quad (6)$$

If DOSA is not employed, the system-level average capacity, SE, and EE of all MNOs for SESA are given, respectively, by,

$$\sigma_{\mathrm{SESA},O} = \sum_{o=1}^{O} \left(\sigma_o^{\mathrm{MC}} + L \sum_{s=1}^{S_{\mathrm{F}}} \sum_{t \in \boldsymbol{T}} \sum_{i=1}^{M} \sigma_{o,s,t,i}(\rho_{o,s,t,i}) \right) \quad (7)$$

$$\gamma_{\mathrm{SESA},O} = \frac{\sigma_{\mathrm{SESA},O}}{\left(\left(M_{\mathrm{C}} + \sum_{o=1}^{O} M_o^{\mathrm{MC}} \right) \times Q \right)} \quad (8)$$

$$\varepsilon_{\mathrm{SESA},O} = \frac{O \times (L S_{\mathrm{F}} P_{\mathrm{SC}} + S_{\mathrm{P}} P_{\mathrm{PC}} + S_{\mathrm{M}} P_{\mathrm{MC}})}{\left(\frac{\sigma_{\mathrm{SESA},O}}{Q} \right)} \quad (9)$$

IV. PERFORMANCE RESULT AND COMPARISON

Selected parameters and assumptions are given in Table I. Detailed parameters and assumptions can be found in [1]-[2]. From Figure 2(a) for a single building of SBSs of all MNOs, it can be observed that the proposed DOSA can provide 2.5 times average capacity and SE as compared to that of the traditional SESA. The additional 1.5 times improvement in the performance of the capacity and SE comes from reallocating mutually the licensed mmWave spectrum of one NR MNO to another. Due to the same reason, DOSA improves EE by about 60% as compared to SESA.

TABLE I. DEFAULT PARAMETERS AND ASSUMPTIONS

Parameters and Assumptions	Value
Spectrum bandwidth per MNO	50 MHz (28GHz) and 10 MHz (2GHz)
Number of MNOs (O), Transmission direction	4, downlink
SBSs per building, UE per SBS	48, 1

Figures 2(b)-2(c) show SE and EE responses of DOSA and SESA techniques when reusing the same countrywide mmWave spectrum to more than one building of SBSs (i.e., L>1) located over the macrocell coverage. Note that SE increases linearly, whereas EE improves negative-exponentially, with an increase in L. This can be justified by the expressions of SE and EE in (8) and (9), respectively. Moreover, from Figures 2(b)-2(c), it can be found that the proposed DOSA technique outperforms SESA with a great margin in terms of SE and EE. Furthermore, it can be observed from Figures 2(b)-2(c) that the proposed DOSA technique can achieve both SE (10 times of 5G, i.e., 370 bps/Hz) and EE (10-100 times of 5G, i.e., 0.03μJ/bit) requirements ([6]-[9])

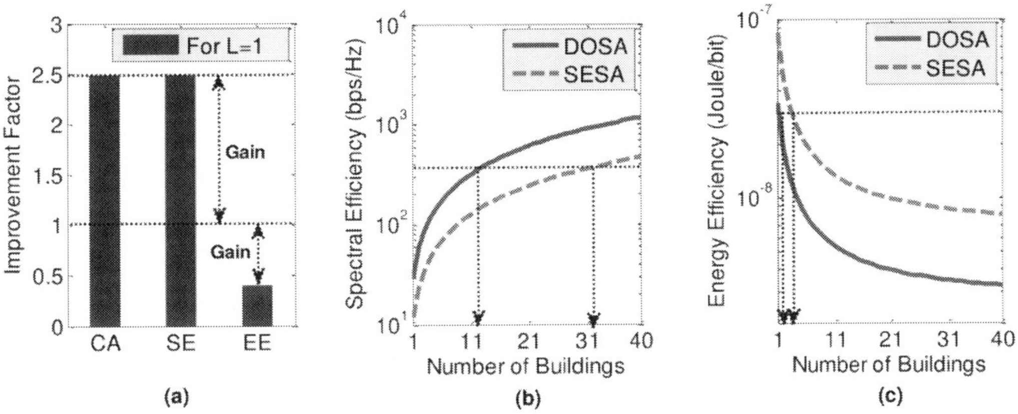

Figure 2. (a) Performance improvement factors, (b) SE, and (c) EE responses.

expected for the 6G mobile networks by reusing the countrywide mmWave spectrum for 46.87% less number of buildings of SBSs than that required by SESA.

V. CONCLUSION

A Dynamic and Opportunistic Spectrum Access (DOSA) technique has been presented to allow opportunistic and dynamic access to the static and equal licensed 28 GHz mmWave spectrum of one NR MNO to that of the other in a country to serve their in-building SCs. System-level Average Capacity (CA), Spectral Efficiency (SE), and Energy Efficiency (EE) performance metrics for an arbitrary number of NR MNOs are derived. For an example case of four NR MNOs, the outperformance of DOSA in CA, SE, EE, as well as satisfying both SE and EE requirements expected for the future 6G mobile networks, over that of SESA have been shown.

REFERENCES

[1] R. K. Saha, "Underlay Cognitive Radio Millimeter-Wave Spectrum Access for In-Building Dense Small Cells in Multi-Operator Environments Toward 6G," Proc. 2020 23rd International Symposium on Wireless Personal Multimedia Communications (WPMC), Okayama, Japan, 2020, pp. 1-6, doi: 10.1109/WPMC50192.2020.9309471.

[2] R. K. Saha, "Interweave Shared-Use Model for Dynamic Spectrum Access in Millimeter-Wave Mobile Systems for 6G," Proc. 2020 IEEE 92nd Vehicular Technology Conference (VTC2020-Fall), Victoria, BC, Canada, 2020, pp. 1-6, doi: 10.1109/VTC2020-Fall49728.2020.9348671.

[3] G Kallós, "A Generalization of Pascal's Triangle using Powers of Base Numbers," Annales Mathematiques Blaise Pascal, vol. 13, pp. 1-15, 2006.

[4] J. Ellenbeck, J. Schmidt, U. Korger, and C. Hartmann, "A Concept for Efficient System-Level Simulations of OFDMA Systems with Proportional Fair Fast Scheduling," Proc. 2009 IEEE Globecom Workshops, Honolulu, HI, 2009, pp. 1-6, doi: 10.1109/GLOCOMW.2009.5360729.

[5] R. K. Saha, "Dynamic Allocation and Sharing of Millimeter-Wave Spectrum with Indoor Small Cells in Multi-Operator Environments Toward 6G" unpublished.

[6] Z. Zhang et al., "6G Wireless Networks: Vision, Requirements, Architecture, and Key Technologies," IEEE Vehicular Technology Magazine, vol. 14, pp. 28-41, 2019, doi: 10.1109/MVT.2019.2921208.

[7] S. Chen, Y. -C. Liang, S. Sun, S. Kang, W. Cheng, and M. Peng, "Vision, Requirements, and Technology Trend of 6G: How to Tackle the Challenges of System Coverage, Capacity, User Data-Rate and Movement Speed," IEEE Wireless Communications, vol. 27, no. 2, pp. 218-228, April 2020, doi: 10.1109/MWC.001.1900333.

[8] C.-X. Wang et al., "Cellular Architecture and Key Technologies for 5G Wireless Communication Networks," IEEE Communications Magazine, vol. 52, no. 2, pp. 122-130, February 2014. doi: 10.1109/MCOM.2014.6736752.

[9] G. Auer et al., "How Much Energy is Needed to Run a Wireless Network?," IEEE Wireless Communications, vol. 18, no. 5, pp. 40-49, October 2011, doi: 10.1109/MWC.2011.6056691.

On Operating 5G New Radio Indoor Small Cells in the 60 GHz Unlicensed Band

Rony Kumer Saha
Radio and Spectrum Laboratory
KDDI Research, Inc.
2-1-15 Ohara, Fujimino-shi, Saitama, Japan
email: ro-saha@kddi-research.jp

***Abstract*—In this paper, we present a time-domain coexistence technique to operate small cells of a Fifth-Generation (5G) New Radio (NR) operator in the 60 GHz band with the access points (APs) of an IEEE 802.11ad/ay, also termed as Wireless Gigabit (WiGig), operator located within a multistory building. Small cells are dual-band enabled operating in the 60 GHz unlicensed and 28 GHz licensed bands. Moreover, we assume that small cells are not Listen-Before-Talk (LBT) feature enabled. Hence, to avoid blocking the transmission of APs of the WiGig operator, an interference avoidance scheme is developed in the time-domain that divides the air time in the 60 GHz band between the incumbent WiGig APs (WiAPs) and 5G NR Unlicensed (NR-U) small cells. We derive average capacity, Spectral Efficiency (SE), and Energy Efficiency (EE) metrics for 5G NR-U small cells. With system-level simulation results, the average capacity, SE, and EE responses for three variants of the 5G NR, namely 5G NR Standalone, 5G NR-U Standalone, and 5G NR-U Anchored are evaluated. It has been shown that NR-U Anchored can achieve the maximum average capacity and EE, whereas NR-U Standalone can achieve the maximum SE when coexisting with a WiGig operator. Because the 60 GHz unlicensed band is present in both schemes, this signifies the importance of operating a 5G NR operator in the unlicensed bands.**

Keywords*—*5G; 28 GHz; 60 GHz; millimeter-wave; unlicensed band; new radio; small cell; coexistence.

I. Introduction

Introduction of the Fifth-Generation (5G) New Radio (NR) to serve a large volume of data traffic has increased the burden on the licensed spectrum of a Mobile Network Operator (MNO) [1]. An effective solution to address this problem is to serve data traffic in the unlicensed bands along with the existing licensed bands. The 3rd Generation Partnership Project (3GPP) has recently taken initiatives to operate cellular networks in the unlicensed bands with the Long-Term Evolution (LTE) [2]. However, technologies such as the IEEE 802.11 based WiFi have already been in operation globally over a wide range of unlicensed bands, including 2.4 GHz, 5 GHz, and 60 GHz bands [3]. This necessitates developing a technique that can allow both cellular networks and incumbent WiFi networks to coexist.

So far now, several research studies have addressed WiFi and cellular network coexistence such as LTE and 5G NR. For example, the authors in [4] addressed the coexistence of 5G NR Unlicensed (NR-U) and WiFi in the 6 GHz band, and in [5], the authors addressed the coexistence of WiFi with the beam based 5G NR-U in the millimeter-wave (mmW) bands. Moreover, in [1], by implementing a mode selection procedure in 5G NR, the authors investigated the coexistence performance of the 5G NR-U and WiFi networks. Moreover, to address the coexistence between WiFi and cellular systems, several studies proposed to apply the Almost Blank Subframe (ABS) based Enhanced Intercell Interference Coordination (eICIC) technique. For example, using the concept of ABS, the authors in [6] proposed a scheme to coexist LTE with WiFi systems in an unlicensed band. Similarly, the authors in [7] proposed the LTE muting mechanism to mute the transmission of LTE in *a* certain number of subframes of every 5 subframes during which the channel can be used by WiFi users. Furthermore, an ABS-based coexistence scheme to avoid co-channel interference between small cells and WiFi systems was presented by the authors in [8].

However, to operate in unlicensed bands, certain regulatory requirements, for example, using Listen-Before-Talk (LBT) and transmission power limits, are needed to be maintained [3]. Hence, to address the transmission power requirement in the unlicensed bands, 5G NR-U is expected to be operated in the small cells deployed indoors. In this regard, 60 GHz unlicensed band is considered an attractive unlicensed band for NR-U [5] [9] due to its wider contiguous bandwidth availability. This implies that NR-U will aggregate the licensed 28 GHz or 38 GHz spectrum and the 60 GHz unlicensed spectrum [9]. However, studies on the NR-U operating in both the licensed and unlicensed mmW spectra for in-building small cells are in the early stage, and detailed analysis and evaluation of major performance metrics, including capacity, Spectral Efficiency (SE), and Energy Efficiency (EE), for NR-U is yet to be addressed, which we aim to contribute in this paper.

In line with so, we derive and evaluate average capacity, SE, and EE responses of in-building 5G NR-U small cells that are considered coexisting with the IEEE 802.11ad/ay, also termed as Wireless Gigabit (WiGig), where each small cell operates in both the 28 GHz licensed and the 60 GHz unlicensed bands. In doing so, we present a time-domain coexistence technique to avoid co-channel interference by modifying the concept of ABS. A system-level performance analysis is carried out for a number of variants of 5G NR, including 5G NR Standalone operating only in the 28 GHz band, 5G NR-U Standalone operating only in the 60 GHz band, and 5G NR-U Anchored operating in both the 28 GHz and 60 GHz bands.

We organize the paper as follows. in Section II, system architecture and time-domain coexistence techniques are discussed. In Section III, we derive average capacity, SE, and EE metrics for each variant of 5G NR-U. In Section IV, we carry out system-level performance analysis in terms of average capacity, SE and EE by varying the amount of transmission time of small cells under each variant of 5G NR-U. We conclude the paper in Section V. A list of notations is given in Table I.

TABLE I. A LIST OF NOTATIONS.

Notation	Description
T_1 and T_2	The optimum value of the number of FBSs for NR-U and WiGig, respectively
λ_1 and λ_2	The average rate of arrival of NR-U and WiGig, respectively
T_{FPP}	An FBS Pattern Period
t and i	Index of a transmission time interval and a resource block, respectively
T	Simulation run time
σ_{MB}	Total capacity served by transceiver 1 and transceiver 2 of all SBSs in the building of operator NR-U
$\sigma_{cap}^{NR\text{-}U,Anch}$, $\sigma_{SE}^{NR\text{-}U,Anch}$, and $\sigma_{EE}^{NR\text{-}U,Anch}$	The system-level aggregate capacity, SE, and EE for NR-U Anchored, respectively
$\sigma_{cap}^{NR,Std}$ and $\sigma_{cap}^{NR\text{-}U,Std}$	The system-level average capacity for NR Standalone and NR-U Standalone, respectively
P_{28GHz} and P_{60GHz}	The transmission power of transceiver 1 and transceiver 2, respectively, of each SBS
$P_{2GHz,MC}$ and $P_{2GHz,PC}$	The transmission powers of a macrocell and a picocell, respectively
M_{2GHz} , M_{28GHz} , and M_{60GHz}	The number of resource blocks of 2 GHz, 28 GHz, and 60 GHz spectra, respectively, of the NR-U operator
S_F	The number of SBSs of the NR-U operator
S_M	The number of macrocell base stations of the NR-U operator
S_P	The number of picocell base stations per macrocell of the NR-U operator

II. SYSTEM ARCHITECTURE AND TIME-DOMAIN COEXISTENCE

Figure 1 shows the system architecture consisting of a 5G NR-U operator and a WiGig operator. Each NR-U operator has three types of base stations (BSs), namely macrocell BSs (MBSs), picocell BSs (PBSs), and small cell BSs (SBSs). We assume that all SBSs and WiGig Access Points (APs) are deployed only within a building, one per apartment per operator. An SBS or a WiGig Access Point (WiAP) serves only one User Equipment (UE) at a time. Each SBS is dual-band enabled such that the 28 GHz licensed band operates at its transceiver 1, and the 60 GHz unlicensed band operates at its transceiver 2. Note that each WiAP operates at the 60 GHz band. Moreover, we assume that any MBS or any PBS of the NR-U operates in the 2 GHz band.

Since both SBSs and WiAPs operate in the 60 GHz unlicensed band, co-channel interference is generated. To coexist both SBSs and WiAPs in the 60 GHz unlicensed band, we present the following coexistence technique. An SBS can share the 60 GHz spectrum with an incumbent WiAP by allocating them in different time slots to avoid simultaneous access by either the SBS or the WiAP to the 60 GHz spectrum using the well-established concept termed as ABS in LTE. We consider modifying ABSs to avoid transmitting control signals as well during ABSs resulting in Fully Blank Subframes (FBSs) as shown in Figure 2.

An optimal amount of time to transmit data by NR-U operator in terms of Transmission Time Intervals (TTIs) can be defined by considering the average number of UEs of each operator over a certain time period T. According to [10], the arrival process of UEs of NR-U and WiGig operators can be assumed to follow the Poisson processes with a mean λ_1 and λ_2 , respectively, over T. An optimum value of the number of FBSs (which is strictly a positive integer) over an FBS pattern period (FPP) T_{FPP} of 5G NR-U operator can be obtained as follows.

$$T_1 = \left\lceil (\lambda_1 / (\lambda_1 + \lambda_2)) T_{FPP} \right\rceil \quad (1)$$

Since UEs of different Radio Access Technologies (RATs) are allocated orthogonally in the time-domain, i.e., in different TTIs, no collision from simultaneous transmissions from UEs of both RATs occurs. Moreover, cellular technologies use a centralized scheduling-based approach to transmit continuously without sensing the channel status such that, based on the values of λ_1 and λ_2 over T, an effective allocation of FBSs using (1) can be performed for UEs of both NR-U and WiGig operators. Furthermore, (1) can be generalized for any arbitrary number of NR-U and WiGig operators, which we show in Appendix I. In general, an increase in the number of active operators, either NR-U or WiGig, causes a corresponding decrease in the number of subframes allocated to each operator for a given T_{FPP} and vice versa.

Remark 1: The value of T_{FPP} plays a significant role in the allocation of subframes to each operator. If T_{FPP} is less than the total number of NR-U and WiGig operators, there would be a high probability that one or more operators might not get scheduled over each T_{FPP}. This problem would get worsen if all operators are active over any T_{FPP}, particularly, for delay-sensitive traffic. Hence, to ensure that each active NR-U, as well as WiGig, operator is scheduled in every T_{FPP} to address the delay-sensitive traffic, it is recommended that the value of T_{FPP} should be chosen such that each active operator is scheduled at least once per T_{FPP}, i.e., T_{FPP} (in terms of TTIs) should be at least equal to the sum of the number of NR-U and WiGig operators. As a general rule, a higher value of T_{FPP} with respect to the total number of operators results in a better performance in subframe allocations to NR-U and WiGig operators.

III. PERFORMANCE METRICS ESTIMATION

Let S_F denote the maximum number of SBSs of the NR-U operator in the building. Assume that there are S_M macrocells and S_P picocells per macrocell. Let M_{2GHz} , M_{28GHz} , and M_{60GHz} denote, respectively, the number of Resource Blocks (RBs) of 2 GHz, 28 GHz, and 60 GHz spectra of NR-U operator where an RB is equal to 180 kHz. Let transceiver 1 and transceiver 2 of each SBS operate at the transmission power of $P_{28\text{GHz}}$ and $P_{60\text{GHz}}$, respectively, whereas the transmission powers of a macrocell and a picocell are denoted as $P_{2\text{GHz,MC}}$ and $P_{2\text{GHz,PC}}$, respectively.

Let $\boldsymbol{T}$ denote simulation run time with the maximum time of Q (in time step each lasting 1 ms) such that $\boldsymbol{T}=\{1, 2, 3, \ldots, Q\}$ and hence $|\boldsymbol{T}|=Q$. Let $\boldsymbol{T}_1$ denote the number of FBSs of NR-U operator over $\boldsymbol{T}$. Let t_1 denote an FBS of NR-U operator such that $t_1 \in \boldsymbol{T}_1$. Using Shannon's capacity formula, a link throughput at RB=i in TTI=t for NR-U operator in bps per Hz for the Signal-to-Noise-Plus-Interference Ratio (SINR) $\rho_{t,i}$ is given by [11],

$$\sigma_{t,i}\left(\rho_{t,i}\right)=\begin{cases}0, & \rho_{t,i}<-10\,\text{dB}\\ \beta\log_2\left(1+10^{\left(\rho_{t,i}(\text{dB})/10\right)}\right), & -10\,\text{dB}\le\rho_{t,i}\le 22\,\text{dB}\\ 4.4, & \rho_{t,i}>22\,\text{dB}\end{cases} \quad (2)$$

where β=0.6 denotes the implementation loss factor that takes into account modulation and coding schemes, for example.

The capacity of macrocell UEs of NR-U operator can be expressed as

$$\sigma_{2\text{GHz}}=\sum_{t=1}^{Q}\sum_{i=1}^{M_{2\text{GHz}}}\sigma_{t,i}\left(\rho_{t,i}\right) \quad (3)$$

where σ and ρ are the throughput and the corresponding SINR responses over $M_{2\text{GHz}}$ RBs of all macro UEs in $t\in\boldsymbol{T}$ for NR-U operator.

Now, transceiver 1 of all SBSs in the building operates at the 28 GHz spectrum in $t\in\boldsymbol{T}$ such that the capacity served by transceiver 1 of all SBSs in the building is given by,

$$\sigma_{28\text{GHz}}^{\text{Trans 1}}=\sum_{s=1}^{S_F}\sum_{t\in\boldsymbol{T}}\sum_{i=1}^{M_{28\text{GHz}}}\sigma_{s,t,i}\left(\rho_{s,t,i}\right) \quad (4)$$

Similarly, transceiver 2 of all SBSs in the building operates at the 60 GHz spectrum in $t_1\in\boldsymbol{T}_1$ such that the capacity served by transceiver 2 of all SBSs of NR-U is given by,

$$\sigma_{60\text{GHz}}^{\text{Trans 2}}=\sum_{s=1}^{S_F}\sum_{t_1\in\boldsymbol{T}_1}\sum_{i=1}^{M_{60\text{GHz}}}\sigma_{s,t,i}\left(\rho_{s,t,i}\right) \quad (5)$$

So, the total capacity served by transceiver 1 and transceiver 2 of all SBSs in the building of operator NR-U is given by,

$$\sigma_{\text{MB}}=\sigma_{28\text{GHz}}^{\text{Trans 1}}+\sigma_{60\text{GHz}}^{\text{Trans 2}} \quad (6)$$

Due to a short distance between a UE and its SBS and a low transmission power of an SBS, we assume similar indoor signal propagation characteristics for both mmWs of the NR-U operator. So, by linear approximation, the system-level average aggregate capacity for the 5G NR-U Anchored is given by,

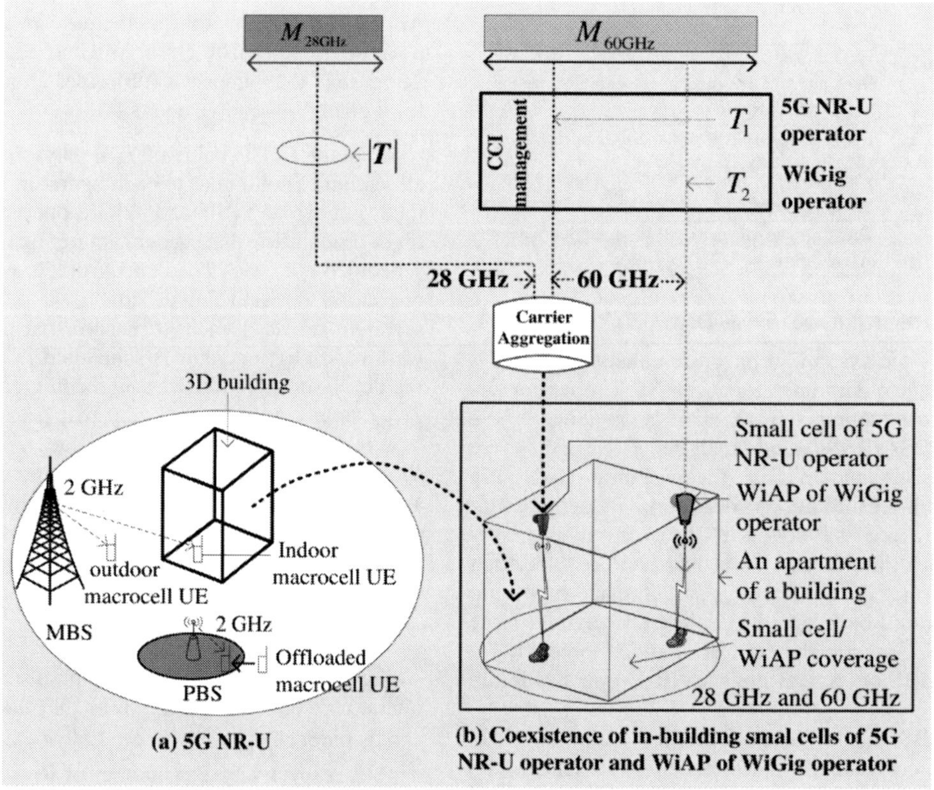

Figure 1. System architecture for the coexistence of small cells of a 5G NR-U operator with WiAPs of a WiGig operator.

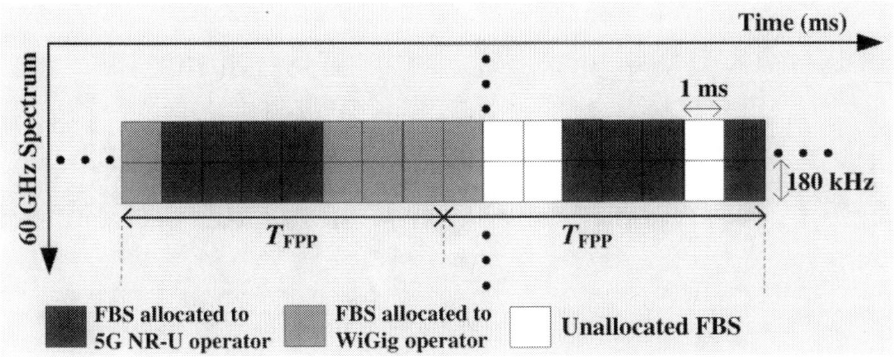

Figure 2. CCI avoidance in time-domain using FBSs.

$$\sigma_{cap}^{NR\text{-}U,Anch} = \sigma_{2GHz} + \sigma_{MB} \quad (7)$$

The SE is then given by,

$$\sigma_{SE}^{NR\text{-}U,Anch} = \sigma_{cap}^{NR\text{-}U,Anch} \Big/ \left(\left(M_{2GHz} + M_{28GHz} \right) \times Q \right) \quad (8)$$

Similarly, the EE (i.e., the energy required per bit transmission) is given by,

$$\sigma_{EE}^{NR\text{-}U,Anch} = \left(\begin{array}{l} \left(L \times S_F \times \left(P_{28GHz} + P_{60GHz} \right) \right) + \\ \left(S_P \times P_{2GHz,PC} \right) + \left(S_M \times P_{2GHz,MC} \right) \end{array} \right) \Big/ \left(\sigma_{cap}^{NR\text{-}U,Anch} / Q \right) \quad (9)$$

It is to be noted that for the SE estimation, only the licensed spectra, i.e., 2 GHz and 28 GHz spectra, of the NR-U operator are considered due to paying the licensing fee by the respective operator to use these bands. Now, 5G NR Standalone and 5G NR-U Standalone operate only in the licensed and unlicensed bands, respectively. The system-level average capacity for NR Standalone and NR-U Standalone can be expressed, respectively, as follows.

$$\sigma_{cap}^{NR,Std} = \sigma_{2GHz} + \sigma_{28GHz}^{Trans\ 1} \quad (10)$$

$$\sigma_{cap}^{NR\text{-}U,Std} = \sigma_{2GHz} + \sigma_{60GHz}^{Trans\ 2} \quad (11)$$

Now, following (8) and (9), SE and EE can be expressed using (10) for NR Standalone and (11) for NR-U Standalone.

IV. Performance Result and Evaluation

Table II shows selected simulation parameters and assumptions. Detailed parameters and assumptions can be found in [12] [13]. Transmission time is varied to evaluate the performance of 5G NR-U small cells when applying the proposed technique as given below.

TABLE II. SIMULATION PARAMETERS AND ASSUMPTIONS

Parameters and Assumptions			**Value**
Number of 5G NR-U and WiGig operators, respectively			1, 1
Spectrum bandwidth of 5G NR-U operator		2 GHz	10 MHz (for an MBS and PBSs)
		28 GHz	50 MHz (for transceiver 1 of all SBSs)
		60 GHz	100 MHz (for transceiver 2 of all SBSs and WiAPs)
Number of cells	Macrocells, picocells, and small cells		1, 2, and 48
Path loss	MBS and a UE[1]	Outdoor macrocell UE	PL(dB)=15.3 + 37.6 $\log_{10}R$, R is in m
		Indoor macrocell UE	PL(dB)=15.3 + 37.6 $\log_{10}R + L_{ow}$, R is in m and L_{ow}=20 dB
	PBS and a UE[1]		PL(dB)=140.7+36.7 $\log_{10}R$, R is in km
	SBS and a UE[1,2]	28 GHz	PL(dB)=61.38+17.97 $\log_{10}R$, R is in m
		60 GHz	PL(dB)=68+21.7$\log_{10}(R)$, R in m
Total base station transmit power (dBm)	Macrocell[1] and picocell[1]		46 and 37
	Small cell operating in 28 GHz[1]		19
	Small cell operating in 60 GHz[1]		17.3
Co-channel small-scale fading model[1]	2 GHz		Frequency selective Rayleigh
	28 GHz		no small-scale fading effect
	60 GHz		no small-scale fading effect
3D multistory building and SBS models (square-grid apartments)			A single building, 6 floors, 8 apartments per floor, 1 SBS and 1 WiAP per apartment, and 10×10 m² area of an apartment
Scheduler, traffic model[2], Type of SBSs			Proportional Fair, full buffer, and Closed Subscriber Group femtocell BSs
TTI[1], FPP, and PF scheduler time constant (t_c)			1 ms, 8 ms, and 100 ms
Total simulation run time			8 ms

taken [1]from [12], [2]from [13].

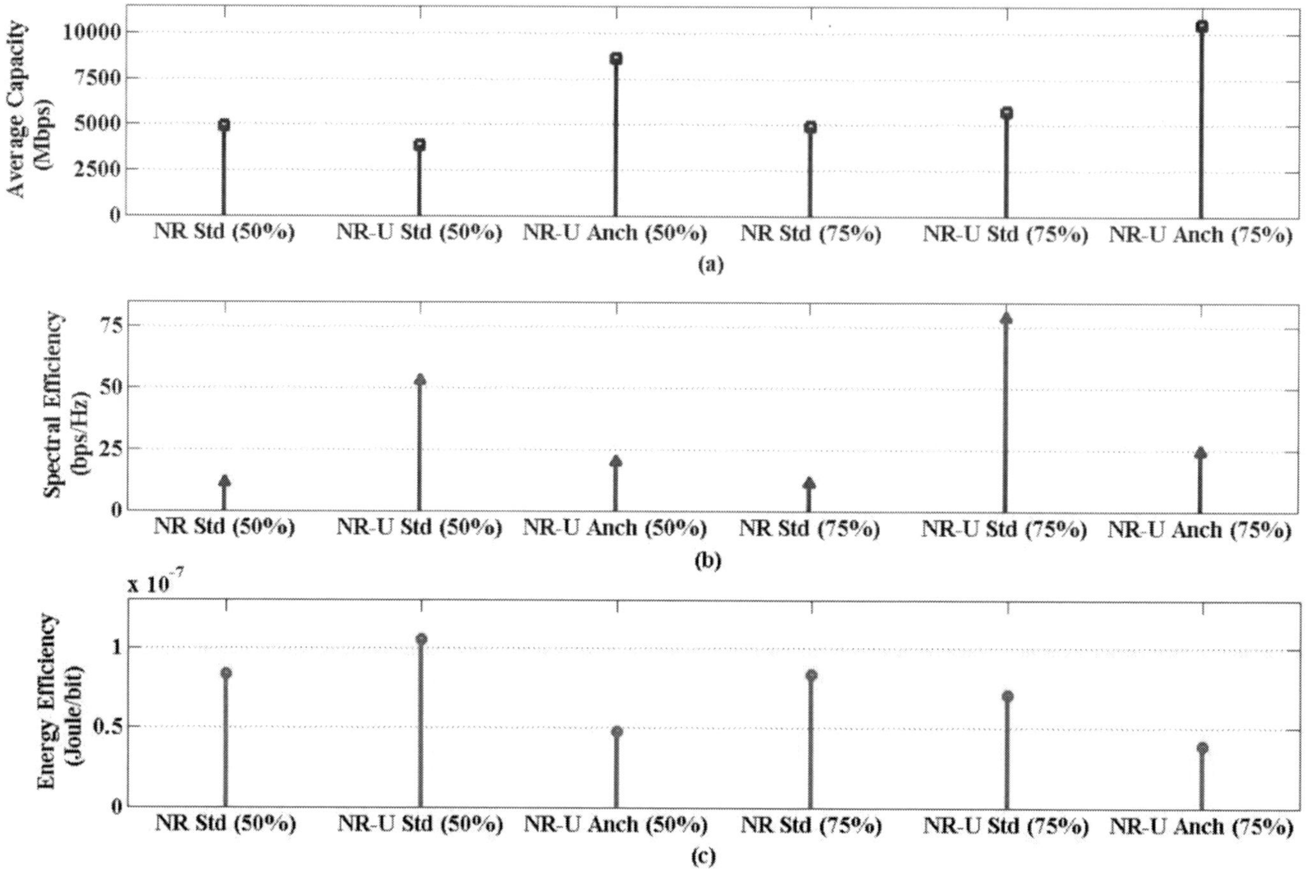

Figure 3. Average capacity, spectral efficiency and, energy efficiency responses of small cells of a single operator of 5G NR Standalone (Std), 5G NR-U Std, and 5G NR-U Anchored (Anch) with the variation of the number of FBSs (i.e., its transmission time) per FPP, including 50% and 75% of FPP, which coexists with a single WiGig operator in a building of small cells. (a) average capacity, (b) spectral efficiency, and (c) energy efficiency.

We vary the transmission time (i.e., the number of allocated FBSs) per FPP (including 50% and 75% of FPP) of small cells of a 5G NR operator coexisting with a single WiGig operator within a building. Figure 3 shows the average capacity, SE, and EE responses for three variants of the 5G NR operator, namely 5G NR Standalone, 5G NR-U Standalone, and 5G NR-U Anchored (Anch), which can be summarized as follows.

- Since 5G NR Standalone operates only in the 28 GHz licensed spectrum, which is allocated exclusively to it only, no changes in capacity, SE, and EE occur with a change in the number of FBSs over an FPP.
- Since 5G NR-U Standalone operates only in the 60 GHz unlicensed spectrum, which is shared as well by the WiGig operator, the capacity, SE, and EE responses increase with an increase in the transmission time from 50% FPP to 75% FPP due to having more time to transmit by the small cells.
- Since 5G NR-U Anchored operates both in the 28 GHz licensed spectrum, as well as in the 60 GHz unlicensed spectrum, with an increase in the transmission time, the average capacity response increases more than that of NR Standalone, as well as NR-U Standalone, operators due to operating in both the 28 GHz licensed and the 60 GHz unlicensed spectra. However, SE is a function of both achievable capacity and system bandwidth. Particularly, though SE is directly proportional to the achievable capacity, it is also inversely proportional to the effective licensed spectrum as given by (8). Due to this reason, SE for the 5G NR-U Anchored does not improve proportionately with its achievable capacity as the transmission time increases from 50% FPP to 75% FPP. Rather, 5G NR-U Standalone achieves the maximum SE due to requiring the least amount of the effective licensed spectrum. However, since EE is a function of transmission energy (Joule/bit), as well as achievable capacity (bits/s), the increase in the achievable capacity due to increasing the transmission time from 50% FPP to 75% FPP is significant enough to exceed the increase in the transmission energy for the NR-U Anchored as given by (9) in the same duration. This results in the minimum average energy required per bit transmission for the NR-U Anchored.

Overall, NR-U Anchored can achieve the maximum average capacity and EE, whereas NR-U Standalone can achieve the maximum SE when coexisting with a WiGig operator. Because in NR-U standalone, as well as NR-U Anchored, the 60 GHz unlicensed spectrum plays a role, this implies the importance of operating the 5G NR operator in the unlicensed bands.

V. Conclusion

In this paper, we have presented a time-domain coexistence technique for small cells of a 5G NR located within a building to coexist with a WiGig operator in the 60 GHz band. Each small cell has been considered dual-band enabled, operating in both the 60 GHz unlicensed and 28 GHz licensed bands. Because each small cell has not been considered Listen-Before-Talk (LBT) feature enabled, to avoid complete blockage of the transmission of WiGig Access Points (APs), an interference avoidance scheme has been proposed in the time-domain to divide the air time in the 60 GHz band between the incumbent WiGig APs (WiAPs) and small cells. We have derived average capacity, Spectral Efficiency (SE), and Energy Efficiency (EE) performance metrics for in-building small cells of the NR-U. With system-level simulation results, by varying the number of allocated FBSs per FPP the 5G NR operator, the average capacity, SE, and EE responses for three variants of the 5G NR, namely 5G NR Standalone, 5G NR-U Standalone, and 5G NR-U Anchored (Anch) have been evaluated. It has been shown that NR-U Anchored can achieve the maximum average capacity and EE, whereas NR-U Standalone can achieve the maximum SE when coexisting with a WiGig operator. Because the 60 GHz unlicensed band is present in both schemes, this signifies the importance of operating a 5G NR operator in the unlicensed bands.

Appendix I

Let X_1 and X_2 be the maximum number of NR-U operators and WiGig operators, respectively, such that $x_1 \in \{0,1,\dots,X_1\}$ with a corresponding average rate of arrivals $\lambda_{n,x_1} \in \{0,\lambda_{n,1},\dots,\lambda_{n,X_1}\}$, whereas $x_2 \in \{0,1,\dots,X_2\}$ corresponding to $\lambda_{w,x_2} \in \{0,\lambda_{w,1},\dots,\lambda_{w,X_2}\}$. Then, (1) can be expressed for NR-U operators as follows.

$$T_{n,x_1} = \left\lceil \left(\lambda_{n,x_1} \Big/ \left(\sum_{x_1=0}^{X_1} \lambda_{n,x_1} + \sum_{x_2=0}^{X_2} \lambda_{w,x_2} \right) \right) T_{\text{FPP}} \right\rceil$$

Similarly, for WiGig operators, (1) can be expressed as follows.

$$T_{w,x_2} = \left\lceil \left(\lambda_{w,x_2} \Big/ \left(\sum_{x_1=0}^{X_1} \lambda_{n,x_1} + \sum_{x_2=0}^{X_2} \lambda_{w,x_2} \right) \right) T_{\text{FPP}} \right\rceil$$

where $T_{\text{FPP}} = \left(\sum_{x_1=0}^{X_1} T_{n,x_1} + \sum_{x_2=0}^{X_2} T_{w,x_2} \right)$. ■

References

[1] Y. Jiang, J. Guo, and Z. Fei, "Performance Analysis of the Coexistence of 5G NR-Unlicensed and Wi-Fi with Mode Selection," Proc. 2020 IEEE/CIC International Conference on Communications in China (ICCC), Chongqing, China, 2020, pp. 953-958, doi: 10.1109/ICCC49849.2020.9238800.

[2] R. Zhang, et al., "LTE-unlicensed: The Future of Spectrum Aggregation for Cellular Networks," IEEE Wireless Communications., vol. 22, no. 3, pp. 150-159, June 2015, doi: 10.1109/MWC.2015.7143339.

[3] S. Lagen, N. Patriciello, and L. Giupponi, "Cellular and Wi-Fi in Unlicensed Spectrum: Competition Leading to Convergence," Proc. 2020 2nd 6G Wireless Summit (6G SUMMIT), Levi, Finland, 2020, pp. 1-5, doi: 10.1109/6GSUMMIT49458.2020.9083786.

[4] G. Naik, J. -M. Park, J. Ashdown, and W. Lehr, "Next Generation Wi-Fi and 5G NR-U in the 6 GHz Bands: Opportunities and Challenges," IEEE Access, vol. 8, pp. 153027-153056, 2020, doi: 10.1109/ACCESS.2020.3016036.

[5] S. Lagen et al., "New Radio Beam-Based Access to Unlicensed Spectrum: Design Challenges and Solutions," IEEE Communications Surveys and Tutorials, vol. 22, no. 1, pp. 8-37, Firstquarter 2020, doi: 10.1109/COMST.2019.2949145.

[6] E. Almeida et al., "Enabling LTE/WiFi Coexistence by LTE Blank Subframe Allocation," Proc. 2013 IEEE International Conference on Communications (ICC), Budapest, 2013, pp. 5083-5088, doi: 10.1109/ICC.2013.6655388.

[7] T. Nihtilä et al., "System Performance of LTE and IEEE 802.11 Coexisting on a Shared Frequency Band," Proc. 2013 IEEE Wireless Communications and Networking Conference (WCNC), 2013, pp. 1038-1043, doi: 10.1109/WCNC.2013.6554707.

[8] H. Zhang, X. Chu, W. Guo, and S. Wang, "Coexistence of Wi-Fi and Heterogeneous Small Cell Networks Sharing Unlicensed Spectrum," IEEE Communications Magazine, vol. 53, no. 3, pp. 158-164, March 2015, doi: 10.1109/MCOM.2015.7060498

[9] X. Lu, M. Lema, T. Mahmoodi, and M. Dohler, "Downlink Data Rate Analysis of 5G-U (5G on Unlicensed Band): Coexistence for 3GPP 5G and IEEE802.11ad WiGig," Proc. 23th European Wireless Conference, Dresden, Germany, 2017, pp. 1-6.

[10] J. D. Chimeh, M. Hakkak, and S. A. Alavian, "Internet Traffic and Capacity Evaluation in UMTS Downlink," Proc. Future Generation Communication and Networking (FGCN 2007), 2007, pp. 547-552, doi: 10.1109/FGCN.2007.154.

[11] J. Ellenbeck, J. Schmidt, U. Korger, and C. Hartmann, "A Concept for Efficient System-Level Simulations of OFDMA Systems with Proportional Fair Fast Scheduling," Proc. 2009 IEEE Globecom Workshops, Honolulu, HI, 2009, pp. 1-6, doi: 10.1109/GLOCOMW.2009.5360729.

[12] Evolved Universal Terrestrial Radio Access (E-Utra); Radio Frequency (RF) System Scenarios. Document 3GPP TR 36.942, V.11.0.0, 3rd Generation Partnership Project, September 2012. Available online: https://arib.or.jp/english/html/overview/doc/STD-T63v11_00/5_Appendix/Rel11/36/36942-b00.pdf [retrieved: June, 2021]

[13] Simulation Assumptions and Parameters for FDD HeNB RF Requirements. Document TSG RAN WG4 (Radio) Meeting #51, R4-092042, 3GPP, May 2009. Available online: https://www.3gpp.org/ftp/tsg_ran/WG4_Radio/TSGR4_51/Documents/ [retrieved: June, 2021]

Use of Augmented Reality (AR) and Virtual Reality (VR) to address four of the "National Academy of Engineering Grand Challenges for Engineering in the 21st Century"

Bibhav Bhattarai
Computer Science & Software Engineering
Auburn University
Auburn, USA
bzb0079@auburn.edu

Daniela Marghitu
Computer Science & Software Engineering
Auburn University
Auburn, USA
marghda@auburn.edu

Abstract— **The National Academy of Engineering's "Fourteen Grand Challenges for Engineering in the Twenty-First Century" identifies challenges in science and technology that are both feasible and sustainable to help people and the planet prosper. Four of these challenges are: advance personalized learning, enhance virtual reality, make solar energy affordable and provide access to clean water. In this work, the authors discuss developing of applications using immersive technologies, such as Virtual Reality (VR) and Augmented Reality (AR) and their significance in addressing four of the challenges. The Drinking Water AR mobile application helps users easily locate drinking water sources inside Auburn University (AU) campus, thus providing easy access to clean water. The Sun Path mobile application helps users visualize Sun's path at any given time and location. Students study Sun path in various fields but often have a hard time visualizing and conceptualizing it, therefore the application can help. Similarly, the application could possibly assist the users in efficient solar panel placement. Architects often study Sun path to evaluate solar panel placement at a particular location. An effective solar panel placement helps optimize solar energy cost. The Solar System Oculus Quest VR application enables users in viewing all eight planets and the Sun in the solar system. Planets are simulated to mimic their position, scale, and rotation relative to the Sun. Using the Oculus Quest controllers, disguised as human hands in the scene, users can teleport within the world view, and can get closer to each planet and the Sun to have a better view of the objects and the text associated with the objects. In a camp held virtually, due to Covid-19, K12 students were introduced to the concept and usability of the applications. Likert scales metric was used to assess the efficacy of application usage. The data shows that participants of this camp benefited from an immersive learning experience that allowed for simulation with inclusion of VR and AR.**

Keywords-Augmented Reality; Engineering Challenges; Immersive Technology; Virtual Reality.

I. INTRODUCTION

The National Academy of Engineering's "Fourteen Grand Challenges for Engineering in the Twenty-First Century" identifies challenges in science and technology that are both feasible and sustainable to help people and the planet prosper. The grand challenges of engineering were announced in 2008 by a committee of leading technological thinkers. These challenges were broadly classified into fourteen game-changing goals. Working towards these goals, as per the committee, is a way for improving life on the planet [1]. This research makes use of immersive technologies to addresses four of such challenges: 1. Advance personalized learning, 2. Enhance virtual reality, 3. Make solar energy affordable, and 4. Provide access to clean water.

AR and VR are two emerging, immersive technologies in recent times. AR creates a composite view by adding digital content to a real-world view, often by using the camera of a smartphone while VR creates an immersive view where the user's view is often cut off from the real world. In AR, users' world views remain intact and virtual objects simply augment the reality, whereas, in VR, users' world views are totally altered, and they can no longer see their actual surroundings.

In this research, a VR application aims to address the first two challenges while two AR applications aim to address the last two challenges. The VR application assists users in visualizing and understanding our solar system by using a VR headset. Users can take an immersive, virtual tour of the solar system. This virtual simulation closely parallels the movements of the planets, as well as their form, scale, and location in relation to the Sun. Thus, this application enables users to view our solar system in an immersive environment, which could be helpful in visualizing and comprehending a system that is not easily observable. The Drinking Water AR application displays information on drinking water accessibility and the environmentally sustainable use of water bottles rather than plastic cups. The application can be used to locate drinking water related information by simply pointing the device camera towards a Point of Interest (POI). Also, it can be used to file and view water-related complaints. Thus, the application helps users to conveniently identify drinking water related information inside AU, thus providing easy access to clean drinking water. The Sun Path AR application helps users visualize Sun's path at a selected date and location. Students study the Sun's path in several areas, but they often fail to visualize and comprehend it. Architects often analyze the sun's path to evaluate the positioning of solar panels at a particular location. An effective solar panel placement helps optimize solar energy cost. Thus, the application could possibly assist the users in efficient solar panel placement.

Empirical studies on the effectiveness of adding mobile game-based augmented reality into basic education suggests that AR techniques can boost student learning [2]. Similarly, there is an AR application to hydrate dementia-affected older adults [3]. The application reminds, inspires, directs, and monitors hydration among those adults. Likewise, students were readily engulfed in AR and their ability to interact with the interface and control virtual objects helped them to understand more advanced concepts of Earth-Sun relationships [4]. All the above-mentioned works in the literature back up this study's argument that AR can help with customized learning, resource access, and visualizing abstract concepts.

In conclusion, the applications serve as a proof of concept for use of immersive technology in addressing engineering concerns. In addition, K-12 students were introduced to the concept and usability of applications at a camp held virtually due to Covid-19. Likert scales metric was used to assess the efficacy of application usage.

In section 2, the paper discusses previous work by other authors related to this research. The project architecture used in the research is then presented in section 3. In section 4, the paper depicts the usability study of the research. In section 5, the result of the study is reported. Finally, in section 6, the authors provide conclusions and future work briefings.

II. RELATED WORK

A. *AR/VR Modes and Characteristics*

Virtual reality and augmented reality are two different types of immersive technology. Virtual reality (VR) fully takes over one's vision, giving users the feeling of being transported from the physical world to a virtual one. On the other hand, augmented reality (AR) simply overlays virtual objects onto the user's view of the real world. Based on the underlying implementation scheme, AR is classified into three different categories: Marker-less AR, Mark-based AR, and Location-based AR. In the same way, VR is classified in 3 Degrees of Freedom (DoF) and 6DoF based on user's degree of freedom.

Augmented Reality creates a composite view by adding virtual components to users' real view. AR is quite popular these days in various fields such as social media, learning, shopping and so forth. With the advent of Snapchat filters, AR became quite popular in social media. Soon after Facebook too integrated filter-based AR functionalities in many of its applications. Similarly, Ikea has AR features in its shopping application with the help of which customers can pick a product and place it at different points in their world view to see how the virtual product fits in their world view. Likewise, various apps such as Quiver, Blippar and Aurasma use AR to help student with learning [5]. There are basically 3 types of AR: Marker-based AR, Marker-less AR, and Location-based AR.

Marker-based AR uses pre-defined markers set by the developer of the application. When the markers are detected in the real world, virtual objects are augmented to the scene. Markers may be any form of 2D image, including black-and-white and color images. Figure 1 depicts AR content overlay over a pre-defined marker.

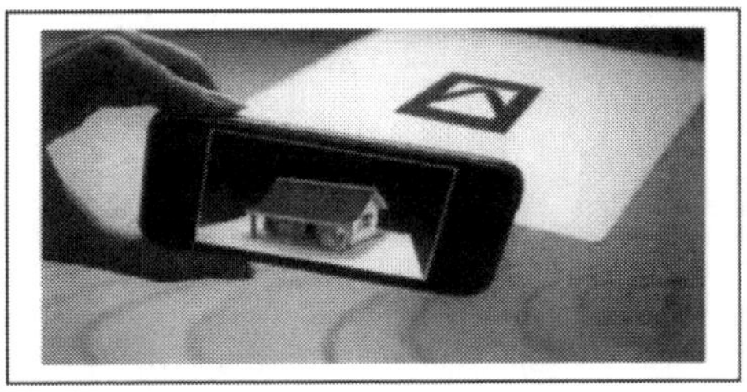

Figure 1. Marker based AR [6].

Marker-less AR is not bounded to a particular marker, but rather allows users to position objects anywhere they want within their real-world view. After placing an object, even if the device camera is removed from the line of sight, the application still remembers the position of the object using a method called Simultaneous Localization and Mapping (SLAM), and so when the device is brought back into line of sight the object is once again visible [7]. Figure 2 is an AR enabled retail application by Ikea. It is a marker-less AR app that allows users to place virtual products at desired position before buying them, thus assisting users with product selection and decision-making.

Figure 2. IKEA AR app example [8].

Location-based AR enables the ability to place virtual objects at various GPS coordinates. Location-based AR, in its simplest form, collects data from device components such as GPS, accelerometer and digital compass to identify the device location and position. The application then compares device data to POI information and adds virtual objects to the real environment accordingly [9]. An example of one of the most popular location-based AR apps is Pokémon Go. Figure 3 depicts another location- based AR application where different points of interest objects are overlaid as per their corresponding GPS coordinates.

Figure 3. Location based AR app [10].

VR is an immersive technology that allows users to interact with a virtual environment as if it were the reality. In virtual reality, Head-Mounted Displays (HMDs) are important for bringing the technology to life. An HMD is worn over the head, with the user's world view entirely obscured and only the screen displays visible in front of their eyes. The display supports a stream of data, images, and other such material. Currently, there are several powerful 3DoF and 6DoF HMDs available on the market. Google Cardboard is an example of a 3DoF headset and supports 3DoF (rotational movement around the x, y, and z axes). Similarly, Oculus Quest by Facebook, illustrated in Figure 4, is an example of a 6DoF headset and supports 6DoF (rotational movement around the x, y, and z axes, up, down forward, and backward).

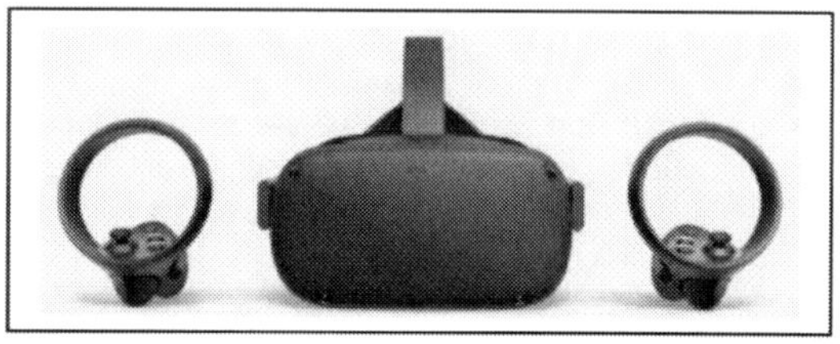

Figure 4. Oculus Quest headset [11].

6DoF tracking ensures a higher level of immersion than 3DoF as the user presence is more authentic. Figure 5 illustrates 3DoF and 6DoF tracking.

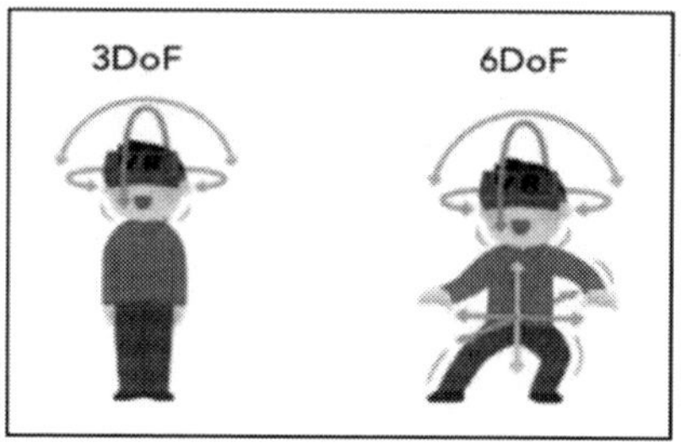

Figure 5. 3DoF and 6DoF [12].

B. *Applications in Academic Settings*

A survey study regarding use of augmented reality provided a scenario in which enabled mobile devices were used for learning and the associated pros and cons of the device usage was evaluated [2]. The questionnaire type survey is based on one single application – EduPARK – which analyzes mobile learning via students' opinion regarding the use of mobile devices for learning. The survey considers a total of 244 students at primary Portuguese Education System. The study participants consisted of students aged 10-16 years old among which 51.6 percent were girls and 48.4 percent were boys. The EduPARK application is designed for a specific urban park in Portugal.

The application uses Augmented Reality (AR) to provide various biological and historical references of the local park. The app was developed in Unity 5 using Vuforia framework and makes use of Vuforia's 2D marker-based technology. The marker-based technology allows the app to detect images/markers, pre-defined by the app creator, and overlay AR contents when the markers are detected by the device camera. As per the paper, the markers were manually installed in either tiles already existing in the park, or on plaques positioned for the purpose of sticking the markers onto them. The authors of the paper weigh in on students' perspective with the application usage. The findings of the paper suggest that the overall perspective remained positive with application usage amongst the students. The study also suggests that students believe that mobile devices, in general, are beneficial when they want to quickly find up-to- date information. However, students had their concerns with some of the external aspects of the application usage such as unstable, slow access to internet connectivity, restrictions forbidding them from carrying mobile devices to the classroom and ease of distraction by other applications in the mobile device. All in all, this paper suggests that use of AR mobile applications in learning can be beneficial.

A study was done that proposed an AR app that helps cognitively impaired elderly people with hydration [3]. Even though a significant number of older adults are capable of drinking water/fluid by themselves, several cognitive deficits such as poor initiation, decreased motivation, amnesia, and premature decay of intention may hinder their capability [13]. Poor Initiation in older adults is observed when they fail to recall, and this deficit is common in elderly people with dementia [14]. Due to poor initiation, old adults fail to recall where and how to fetch water. Often, older adults have a degraded sense of taste and smell due to which drinking water might not be as quenching. Thickening of orbitofrontal cortex, a part of the brain that pleases and is activated after drinking water [14], when medically observed in older adults, results in lack of fulfillment and delight that follows water intake [15]. Premature decay of intention occurs when a certain activity takes longer than anticipated time to fulfil, or when an activity is thought of, but execution is hindered by some other distraction. Decay in intention is significantly higher in elderly people with cognitive defects [16]. The paper claims that the AR app proposed has advantages over existing water drinking reminder apps when it comes to helping cognitively impaired old adults to stay hydrated [3]. The app makes use of Vuforia marker- based technology and a game like activity to motivate users to meet/increase water intake. Furthermore, it also mentions carrying out a feasibility study of two versions of the app- basic and advanced - with elderly people (in assistance with their caregivers) to find out which of the two could be more suitable. It is, therefore, clear from the paper that the proposed AR game is beneficial for hydration amongst elderly people since it assists them to cope with their cognitive disabilities.

In the application-based paper, the authors use AR involving exercises designed to teach spatial concepts of rotation/revolution, solstice/equinox, and seasonal variation of light and temperature [4]. It utilizes ARToolkit to teach about earth-sun relationships to thirty undergraduate geography students. Users utilized a lightweight Cy-Visornf DH-440 head mounted display (HMD) with a Logitech QuickCam Pro 3000 video camera attached. The HMD and camera were connected to a laptop running Windows XP and ARToolkit version 2.52 software. The paper claims that students find it challenging to understand spatial concepts and phenomena that are complex, and the use of AR based application resulted in a significant improvement in student understandings along with reduction in misunderstandings. Often, teachers use 3d objects or props available in the classroom to explain complex concepts but both teacher and students struggle since the available objects often fail to mimic the actual concept. AR based applications usually come in handy at such scenario and eradicate the need for props. The research made use of pre- and post-assessment worksheets, and the analysis of the assessment resulted in some definitive statistics as follows:

- In general, conceptual, and factual understanding ofthe concepts improved in all cases.
- The most significant improvement was seen in those with lower pre-assessment scores.
- Most of the students resorted to pictorial descriptions to help illustrate their understanding on both pre and post assessment which further fortified the stance on use of pictures being more intuitive when it comes to understanding and explaining complex spatial concepts

The research also made some qualitative analyses and drew some definitive conclusions as stated below:

- Ability to interact with the interface and control over virtual objects helped students to understand more advanced concepts.
- In some cases, the students could no longer distinguish the difference between real and superimposed virtual objects. In no time, they felt like all virtual objects were assimilated in the real world.

The paper, thus, explores AR's potential to help student visualize complex spatial concepts, and puts forth a definitive conclusion that AR rightly assists students with their learning and understanding.

III. PROJECT ARHITECTURE

A. *Approaches to Deployment*

The approach to deployment depends on the wireframes of the applications.

Wireframes for Drinking Water AR Application: The welcome activity is a splash screen that shows the logo of the application and lets users know that the application is starting up. After the splash screen is successfully rendered, if it is the first time that the user is using the app then the app will ask the user for device camera and GPS permissions. When and if the user allows all required permissions, then the loading device location dialog is shown while device GPS is asynchronously being fetched by a background thread. After the location is fetched the app makes use of ARCoreLocation to fetch and position the water marker overlay on the device camera view. The main activity also has a view/file complaint button which can be used by general users to file complaint and admin users to view and resolve the complaints. The user authentication and data storage functionalities are achieved using Google's Firebase (a cloud database). The application wireframes are illustrated in Figure 6.

Figure 6. Drinking Water AR application wireframe

Wireframes for Sun Path AR Application: The welcome activity is a splash screen that shows the logo of the application and lets the user know that the application is starting up. After the splash screen is successfully rendered, if it is the first time that the user is using the app then the app will ask the user for device camera permission. When and if the user allows camera access, the user is taken to the main activity of the application. All other functionalities of the application is found in the main screen of the app. The application wireframes are illustrated in Figure 7.

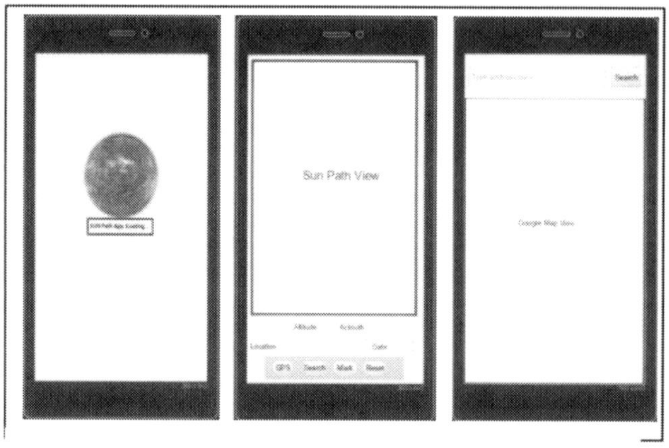

Figure 7. Sun Path AR application wireframe

Wireframes for Solar System VR Application: The main screen is the world space view for the user. The view includes all eight planets and the Sun in the solar system. All planets are simulated to mimic their position, scale, and rotation relative to the Sun. Users can use the Oculus Quest controllers to teleport within the world view. To give users a more realistic feel, the controllers are disguised as human hands in the scene. Users can get closer to each planet and the Sun to have a better view of the objects and the text associated with the objects. The application wireframe is illustrated in Figure 8.

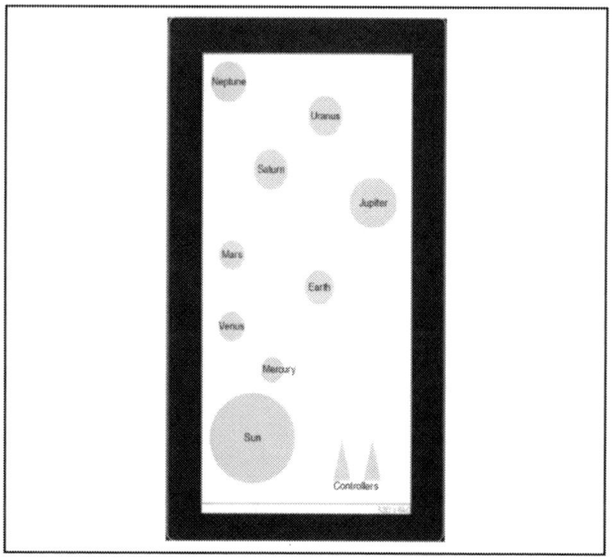

Figure 8. Solar System VR application wireframe

B. *Equipment Selection*

Software & hardware requirements stay the same for AR applications and differ with the VR application.

AR applications software requirements:

- Minimum Android version: 7 (API level 24).
- Target Android version: 9 (API level 28)

AR applications hardware requirements:

- ARCore supported Android mobile devices.
- Target Android version: 9 (API level 28)

VR application software requirements:

- Quest builds 20.0 release

VR application hardware requirements:

- Oculus Quest.

C. *Drinking Water AR Application*

The pictorial representation in Figure 9 is the flowchart that depicts the runtime flow of the water application. When the application is started it first checks to see whether the device is supported. If the device is supported, then the application seeks user permission to use device camera and GPS coordinates since both components are required for the application to run. Once the permissions are granted then the application initializes ARCore and ARCorelocation functionalities asynchronously. After the asynchronous methods return Future objects, the application renders the location markers.

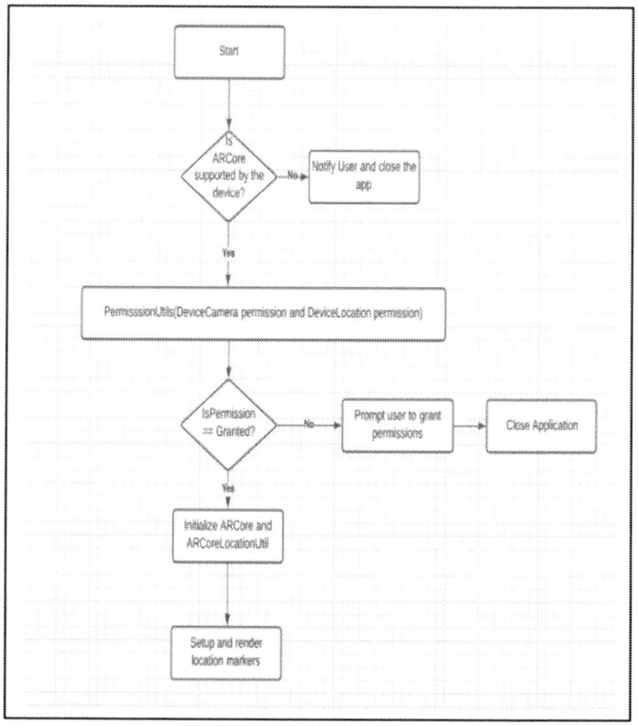

Figure 9. Solar System VR application wireframe

The water AR application is developed in Android Studio using Java programming language, and libraries such as Google's ARCore, Google's FireBase and ARCoreLocation by APPoly. ARCore is Google's platform for building AR experiences. It assists a device to understand its real environment so that it can augment it. Two fundamental features of ArCore are as follows:

- Motion tracking: allows tracking position of the

mobile device relative to the world.

- Understanding of the real world: Allows devices to understand vertical and horizontal surfaces and planes [17]

ARCore API which handles session lifecycle, access to device camera and pose is instantiated using ARCore session class. While this session is running ARCore holds exclusive access to device camera. Since this class consumes a significant amount of heap memory of the device, it is essential to call close method to release memory while not using the session. Failure to close may result in app crashing [18]. Similarly, ArSceneView is a SurfaceView which integrates with ARCore to render a scene [19].
Two of the methods from the ArSceneView class that have significant implementation in the application are getArFrame method which returns the most recent ARCore Frame, if available, and getSession method which returns the ARCore Session used by the view. Likewise, Frame class in ARCore captures the state and changes to the AR system by making a call to session object. It makes use of the getCamera method of the class to get the camera object [20]. Once the libraries are imported, to place a virtual object in a scene, anchor must be defined. Anchor class describes a fixed location and orientation in the real world [21].

Anchor in the application is obtained from the ArCoreLocation library by APPoly. APPoly is a software company based in the United Kingdom and contributes to the open-source community with various software packages. One such software package is ARCoreLocation. Since ARCore does not support use of real-world coordinates in its AR space [22], this application makes use of the ARCore Location library to realize the location-based functionality in the app. The location library used to realize location- based AR is ARCore-Location: 1.2 [23]. ARCoreLocation allows the water app to position AR objects at real-world GPS coordinates. The real-world GPS coordinates (longitude and latitude) are provided to the application by making use of a JSON file.

The application data related to users and complaints is handled using Google's Firebase – a cloud service that is used to authenticate users and store data in Cloud Firestore. Cloud Firestore is a NoSQL database that can be used to easily store, sync and query data for applications.

D. Sun Path AR Application

The pictorial representation in Figure 10 is the flowchart that depicts the runtime flow of the sun path application. When the application is started, it seeks user permission to use device camera since the component is required for the application to run. Once the permission is granted then it initializes the default scene and overlays the sun path on top of the device camera view. The user then can select custom location, date and time and the application will update the scene accordingly. Figure 10 depicts the flowchart for the application.

The Sun path AR application is developed in visual studio using JavaScript programming language and React Native framework. React Native provides developers with a community of open-source modules that can be readily incorporated in app development. An overview of components is as illustrated in Figure 11. This application is realized into three main custom components: 1. Location Component 2. Display Component, and 3. Main Component. Each of these components make use of core components and community components and interact with one another. Location Component: This is the component where location-based logic and code is written. This component makes use of following community components:

- @react-native-community/geolocation
- react-native-google-places-autocomplete
- react-native-maps

Display Component: This is the main user interface component where UI logic and code is written. This component mainly comprises of core components such as View, Text and ScrollView. The community components used are:

- @react-native-community/datetimepicker
- react-native-vector-icons/MaterialCommunityIcons

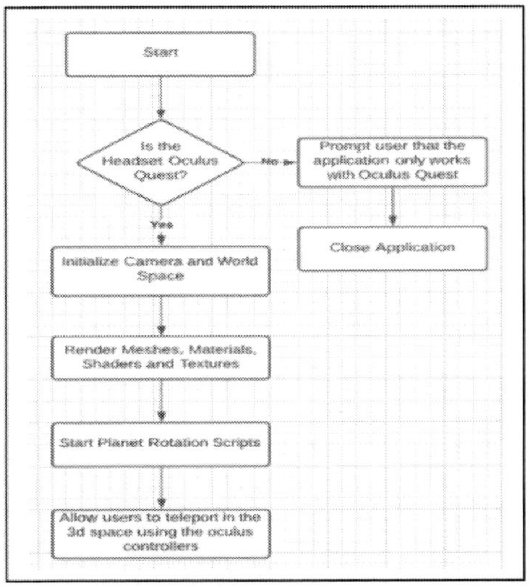

Figure 10. Solar System VR application wireframe

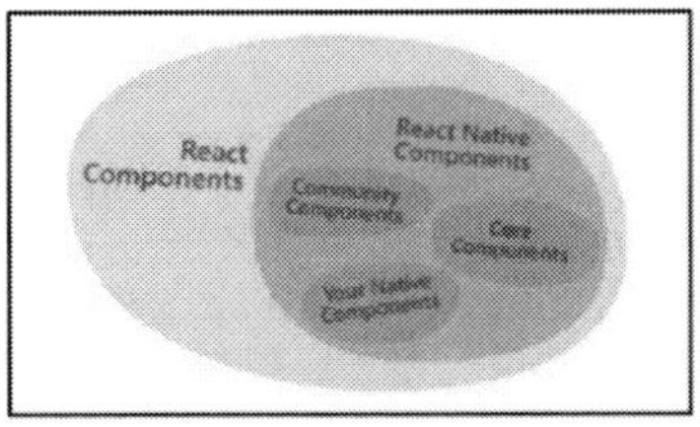

Figure 11. React Native overview [24].

Main Component: Is the engine of the application. All custom components are called here along with the following community components:

- react-native-WebView
- react-native-camera

Amongst various sun position calculation algorithms (such as Spencer, Pitmann and Vant-Hull, Walraven, PSA, and Michalsky), PSA has superior accuracy and performance [25]. Figure 12 illustrates PSA algorithm's performance in terms of accuracy in calculating zenith distance, azimuth, and sun vector deviation. User provided GPS coordinates, date and time is fed into the PSA algorithm function. The function returns Sun spherical coordinates and that is used in a projection matrix to visualize the sun path and overlay it on top of the world view.

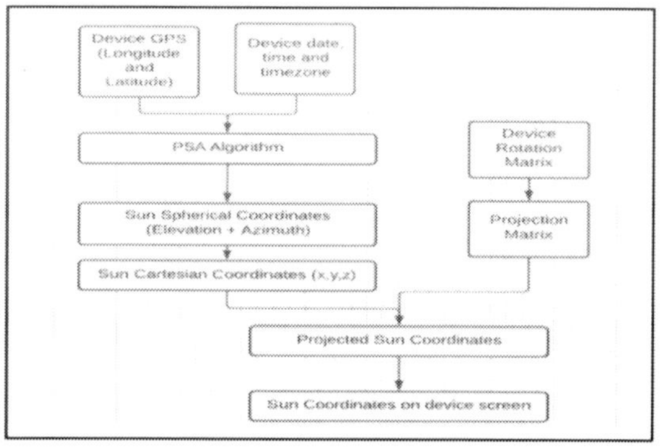

Figure 12. PSA algorithm

E. *Solar System VR Application*

Figure 13 shows the flowchart of the runtime flow of the Solar System VR application, developed in Unity using C# programming language. When the application is started, it first checks to see if the headset in which the application is being run is compatible. The application currently only supports Oculus Quest, and so trying to run it on other headset will cause the application to crash. After the initial validation is successful, the app will then initialize the camera component and the world space/scene of the application. Immediately after, the application will render all GameObjects of the scene and start the planetary rotation script (which is used to simulate planet revolution around the Sun). While in the world space of the application, the user can use controllers to teleport to different areas in the solar system and have a closer look at each of the planets. As illustrated in Figure 14, a scene in Unity can have objects that are called GameObjects. GameObjects serve as containers for components. Depending on the type of object desired, various combinations of components can be added to a GameObject. Developers can either use in-built components or create a custom component using Unity Scripting API [26]. Transform component, which defines position and orientation of the object it is attached to, is the only indispensable component in a GameObject. All other components either default or custom can be attached or detached from a GameObject.

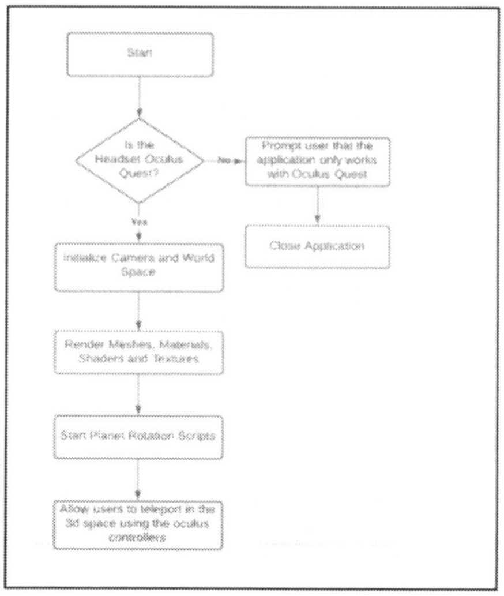

Figure 13. Flowchart of Solar System VR Application

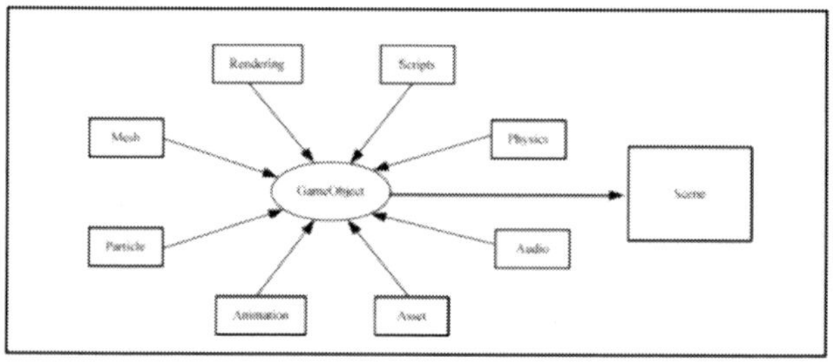

Figure 14. Unity3D GameObject Component Model

IV. USABILITY STUDY

A. *Virtual Educational K12 Camp*

Research in the Formation of Engineers (RFE) computing virtual camp was conducted for K-12 students, in which, students from grade 9 to 11 participated. These students were instructed on important topics of AR/VR and were also asked to use the applications. The following observations were gathered from students' responses:

- All the students were unsure if they had used AR/VR applications before, as shown in Figure 15.
- Many students indicated that the use of AR/VR functionalities helped them in better understanding of subject topics.
- Students equivocally agreed that the apps were easier to use and that they were able to effortlessly determine drinking water sources and sun location.

Pre-survey and post-survey detail the discrepancies in subjects' comprehension before and after using the AR/VR applications developed for this research. Students developed a greater understanding of the technology by using the applications. According to the post-survey findings, as depicted in Figure 16, 50 percent of the students strongly agreed, and the other 50 percent agreed that using such technologies was interesting. The Drinking Water AR app made it easy to find drinking water places, according to 50 percent who agreed somewhat, 25 percent who agreed, and the remaining 25 percent who strongly agreed. Similarly, 50 percent strongly agreed, 25 percent agreed, and 25 percent slightly agreed that determining the sun's location using the Sun Path AR app was simpler.

B. *Pre-Survey*

According to the pre-survey findings, as shown in Figure 15, 100 percent of the students were unaware of the AR/VR technology prior to being introduced in this study.

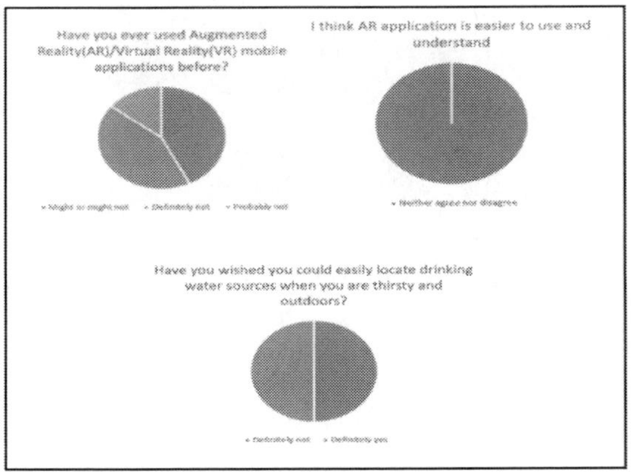

Figure 15. Pre-Survey results

C. *Post Survey*

According to the Post Survey findings, as shown in Figure 16, 100 percent of the students agreed that using AR/VR technologies is interesting.

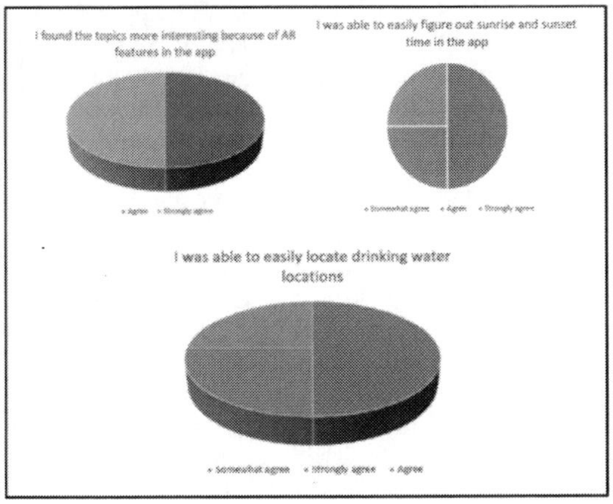

Figure 16. Post Survey results

V. RESULTS

A. *Drinking Water AR Application*

The application makes use of location-based AR to overlay virtual objects when the device is pointed towards the line of sight of POIs. Currently, Haley building and Shelby Engineering buildings are the POIs for the application. Figure 17 shows the overlay when the app is brought to the line of sight of one of the coordinates. By pointing their phones towards the POIs, users can quickly identify drinking water sources and related information. In addition, the app also promotes civic engagement. Users can register/sign into the program and then file complaints about water supplies. Also, the application has provisions to add admin users. Admin users can look at the complaints and mark them resolved when accomplished. Currently, people on campus can use Google Maps to locate buildings but they do not have access to building related information. In the future, the application could be expanded to provide users with not only water information about the buildings, but also information about the buildings' internal mappings.

The application makes use of marker-less AR to overlay virtual objects in device's camera view. The main scene of the app displays Sun's path at a given date, time, and location, as illustrated in Figure 18. Sun is the major source of energy to our planet, and examining its path is essential for better harvesting its energy. Sun path diagrams provide a wealth of information on how the sun can affect a site and structure over the year. The solar azimuth and altitude for a given position can be determined using the diagram. A conventional way of examining its path is by manually plotting points/lines in the diagram to get solar azimuth and altitude. Accurate and timely analysis of Sun's path plays a significant role in multitude of sectors. This app eliminates the need to manually measure the position of the sun at aspecific date, time, and place.

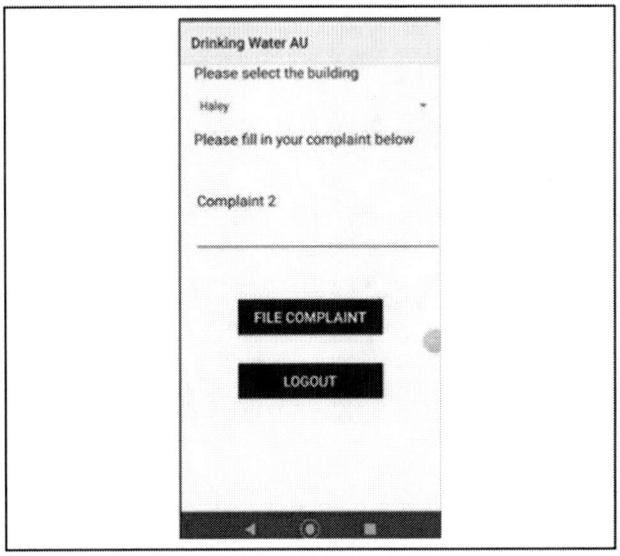

Figure 17. Drinking Water AR Application prototype

B. *Sun Path AR Application*

Users can easily access sun related information such as sun position, sunrise time and sunset time. Users can use the search functionality in the app to visualize Sun's path in any coordinates searchable in Google Maps API, as demonstrated in Figure 18. Practical uses, such as estimating solar power and solar water capacity, as well as agricultural applications, are possible with this app.

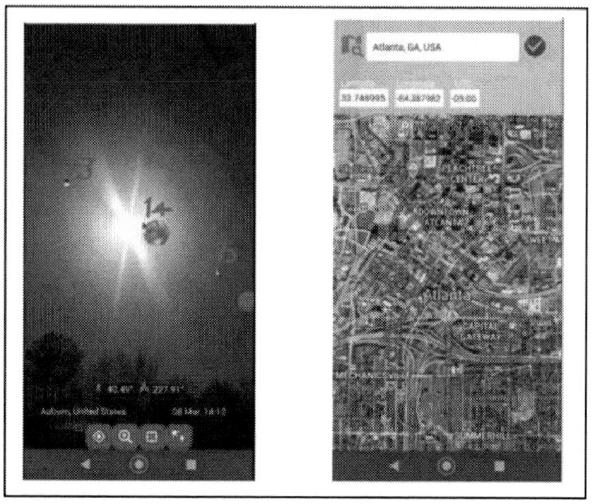

Figure 18. Sun Path AR Application prototype

C. *Solar System VR Application*

The application makes use of VR to simulate our solar system. In the main scene, users can see the movements of the planets, as wells as their form, scale, and location in relation to the Sun. Users can use controllers as their hands to teleport within the app and have a better visual of the Sun and planets, as illustrated in Figure 19. This can be useful to K-12 education as it provides an immersive, interactive way to visualize and comprehend the solar system. This way of teaching using VR could be extended to other subjects.

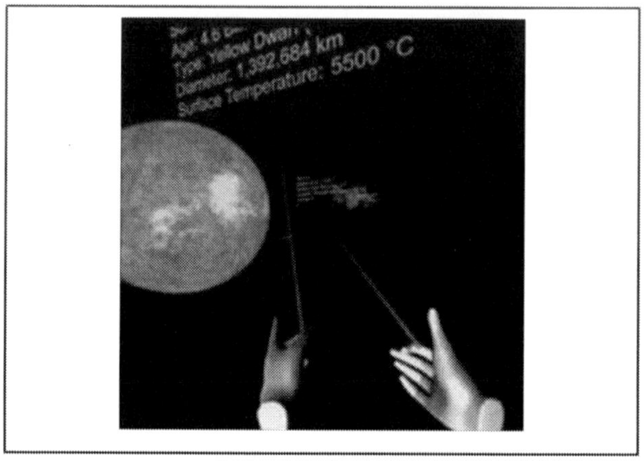

Figure 19. Solar System VR Application prototype

VI. CONCLUSIONS AND FUTURE WORK

The Drinking Water AR app served as a prototype to resolve the issue of access to safe drinking water while also encouraging public participation by enabling users to file water-related complaints. By assisting users in visualizing sun path at a given time, date, and place, the Sun Path AR application served as a prototype to help users learn about sun path and its role in making solar energy affordable. It provides solar azimuth and altitude information to the user, eliminating the need to manually calculate the values using a sun path diagram. The Solar System VR app acted as a model for enhancing virtual reality by creating an immersive and interactive solar system application. The app aided the user in visualizing a concept which is not readily apparent.

The effectiveness of apps was also evaluated among K- 12 students using a Likert scale-based pre- and post-survey metric. The study included twelve students from various schools across the United States. Based on the user reviews, it is fair to say that the applications were effective in terms of interaction, functionality, usability, and user experience.

However, the implementations and evaluations had some limitations that could be addressed in the future. A virtual camp, conducted online due to Covid-19, was not quite effective to quantitatively evaluate the effectiveness of the work. In the future, the authors propose evaluating the application in an in-person camp with greater number of participants. Besides, following changes to the applications is proposed:

- Currently, the water application only supports two of

the buildings inside Auburn University, and so scaling it to add more buildings is proposed.

- The mock data used for drinking water application could be replaced with actual data from the university.
- Both the sun path application and the water application are developed for android phones only. So, equivalent versions of the applications compatible to iPhone could be developed.
- Similarly, solar system VR application is only runnable in Oculus Quest Headset and could be built to support a greater number of headsets.

ACKNOWLEDGMENT

This work is made possible due to an NSF Grant # 1826181.

REFERENCES

[1] "Grand Challenges - 14 Grand Challenges for Engineering." http://www.engineeringchallenges.org/challenges.aspx (retrieved: Jan. 24, 2021).

[2] L. Pombo and M. M. Marques, "Improving students' learning with a mobile augmented reality approach – the EduPARK game," ITSE, vol. 16, no. 4, pp. 392–406, Nov. 2019, doi: 10.1108/ITSE- 06-2019-0032.

[3] S. Lehman, J. Graves, C. Mcaleer, T. Giovannetti, and C. C. Tan, "A Mobile Augmented Reality Game to Encourage Hydration in the Elderly," in Human Interface and the Management of Information. Information in Applications and Services, vol. 10905, pp. 98–107, 2018.

[4] S. Yamamoto and H. Mori, Eds. Cham: Springer International Publishing, 2018, pp. 98–107.

[5] B. E. Shelton and N. R. Hedley, "Using augmented reality for teaching Earth-Sun relationships to undergraduate geography students," in The First IEEE International Workshop Augmented Reality Toolkit, Sep. 2002, p. 8 pp.-, doi: 10.1109/ART.2002.1106948.

[6] "6 Exciting AR Apps for Student Learning," Edutopia. https://www.edutopia.org/blog/ar-apps-for-student-learning-monica-burns (retrieved: Mar. 10, 2021).

[7] Y. El Filali and K. Salah-ddine, "Augmented Reality Types And Popular Use Cases," vol. 8, pp. 91–97, Apr. 2019.

[8] K. Ahir, "What is the difference between Marker based and Markerless AR?," Medium, Sep. 03, 2019. https://kumar-ahir.medium.com/what-is-the-difference-between-marker-based- and-markerless-ar-192fb9fa09c5 (retrieved: Mar. 10, 2021).

[9] A. Ayoubi, "IKEA Launches Augmented Reality Application," Architect, Sep. 21, 2017. https://www.architectmagazine.com/technology/ikea-launches-augmented-reality-application_o (retrieved: Mar. 10, 2021).

[10] L. H., "Location-Based AR Apps: Best Examples and Guide on How To Build," Cleveroad Inc. - Web and App development company, Jul. 17, 2018. https://www.cleveroad.com/blog/location- based-ar-apps-best-examples-and-guide-on-how-to-build (retrieved: Mar. 10, 2021).

[11] Locatify, "Location Based Augmented Reality Apps (AR & RTLS)," Locatify. https://locatify.com/blog/location-based-augmented-reality-apps-2017-rtls-ar/ (retrieved: Mar. 10, 2021).

[12] "Oculus Headsets: The Original Quest is Back | Oculus." https://www.oculus.com/quest/ (retrieved: Mar. 10, 2021).

[13] D. Heaney, "How virtual reality positional tracking works," VentureBeat, May 05, 2019. https://uploadvr.com/how-vr-tracking-works/ (retrieved: Mar. 10, 2021).

[14] J. C. Mentes, "A typology of oral hydration problems exhibited by frail nursing home residents," J Gerontol Nurs, vol. 32, no. 1, pp. 13–19; quiz 20–21, Jan. 2006, doi: 10.3928/0098- 9134-20060101-09.

[15] I. E. T. de Araujo, M. L. Kringelbach, E. T. Rolls, and F. McGlone, "Human cortical responses to water in the mouth, and the effects of thirst," J Neurophysiol, vol. 90, no. 3, pp. 1865–1876, Sep. 2003, doi: 10.1152/jn.00297.2003.

[16] J. Pacheco, J. O. Goh, M. A. Kraut, L. Ferrucci, and S. M. Resnick, "Greater cortical thinning in normal older adults predicts later cognitive impairment," Neurobiol Aging, vol. 36, no. 2, pp. 903–908, Feb. 2015, doi: 10.1016/j.neurobiolaging.2014.08.031.

[17] G. A. Radvansky, A. K. Tamplin, and S. A. Krawietz, "Walking through doorways causes forgetting: Environmental integration," Psychon Bull Rev, vol. 17, no. 6, pp. 900–904, Dec. 2010, doi: 10.3758/PBR.17.6.900.

[18] "ARCore," Google AR & VR. https://arvr.google.com/arcore/ (retrieved: Mar. 10, 2021).

[19] "Session | ARCore," Google Developers. https://developers.google.com/ar/reference/java/com/google/ar/co r e/Session (retrieved: Mar. 10, 2021).

[20] "ArSceneView | Sceneform (1.15.0)," Google Developers. https://developers.google.com/sceneform/reference/com/google/a r/ sceneform/ArSceneView (retrieved: Mar. 10, 2021).

[21] "Frame | ARCore," Google Developers. https://developers.google.com/ar/reference/java/com/google/ar/co r e/Frame (retrieved: Mar. 10, 2021).

[22] "Anchor | ARCore," Google Developers. https://developers.google.com/ar/reference/java/com/google/ar/co r e/Anchor (retrieved: Mar. 10, 2021).

[23] Appoly, "ARCore Location - Android Studio - Appoly News & Opinions," Appoly, Mar. 28, 2018. https://www.appoly.co.uk/2018/03/28/arcore-location/ (retrieved: Mar. 10, 2021).

[24] Appoly, appoly/ARCore-Location. Appoly, 2021.

[25] "Core Components and Native Components · React Native." https://reactnative.dev/docs/intro-react-native-components (retrieved: Mar. 10, 2021).

[26] M. Blanco-Muriel, D. C. Alarcón-Padilla, T. López-Moratalla, and M. Lara-Coira, "Computing the solar vector," Solar Energy, vol. 70, no. 5, pp. 431–441, Jan. 2001, doi: 10.1016/S0038-092X(00)00156-0.

[27] "Unity - Manual: GameObjects." https://docs.unity3d.com/Manual/GameObjects.html (retrieved: Mar. 10, 2021)

A Direction of Arrival Machine Learning Approach for Beamforming in 6G

Anabel Reyes Carballeira
National Institute of Telecommunications, INATEL
Santa Rita do Sapucai, MG, Brazil
email: anabel.carballeira@mtel.inatel.br

Abel Rodriguez Medel
National Institute of Telecommunications, INATEL
Santa Rita do Sapucai, MG, Brazil
email: abel.medel@mtel.inatel.br

Jose M. Camara Brito
National Institute of Telecommunications, INATEL
Santa Rita do Sapucai, MG, Brazil
email: brito@inatel.br

Abstract—**Beamforming (BF) appropriately weights the amplitude and phase of individual antenna signals to create narrowly focused radiation. This makes it possible to provide better coverage in an indoor environment and at the edge of a cell. To make the best use of this technology, it is important to know the location of the device to direct the antenna beam of the radio Base Station (BS). Consequently, the Direction of Arrival (DOA) method is becoming very crucial and essential in this time. This paper proposes a Machine Learning (ML) based approach for DOA by evaluating three models: *Support Vector Classification* (SVC), *Decision Tree* (DT) and *Bagging Classifier* (BC). These models are trained using a public database built from drone's radio frequency signals. The proposed model significantly outperforms the techniques presented in previous work.**

Index Terms—**Beamforming; Direction of Arrival; Machine Learning.**

I. Introduction

Up to the Fifth Generation Mobile Network (5G), the development of the cellular systems focused on communication aspects, while other services, had low priority. Diverging from current networks, future communication systems will become pervasive across multiple industry verticals by enabling a plethora of services that require location, such as assets tracking, context-aware marketing, transportation and logistics systems, Cross Reality (XR) experiences, and health care.

For location services, the Direction of Arrival (DOA) method estimates the direction angle of a source transmitting a signal to a receiver. DOA is highly applicable in wireless communications, astronomical observations, radar, and sonar [1]. In addition, with the beginning of the studies of the 6G network, the DOA methods assumes a new importance.

One of the key technologies in 6G is expected to be Beamforming (BF), specifically Holographic Beamforming (HBF) [2]–[5]. BF is a technique that focuses a wireless signal towards a specific receiving device, rather than having the signal spread in all directions from a broadcast antenna, as it usually would. Therefore, it is important to know the location of mobile devices and Internet of Things (IoT) terminals to direct the antenna beam of the radio BS. The resulting connection is faster and more reliable than it would be without BF.

The location technique for BF in 6G should be autonomous, reconfigurable, adaptive, and fast responsive. It is impossible to manually adjust the BF direction due to the extensive enhancement of the capacity of communication networks. ML has been considered part of the most important technologies in 6G [2], [6]–[10] due to the high capacity of communication networks and the massiveness of IoT devices.

ML is presented as a promising technology to be used for DOA. ML-based methods are data-driven and it can be more robust than other methods because they adapt better to array geometry imperfections and sensor imperfections. They also do not depend of the array geometry shape [1]. In addition, ML offers low-cost implementation and simplicity.

In [11], the authors propose a new DOA method based on an ML model to estimate the azimuth angle of a signal. The system employs only four antennas to find the direction of eight possible signal provenance angles. With this system was obtained a dataset named as *Dround_Data_New*, which contains well-known signals transmission powers for the eight angles. The authors trained and validated the dataset with a Deep Neural Network (DNN) model. The main goal of this work is to propose another ML model in order to increase the accuracy during prediction and decrease the training time over the same dataset *Dround_Data_New*.

The article is organized as follows. Section II is an overview of the related work. Section III extends the system architecture, the training dataset, the data modification for classification, and the proposed ML model. Section IV compares and discusses the results of the proposed DOA model with the approach presented in [11]. Finally, Section V concludes the paper.

To promote reproducible research, the code to generate the results of this paper is available here: [12].

II. Related work

Inherently multi-channel techniques, Multiple Signal Classification (MUSIC) [13], and Estimation of Signal Parameters Via Rotational Invariance Techniques (ESPRIT) [14], are considered to be the most popular DOA methods. However, there have been many problems associated with their application due to the base-band data from all antenna elements should be extracted simultaneously. A data correlation matrix needs to be formulated. Therefore, calibrating the values of each Radio Frequency (RF) channel becomes necessary to have a coherent multi-channel receiver [11]. A technique that does not require phase calibration is proposed in [15] as a Sparse Signal Representation (SSR) technique. However, this scheme cannot offer adequate accuracy.

In order to avoid the phase synchronization mechanism and antenna calibration mechanism, the authors in [11], [16], [17] used a system consisting of a single channel receiver, an M independent antennas, and a rotating switch similar to the one depicted in Figure 1. The authors in [16], examined the potential in using the different radiation patterns of a Switched Parasitic Antenna (SPA) for DOA. The DOA performance of the SPA is examined by calculating a lower bound on DOA accuracy, which is called the Cramer-Rao lower Bound (CRB). Then, all DOA estimation schemes derived from a general antenna array can also be applied to a parasitic antenna by inserting a new steering matrix. The authors in [17], employ a receiver, which is connected to one of M available sensors. Each sensor is enabled for reception every MT, where T is the time a sensor is enabled. The single-channel receiver has an RF switch that selects one sensor at a time. For the direction estimate, the posterior distribution of DOA is derived. Then, the Bayesian maximum posterior probability is applied to select the direction angle. The results of that work show high accuracy for the direction estimate of signals arriving from 10° and 40° angles simultaneously. However, the convergence time for the estimate is not clear because it is presented as a dimensionless quantity.

In [18], a comprehensive study is conducted to optimize the channel estimation and DOA estimation fields of massive Multiple Input Multiple Output (MIMO) based on the deep learning technique. Simulation results corroborate that the proposed scheme can achieve better performance in terms of DOA estimation compared with conventional methods. However, the system is complex and expensive because it employs 128 antennas. The authors in [19], proposed a cascaded neural network, which can be implemented to estimate the DOA of two closely spaced sources. The cascaded network consists of two parts: a SNR classification network and a DOA estimation network. The latter network contains two estimation subnetworks, which are applied to high and low SNRs to train the noisy data. The results of that work show better performance than other DOA techniques by detecting two signals coming from two directions separated by angles less than 5°. However, the performance is worse than the other techniques for sources with greater separation.

The authors in [11] used a system consisting of a single channel receiver, four antennas, and a rotating switch like the one depicted in Figure 1. There, the receiver sequentially activates the n-th antenna element at a time using the rotating switch, and measures the corresponding received power (P_n) where $n \in \{1, ..., N\}$. Then, the value of the normalized power measured in the n-th antenna will be given as:

$$x_n = \frac{P_n}{\sum_{i=1}^{N} P_i} \quad (1)$$

Next, the obtained normalized power values are fed to a Sparse Denoising Autoencoder (SDAE)-based DNN to find the azimuth angle of the transmitted signals. The SDAE makes compression and later a reconstruction of the power values to obtain a version of the power values with only essential information. Then, it starts the DNN training phase. DNN comprises three fully connected hidden layers and a softmax layer [20] for the classification task. The model achieved an overall accuracy of 96.25%. However, this paper proposes another ML method using the same dataset than in [11] to show improvements in both the overall accuracy and the elapsed training time for DOA.

III. SYSTEM MODEL AND DATASET

A. System overview

The system model consists of a single-channel receiver, and N directional antennas arranged circularly, see Figure 1. The antenna array is connected to the receiver using a non-reflective Single-Pole-N-Throw (SPNT) RF switch, which sequentially activates each antenna, and measures the received power values. The power measurements (P_1, P_2, P_3, ..., P_N) corresponding to each switching cycle are fed to the proposed ML model. Then, it is performed the DOA by exploiting the sparsity property of the incoming signal, and the gain variation property of the directional antenna array.

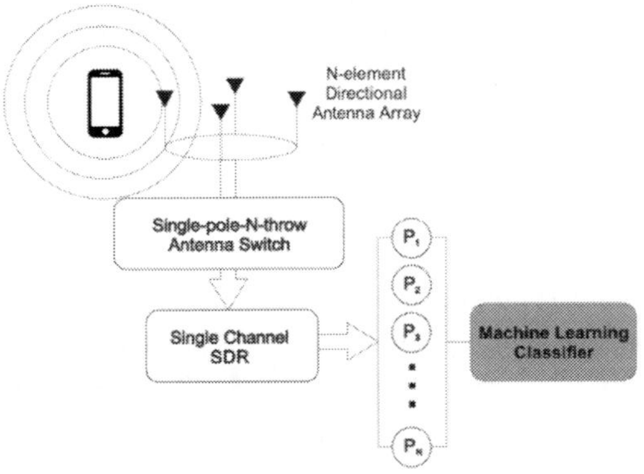

Fig. 1. The System Model.

B. *Dround_Data_New* dataset review

The *Dround_Data_New* dataset was collected by Software Defined Radio (SDR) (USRP B210), and a four-element sector antenna. The authors in [11], use only a single RF receiving channel for the SDR. Thus, the SDR is connected to the antenna using a non-reflective Single-Pole-4-Throw (SP4T) RF switch. The DJI Phantom 3 drone is the device that has been involved in this dataset. It is considered as the target device throughout the experiment. The drone downlink channel occupies the bandwidth from 2.401 GHz to 2.481 GHz. Each drone transmits a 10 MHz bandwidth Orthogonal Frequency Division Multiplexing (OFDM) signal. The OFDM signal transmitted by the drones is the main source to perform the DOA task. Figure 3a in [11] represents the environment that they used for the training data collection. The scenario represents a large ground with an open area. Also, there was a negligible RF intereference on the 2.0401 GHz - 2.481 GHz range due to the experiment occurring in a remote area.

To simplify the experiment, the authors in [11] virtually divided the area into eight octants (see Figure 3b in [11]). Therefore, *Dround_Data_New* is made up of octants. Each octant is considered as one direction (azimuth angle). For example, the first octant is considered as the angle's range 0°-45°, while the second octant is considered as the angle's range 45°-90°, and so on. Therefore, when the drone is flying, its direction is indicated by its corresponding octant. The dataset just has one type of data labeling for the classification of the azimuth angles. The *Dround_Data_New* dataset consists of 120 samples per angle's range. It is important to clarify that in the future more tests can be done and more data can be obtained to achieve a more precise direction. For example, instead of splitting the area into octants it can be splitted into sixteen or sixty-four parts.

C. Dataset modifications

It is common practice when performing a supervised ML experiment to hold out part of the available data as a validation set. The validation dataset is not used for training, instead, it is used to validate the trained model by predicting the labels of those unseen data. In [11], the dataset is divided into data to train and data to validate. The *Dround_Data_New* consists of 110 samples per angle for training and 10 samples for validation (representing approximately 8.33% of the total data). It is not a convincing validation dataset because it is small compared with the entire dataset due to the Pareto principle [21]. Besides, the data to train and validate were divided into different files in a fixed way, which makes it difficult to do different tests with different sizes of data for training and validation. Therefore, this data was joined in the same file and, shuffled, and splitted by using the *train_test_split* [22] method from the *Scikit-Learn (sklearn)* library to readjust dynamically the training and validation dataset sizes. In this work, the *train_test_split* method take as input: an array holding the samples, an array holding the class labels for the samples, a parameter called *test_size* which represents the proportion of the dataset to include in the validation dataset, and the parameter called *random_state* which controls the shuffling applied to the data before applying the split.

D. Classification model

In this subsection, a brief review of the ML model and the ensemble methods used in this work is given.

1) Support Vector Classification (SVC): SVC tries to find the best hyperplane to separate different classes by maximizing the distance between sample points and the hyperplane. The SVC model takes as input the following parameters:

- *kernel*: Selects the type of hyperplane used to separate the data. It must be one of *linear, poly, rbf, sigmoid, precomputed* or a callable.
- *C*: Is the penalty parameter of the error term. It controls the trade off between smooth decision boundary and classifying the training points correctly.
- *gamma*: Kernel coefficient for *rbf, poly* and *sigmoid*.

2) Decision Tree (DT): DT models are one of the simplest and most successful forms of ML models [23]. The goal of DT is to create a model that predicts the value of a target variable by learning simple rules inferred from the data features. The DT models build a tree during training that is the one applied when making the prediction. The input and output values can be discrete or continues. The DT model takes as input the following parameter:

- *max_depth*: This indicates how deep the tree can be.

3) Bagging Classifier (BC): It is an ensemble meta-estimator that fits base classifiers each on random subsets of the original dataset and then aggregates their individual predictions (either by voting or by averaging) to form a final prediction [24]. This work uses the *Bagging Classifier* class from the *sklearn* library and it takes as input the following parameters:

- *base_estimator*: Applied to random subsets of the dataset. The base classifier used was DT [25].
- *n_estimators*: The number of base estimators (in this case, the number of DTs in the ensemble.
- *max_samples*: The number of samples to extract from the training data to train each base estimator.
- *bootstrap*: Defines whether samples are drawn with replacement. If *False*, sampling without replacement is performed.
- *n_jobs*: Tells Scikit-Learn the number of CPU cores to use for training and prediction. *n_jobs* is *None* by default, which means unset; it will generally be interpreted as *n_jobs*=1, which means that only one core will be used by Scikit-Learn. *n_jobs*=-1 tells Scikit-Learn library to use all available cores. For *n_jobs* below -1, number of cores + 1 + *n_jobs* are used. For example, with *n_jobs*=-2, all CPUs but one is used.
- *random_state*: Provided to control the random number generator used. The values of *random_state* can be: *None* (default), an integer, and a *numpy.random.RandomState* instance. *random_state=None* calls the function multiple times. It will reuse the same instance, and it will produce different results. If *random_state* is an integer, it is going to use a new random number generator seeded by the given integer. Using an integer will produce the same results across different calls. Popular integer random seeds are 0 and 42. The *numpy.random.RandomState* instance uses the provided random state, only affecting other users of that same random state instance.

IV. SIMULATION RESULTS

A. Tuning the parameters and the validation set

Figures 2 and 3 show the validation curves and learning curves for SVC and DT respectively. Figure 2a shows the behavior of the training score and validation score against the

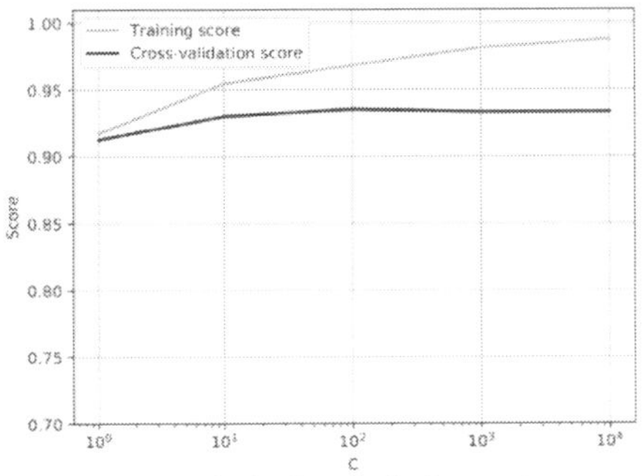

a. Validation Curve for the C parameter.

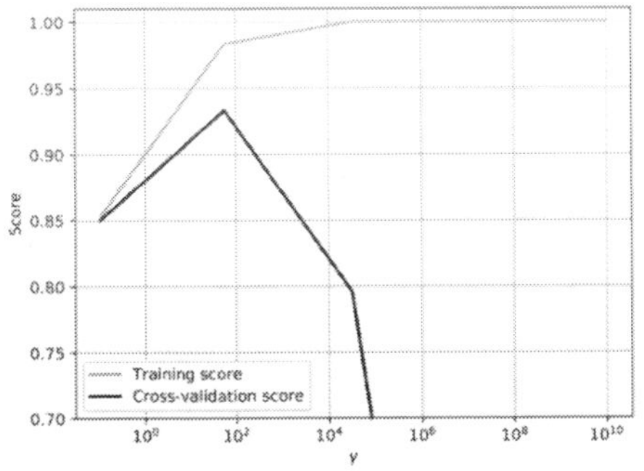

b. Validation Curve for the *gamma* parameter.

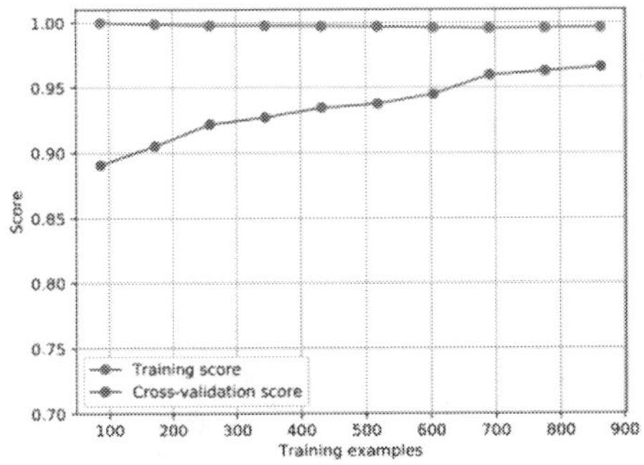

c. Learning Curve.

Fig. 2. Validations curves and Learning curves of SVC.

values of the parameter *C*. It is observed that the training score is always increasing and the validation score decreases slightly for a value of C equal to 100. Therefore, the value of C will be 100 to avoid overfitting, which means that the noise or random fluctuations in the training data is picked up and learned as concepts by the model. Figure 2b shows the training scores and validation scores of an SVC for different values of the kernel parameter *gamma*. Until *gamma* equal to approximately 100, it can be seen that both the training score and the validation score are increasing. After *gamma* equal to 100 the training score keeps increasing but the validation score decreases; therefore, the classifier overfit. The problem is that these concepts do not apply to new data and negatively impact the models ability to generalize.

Figure 3a shows that for low values of *max_depth* the DT model is underfitting, which means that it can neither

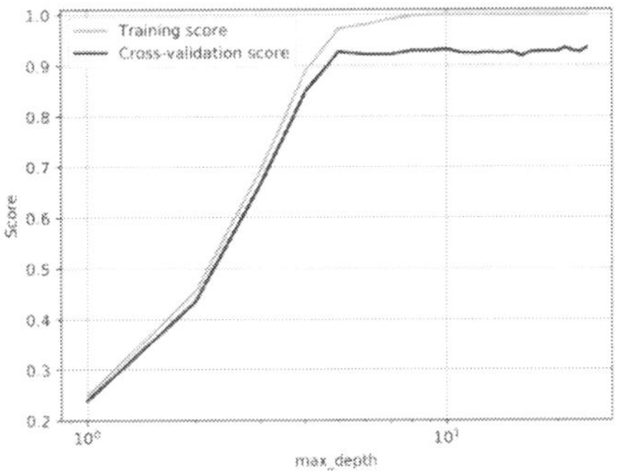

a. Validation Curve for the *max_depth* parameter.

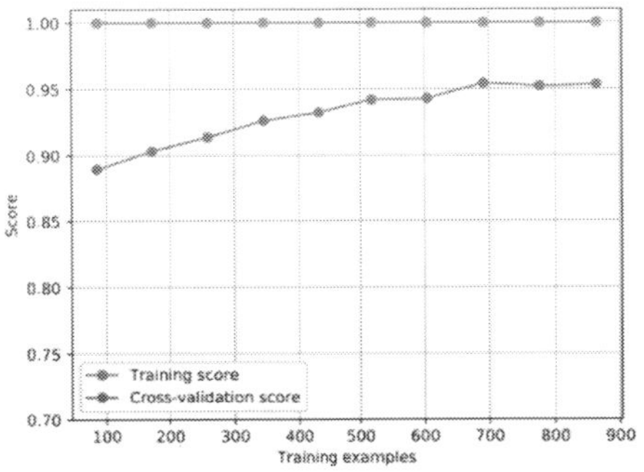

b. Learning Curve.

Fig. 3. Validations curves and Learning curves of DT.

model the training data nor generalize to new data. With the previous analysis and with the use of the search grid provided by *GridSearchCV* [26]—which exhaustively considers all parameter combinations to optimize a model— the best parameters for the SVC and DT models are summarized in Table I.

TABLE I
INPUT PARAMETER VALUES OF THE SCV AND DT MODELS.

Model	Parameters	Value
SVC	*kernel*	*rbf*
	C	100
	gamma	100
DT	*max_depth*	16

Figure 2c shows that the validation score is maximum after approximately 700 training samples and then remains almost constant, and the training score is still around the maximum. Therefore, 700 samples were destined for training, which represents 72.9% of the total samples (the total samples is 960). As a result of the total data, 70% was allocated for training and 30% to validate the SVC model. The same is observed in Figure 3b for the DT model. Therefore, 70% of the samples will also be used for training the DT model.

As BC is designed to reduce the possibility of overfitting complex models there is no need to analyze their validation curves. Table II shows the values given to the BC input parameters. The values of *n_estimators* and *max_samples* have been decided with the use of the search grid provided by *GridSearchCV* [26]. Figure 4 shows the learning curve of the BC model with a behavior similar to that of SVC and DT. Therefore, 70% of the data from *Dround_Data_New* dataset was also used to train the BC model.

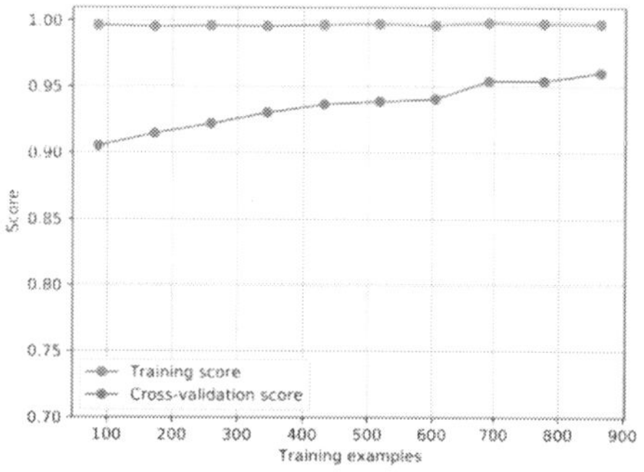

Fig. 4. Learning curves of BC.

TABLE II
INPUT PARAMETER VALUES OF THE *Bagging Classifier*.

base_estimator	*Decision Trees*
n_estimators	300
max_samples	0.55
bootstrap	False
n_jobs	-1
random_state	42

B. Results

The performance of the SDAE-DNN model used in [11], SVC model, DT model and the BC model is shown in Figure 5 by means of confusion matrices and in Table III. It can be concluded that the DT and BC models present a better result than the SDAE based DNN and SVC models despite using less data to train. It can be seen that the BC and DT results are practically the same but with a longer time in BC (which makes sense as it is a more complex method). Therefore, the use of BC in this case does not make sense since DT provides the same results in a shorter time.

TABLE III
COMPARISON BETWEEN MODELS

Model	Validation dataset size	Elapsed time	Accuracy
SDAE-DNN	8.33%	109.29s	96.25%
SVC	10%	0.02s	95.83%
DT	30%	0.0s	98.61%
BC	30%	5.23s	98.61%

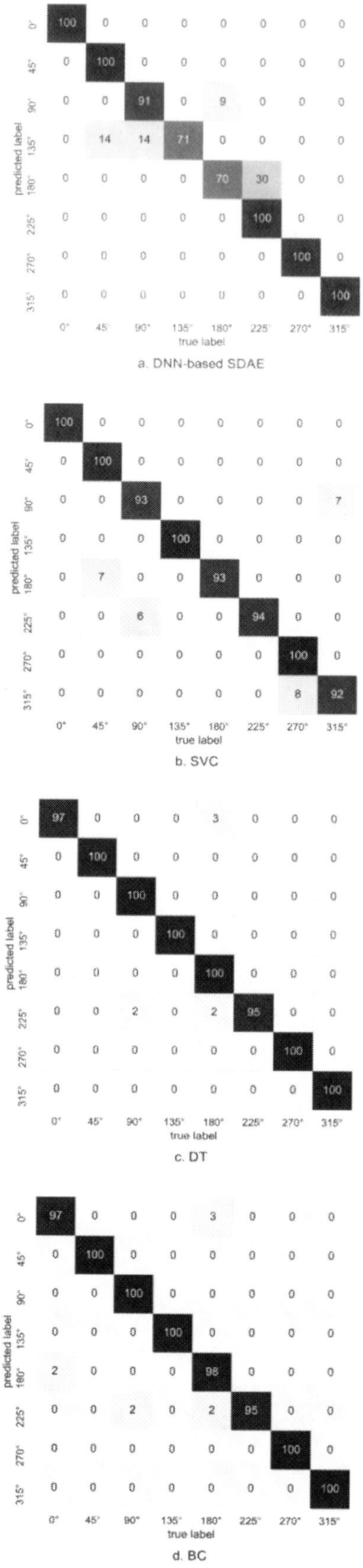

Fig. 5. Confusion matrix.

V. Conclusion

The necessity of having an intelligent system for DOA with reliable accuracy is becoming crucial for Next Generation Mobile Networks techniques like BF in 6G to improve the communication. These systems can integrate well-trained ML models to improve the robustness in performance. In this work, different ML models were trained using a public dataset. The best results were obtained for the DT model, overcoming another model proposed in the literature.

In future works, we will include not only the azimuth angle for DOA but also the elevation angle using the analyzed ML models. It will be considered an angle resolution of 5° instead of 45° to reduce the antenna beam and increase its directivity. The performance of the ML models will be evaluated by simulation results.

Acknowledgment

This work was partially supported by RNP, with resources from MCTIC, Grant No. No 01245.010604/2020-14, under the 6G Mobile Communications Systems project of the Radiocommunication Reference Center (Centro de Referência em Radiocomunicações - CRR) of the National Institute of Telecommunications (Instituto Nacional de Telecomunicações - Inatel), Brazil.

References

[1] Z.-M. Liu, C. Zhang, and S. Y. Philip, "Direction-of-arrival estimation based on deep neural networks with robustness to array imperfections," *IEEE Transactions on Antennas and Propagation*, vol. 66, no. 12, pp. 7315–7327, 2018.

[2] Z. Zhang, Y. Xiao, Z. Ma, M. Xiao, Z. Ding, X. Lei, G. K. Karagiannidis, and P. Fan, "6g wireless networks: Vision, requirements, architecture, and key technologies," *IEEE Vehicular Technology Magazine*, vol. 14, no. 3, pp. 28–41, 2019.

[3] B. Zong, C. Fan, X. Wang, X. Duan, B. Wang, and J. Wang, "6g technologies: Key drivers, core requirements, system architectures, and enabling technologies," *IEEE Vehicular Technology Magazine*, vol. 14, no. 3, pp. 18–27, 2019.

[4] M. Z. Chowdhury, M. Shahjalal, S. Ahmed, and Y. M. Jang, "6g wireless communication systems: Applications, requirements, technologies, challenges, and research directions," *IEEE Open Journal of the Communications Society*, vol. 1, pp. 957–975, 2020.

[5] S. Elmeadawy and R. M. Shubair, "Enabling technologies for 6g future wireless communications: Opportunities and challenges," *arXiv preprint arXiv:2002.06068*, 2020.

[6] K. David and H. Berndt, "6g vision and requirements: Is there any need for beyond 5g?," *IEEE Vehicular Technology Magazine*, vol. 13, no. 3, pp. 72–80, 2018.

[7] S. J. Nawaz, S. K. Sharma, S. Wyne, M. N. Patwary, and M. Asaduzzaman, "Quantum machine learning for 6g communication networks: State-of-the-art and vision for the future," *IEEE Access*, vol. 7, pp. 46317–46350, 2019.

[8] K. B. Letaief, W. Chen, Y. Shi, J. Zhang, and Y.-J. A. Zhang, "The roadmap to 6g: Ai empowered wireless networks," *IEEE Communications Magazine*, vol. 57, no. 8, pp. 84–90, 2019.

[9] E. C. Strinati, S. Barbarossa, J. L. Gonzalez-Jimenez, D. Ktenas, N. Cassiau, L. Maret, and C. Dehos, "6g: The next frontier: From holographic messaging to artificial intelligence using subterahertz and visible light communication," *IEEE Vehicular Technology Magazine*, vol. 14, no. 3, pp. 42–50, 2019.

[10] F. Tariq, M. R. Khandaker, K.-K. Wong, M. A. Imran, M. Bennis, and M. Debbah, "A speculative study on 6g," *IEEE Wireless Communications*, vol. 27, no. 4, pp. 118–125, 2020.

[11] S. Abeywickrama, L. Jayasinghe, H. Fu, S. Nissanka, and C. Yuen, "Rf-based direction finding of uavs using dnn," in *2018 IEEE International Conference on Communication Systems (ICCS)*, pp. 157–161, IEEE, 2018.

[12] (accessed July 5, 2021). https://github.com/anakings/DOA-ML/tree/master/my_solution.

[13] R. Schmidt, "Multiple emitter location and signal parameter estimation," *IEEE transactions on antennas and propagation*, vol. 34, no. 3, pp. 276–280, 1986.

[14] R. Roy and T. Kailath, "Esprit-estimation of signal parameters via rotational invariance techniques," *IEEE Transactions on acoustics, speech, and signal processing*, vol. 37, no. 7, pp. 984–995, 1989.

[15] H. Fu, S. Abeywickrama, C. Yuen, and M. Zhang, "A robust phase-ambiguity-immune doa estimation scheme for antenna array," *IEEE Transactions on Vehicular Technology*, vol. 68, no. 7, pp. 6686–6696, 2019.

[16] T. Svantesson and M. Wennstrom, "High-resolution direction finding using a switched parasitic antenna," in *Proceedings of the 11th IEEE Signal Processing Workshop on Statistical Signal Processing (Cat. No. 01TH8563)*, pp. 508–511, IEEE, 2001.

[17] Q. Gao, Y. Zhao, and D. Hu, "Direction-of-arrival estimation for wideband array signals with a single channel receiver," in *2014 IEEE Radar Conference*, pp. 0809–0812, IEEE, 2014.

[18] H. Huang, J. Yang, H. Huang, Y. Song, and G. Gui, "Deep learning for super-resolution channel estimation and doa estimation based massive mimo system," *IEEE Transactions on Vehicular Technology*, vol. 67, no. 9, pp. 8549–8560, 2018.

[19] Y. Guo, Z. Zhang, Y. Huang, and P. Zhang, "Doa estimation method based on cascaded neural network for two closely spaced sources," *IEEE Signal Processing Letters*, vol. 27, pp. 570–574, 2020.

[20] B. Yuan, "Efficient hardware architecture of softmax layer in deep neural network," in *2016 29th IEEE International System-on-Chip Conference (SOCC)*, pp. 323–326, IEEE, 2016.

[21] R. Sanders, "The pareto principle: its use and abuse," *Journal of Services Marketing*, 1987.

[22] (accessed July 5, 2021). https://scikit-learn.org/stable/modules/generated/sklearn.model_selection.train_test_split.html.

[23] G. Brewka, "Artificial intelligence—a modern approach by stuart russell and peter norvig, prentice hall. series in artificial intelligence, englewood cliffs, nj.," *The Knowledge Engineering Review*, vol. 11, no. 1, pp. 78–79, 1996.

[24] (accessed July 5, 2021). https://scikit-learn.org/stable/modules/generated/sklearn.ensemble.BaggingClassifier.html#:~:text=A%20Bagging%20classifier%20is%20an,to%20form%20a%20final%20prediction.

[25] (accessed July 5, 2021). https://scikit-learn.org/stable/modules/tree.html.

[26] (accessed July 5, 2021). https://scikit-learn.org/stable/modules/generated/sklearn.model_selection.GridSearchCV.html.

Taking into Account Children Accurate Weights during Parent Selection Process in RPL to Extend WSN Lifetime

Doda Afoussatou Rollande Sanou
Lab. of Algebra, Discrete Math. and Computer Science
University Nazi BONI
Bobo-Dioulasso, Burkina Faso
E-mail: sanourollande@gmail.com

Tiguiane Yélémou
Lab. of Algebra, Discrete Math. and Computer Science
University Nazi BONI
Bobo-Dioulasso, Burkina Faso
E-mail: tyelemou@gmail.com

Hamadoun Tall
Lab. of Algebra, Discrete Math. and Computer Science
University Nazi BONI
Bobo-Dioulasso, Burkina Faso
E-mail: hamadoun.tall@gmail.com

Mahamadi Boulou
Lab. of Algebra, Discrete Math. and Computer Science
University Nazi BONI
Bobo-Dioulasso, Burkina Faso
E-mail: mamadiboulou@gmail.com

***Abstract*—Wireless sensor networks (WSNs) are composed of several sensors nodes with limited resources. Nodes can collect data in their deployed area and forward them to the sink using multi-hop communication. WSNs have limited energy and are generally deployed in harsh areas. So, it is not easy for humans to access and replace batteries. Thus, the lifetime of the network must be extended to allow data collection for a long time. To optimize energy consumption in low-power and lossy networks, the Routing Protocol for Low-Power and Lossy Networks (RPL) has been proposed. However, the energy consumption in RPL protocol is not fairly distributed. Some nodes are more solicited to forward data toward the sink node. As a result, the most solicited nodes deplete more quickly their energy, that lead to the network partitioning, data packets lost and more re-transmissions.**

In the literature, most of the proposed optimization techniques are not able to balance both routing load and power consumption. To address this challenge, in this paper, we present a routing technique based on children weights to fairly distribute children nodes among candidate parent nodes. Doing so helps all forwarding nodes in the network to have nearly the same traffic load. That permits to balance routing load and power consumption in the network. Analytical results show that our proposal is better compared to other improved RPL protocols using the Expected Transmission Count (ETX) and number of children metrics.

***Keywords*—Wireless Sensor Network; RPL; load balancing; energy consumption**

I. INTRODUCTION

Wireless Sensor Networks (WSNs) are collections of sensor nodes able to collect data from their deployment environment and transmit them through a multi-hops routing toward the sink.

The miniaturization and low costs of sensor devices have led to the vulgarization of their usage. They have various fields of application, such as monitoring of harmful chemicals, precision agriculture and monitoring of hostile environments. In most cases, sensor nodes operate with batteries that are generally difficult to recharge or replace. These batteries commonly have a limited lifetime. In addition, human intervention ends after the deployment of the sensor network. Most of the time, we would like to be able to collect data over a long period of time. Source nodes need to collect data from their environments, treat and transmit them to the sink. But, due to the short communication range, many of them are out of the communication range of the sink and multi-hop transmissions must be used to forward the collected data. In turn, that may result to a concentration of traffic on nodes closer to the sink and may induce an imbalance load and power consumption. As direct consequence, this may induce a negative impact on the end-to-end delay and increase the packet loss rate due to congestion, affecting the network lifetime.

To optimize the use of these sensors limited resources, Routing Over Low power and Lossy networks (ROLL), an Internet Engineering Task Force (IETF) working group, has developed a Routing Protocol for low-power and Lossy networks (RPL) [1]. The real problem with RPL is the lack of a mechanism to ensure fair balance of traffic among the nodes in the network. Consequently, as the size of the network increases, techniques for optimizing parent selection do not perform well [2].

In a large size network, energy wastage, non-optimal parent selection, slow recovery time after the death of a preferred parent node and imbalanced load are the main factors leading to low performance in WSNs [2]. In this paper, we focus on the problem of traffic load balancing in WSNs. Our contributions are:

1) a critical analysis of existing methods and techniques for traffic load balancing and lifetime optimization of WSNs;
2) a method for balancing traffic load and energy con-

sumption taking into account the number of intermediate nodes during the parent selection phase;
3) an evaluation of this new approach by comparing its performances with those in the literature.

The remainder of the paper is organized as follows. Section II the briefly presents RPL protocol. Section III is dedicated to related work. In Section IV, we present our new parent selection approach and Section V shows an analytical study of the performance of the contribution. Section VI concludes the paper.

II. Brief overview of RPL

RPL is a reactive distance vector routing protocol developed by the Internet Engineering Task Force (IETF) to overcome the problems of Low-power and Lossy Networks (LLNs). It is primarily designed for static lossy networks. It operates on the principle of Destination Oriented Cyclic Graph (DODAG). To form the network topology, a DODAG root broadcasts a first DODAG Information Object (DIO) message to non-root nodes. Thus, when a non-root node wants to join a DODAG, it sends a first DIO message including its rank, identifier and version number of the requested DODAG. On the way to the requested DODAG, each traversed intermediate node updates its view of the topology. This DODAG version number allows the DODAG roots to reset the routing information and starts the DODAG creation process from scratch. Also, each time a non-root node receives a DIO message with a different version number than the previous one, it resets all information and restarts the process of selecting the preferred parent [2].

The process of sending DIO messages is periodic and regulated by the trickle timer algorithm [3]. This algorithm is integrated in RPL to control the DIO messages sending rate in order to minimize the network routing load and thus save energy. However, it has been found that variations in link quality can lead to a long convergence period or sub-optimal routes. Indeed, if after a certain time, the node has received enough coherent DIO messages from its neighbors, it can increase exponentially the DIO message sending period until it reaches a maximum value called *Imax*. Otherwise, it reduces to a minimum value called *Imin* in order to encourage the dissemination of new information.

It is important to notice that DIO messages are not the only control messages. There is also DODAG Information Solicitation (DIS), which is used by nodes that wishe to have information on available routes. We also have DODAG Advertisement Object (DAO) that child nodes send to a parent node as a membership request and when the parent accepts the request, it sends the DAO-Acknowledgement (DAO-ACK) to the child. However, these messages alone do not allow the election of the preferred parent. Thus, the designers of the RPL protocol have implemented two objective functions. They define the routing metrics and the way they is applied to compute the rank and the selection of the preferred parents. The first one is the objective function 0 (OF0) [4], which allows the selection of the path with the lowest rank toward the route. The second is the Minimum Rank Hysteresis Objective Function (MRHOF) [5] the used to select best path according to the number of re-transmissions or the number of hops and energy.

III. Related Work

In this section, we present and discuss existing techniques for traffic load balancing and energy consumption optimization in WSNs.

In [6], Farshid H et al. present an algorithm to identify the quality of all the shortest paths toward the sink using spatio-temporal correlations and constraints-based programming techniques. These allowed to fairly distribute the energy consumption for all nodes in the same rank. However, given the complexity of the exploited spatio-temporal correlation, it could lead to an additional energy consumption.

Ghaleb et al. [7] have designed an objective function to optimize routing load by taking into account the number of children of potential parent nodes. They extended the DIO message with a field, namely, the number of children nodes. Thus, when receiving DIOs, a child compares the number of children of each parent and chooses as parent the one with the lowest number of children. Their proposed approach is not always efficient. The number of one-hop children does not always reflect the data load to be passed to the parent. It is better to take into account the traffic load to the leaf nodes.

In order to increase the stability of the network and extend its lifetime, Iova et al. in [8] have improved the standard Expected Lifetime (ELT) [9] metric to detect bottleneck nodes. The authors estimate the amount of traffic that each node could carry for an fair distribution of the traffic load. However, the proposal is only compared to single and multiple path ETX metric and ELT standards. To further optimize energy consumption, the authors should determine the possible paths towards the sink as a function of the node's traffic load.

Lamaazi et al. [10] have addressed shortcomings associated with the exploitation of singular metrics and proposed a new objective function exploiting a composite metric (ETX, energy consumption and transmission delay). The evaluation and determination of each parameter is quite delicate and may lead to an additional energy consumption cost.

Nassiri et al. [11] proposed a composite metric to efficiently select preferred parents. This proposal consists in forming DoDAGs using the Received Signal Strength Indicator (RSSI) and the metric in DIO messages. To select links with lowest traffic load and lowest latency, they exploit the upstream load estimate and superframe distance. However, the exploitation of DIO and beacon-enabled message at the same time could induce a significant additional routing overhead.

Pereira et al. [12] first proposed a new objective function that helps to discover all potential paths and then selects the preferred parent based on energy. The proposed approach consists in estimating the energy consumed by a node during the transmission and packet re-transmission phase. Then, on the Network Interface Average Power (NIAP), they determined the rank of the potential parent. To optimize the energy consumption, the authors opted to update that metric before updating the tickle timer. However, the estimation made by NIAP is not adaptive because, in some cases, it can not support all the load.

Authors in [13] present a new way to elect cluster heads. Their technique allows to select among several candidate nodes, the one with the smallest distance from the sink and in case of same distances, the one with the highest residual energy. Then by exploiting the Voronoi diagram [14] and the probabilistic perception model, nodes are distributed among clusters. Finally, these nodes will coordinate data sending according to the members of each cluster via Time Division Multiple Access (TDMA). However, nothing has been said about time slot allocation according to the amount of data per cluster and its effect on the network performance.

Sampayo et al. [15] have proposed a technique of duty cycling to optimize energy consumption in the network. When an application wants to send packets, it broadcasts control messages with an unique identifier. Then, upon receipt the message, it compares its rank with the previous one. a node wakes up if the rank of the received message is higher than the previous one. A few moments after sending the control message, the source node broadcasts its data packets. Then, it goes into standby mode and starts a timer to wake up and receive the acknowledgment message. The drawback here is that un-synchronized sleep and wake-up of nodes can cause packet loss leading to re-transmissions.

In [16], Shah et al. proposed a scheduling algorithm for connectivity and node coverage. Then, they balanced the power consumption of the WSNs nodes using the duty cycle technique. To ensure continuous operating of the network, the authors divided the network life into cycles. At the end of each cycle, nodes are allowed to send data with statistics on the different operations to the receiving node. The performance evaluation with ns-2.34 simulator show that the approach outperforms some existing works in terms of energy efficiency. However, their metrics are unrealistic. Since, allowing each node to consume the same amount of energy or imposing an energy threshold is almost impossible. Because, there are nodes that are only within the coverage range of a specific node.

To fairly distribute traffic load and reduce frequency of parents switching, Wang et al. [17] proposed a QoS based method. As QoS metric, they combined the ETX and Packet Transmission Rate (PTR) parameters. Thus, for a node to change its parent, the difference in metrics between it and its current parents must be greater than a defined hysteresis threshold. However, the need to calculate and compare metrics each time a node wishes to change parent shows that the solution will incur an additional energy cost.

The authors in [18] designed a new load balancing routing based on objective function that works as follows. First, this function, exploit the ETX metrics to select best parent node. Then, they used the Packet Re-transmission Rate (PTR) metric to select among these parent nodes the one with the lowest PTR value. However, the PTR creates fluctuations. Also, flow metric is more complex and does not reflect the total number of flows in a node. It does not take into account the numbers of sub-children of a child node in the choice of the parent.

The related work shows that several approaches are proposed in the literature to optimize energy consumption in LLNs networks. The main drawback of these proposed approaches are that, they does not take into account all upstream children when selecting the preferred parent. Also, these proposed approaches lack of method to fairly distribution the traffic load amount parent nodes.

Load balancing techniques based on selecting the preferred parent with the fewest children does not take into account all upstream children when selecting the preferred parent. Indeed, when selecting parent, it is better to choose a parent that has less children and its children also have less children.

IV. Our Proposal

A. *Number of children based algorithm*

The proposed load balancing routing protocol is based on a composite metrics that combines the ETX metric and the number of children. The protocol has two phases: (i) the network construction and the metric designs phase and (ii) the network optimization phase. In this section, we describe in details these two phases.

1) The network construction and the metric design phase: This phase allows the RPL DODAGs construction and the initialization of the routing metric values. The different steps are presented as follows:

1) At the starting of the network, nodes exploit the ETX metric to form DODAGs;
2) Each node periodically broadcasts DIO messages.
3) Nodes receiving the DIO messages may select the transmitting one as its parent toward the sink;
4) Each node evaluates the value of its metric by summing the child metric (the metric, which counts the weight of all upstream nodes from it) communicated by its children. This information is carried by the DIO message and helps parent nodes to have an updated state of its children including the number of children of each child.

Unlike most RPL improvements that take into account the number of children, our approach allows to consider the actual weight of a each child. Indeed, instead of counting a child as weight 1, we take into account its children and grandchildren (more than one hop children of the parent). Therefore, for a given parent node, the children will not have the same weight.

2) The network optimization phase: This phase will permit to fairly distribute the traffic load of each intermediate node toward the sink and works as follows:

1) if a child node receives DIOs messages from multiple parents, it compares the received values of the metric (that has defined early) and selects the parent with the lowest metric value;
2) then, for each node, a DAO message including its weight (its number of children) is transmitted for the selected parent;

3) to avoid fluctuations, a child node can only move to a new parent if the metric value of this parent have two (02) units greater than the old parent;
4) upon receipt of DAO message, the parent node sends a DAO-Ack message to the child node if its membership request is accepted.Then, the parent node increments the number of its children by the weight of this accepted child. The weight of a node is the number of children using it as an intermediary to reach the sink;
5) To have an updated number of children of each parent, a timer is defined. All children that have not transmitted data to the parent node will be removed after the expiration of the timer. So the parent node decrement its weight by the weight of disconnected node;
6) Each time a node receives a DIO message then restart the process from step 1.

B. Analytical study of the performance of our proposal compared to the ETX metric and to the number of children metric

In our evaluated scenarios, nodes have the same packet generation rate of 5 packets each 10 minutes per nodes. Figure 1 represents a network scenario where 6 children nodes (4, 5, 6, 7, 8 and 9) have possibility to choose a parent node among the three nodes that are (1, 2, 3) as the next hop toward the sink. In this scenario, the selection of parent node is based on the link quality metric. Thus, upon receipt of the DIOs, nodes (6, 7, 8 and 9) select node 2 as the preferred parent because it is the best according to the ETX metric. This will create unbalance load because the number of children of node 2 is 7 when nodes 1 and 3 have 3 and 2 respectively. As a consequence, node 2 will run out of energy more quickly than the others.

we supposed that the only obstacle for the communication is the distance. Node 2 is the nearest parent. In the second scenario, Figure 2, parent node selection is based on the number of children. Here, upon receiving the DIOs including the number of children and after comparing its DIOs, nodes 4 and 5 select node 1 as their parent, node 6 and 7 select node 2 as their parent, and nodes 8 and 9 select node 3 as their parent toward the sink. If we evaluate the load on the basis of the number of children metrics only, we notice a fair distribution of the routing load. Because each of parent nodes 1, 2 and 3 have 2 children. Respectively node 4 and 5 for parent 1, nodes 6 and 7 for parent 2 and nodes 8 and 9 for parent 3.

However, the application of this metric results in load unbalance because, in the Figure 2, node 2 support 5 children when nodes 1 and 3 have 4 and 3 children respectively. Doing so, the parent node with the lowest number of children will be more selected by children that increased its number of children (including grandchildren). As its number of children increased it may be overloaded and can quickly run out of energy.

In the third scenario, Figure 3, we have exploited the number of children of the child metric during the preferred parent selection phase. The results show that the data traffic is fairly distributed between the three intermediate nodes 1, 2 and 3. This result is due to the fact that parent nodes (1, 2 and 3) have exactly the same number of one hop children (02) parent nodes that are one hop away from the sink and the same number of two hop children (04) nodes that are upstream of the parent node. In this scenario, all nodes will have to transmit the same number of packets. As a result, all parent nodes will consume the same amount of energy and the network lifetime will be extended.

The results of the analytical evaluations show that the data traffic of scenario 3 is fairly distributed among the three parent nodes. As the parent nodes have the same traffic load, their energy depletion will be similar and the network lifetime can be extended. So the proposed approach optimize the energy consumption compared to the approach based on ETX metric [19] and the number of children metric [20].

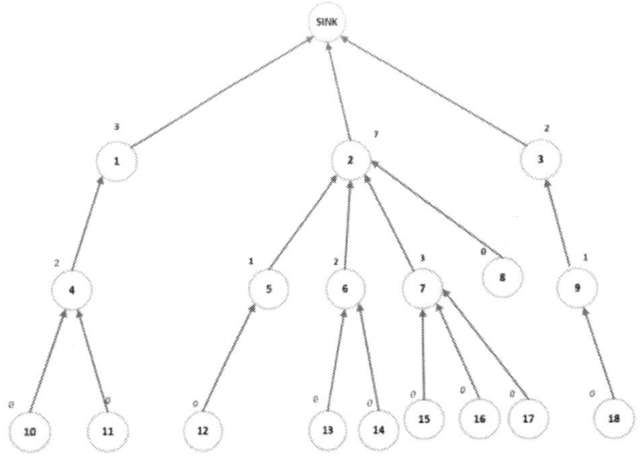

Fig. 1: Network exploiting the ETX metric.

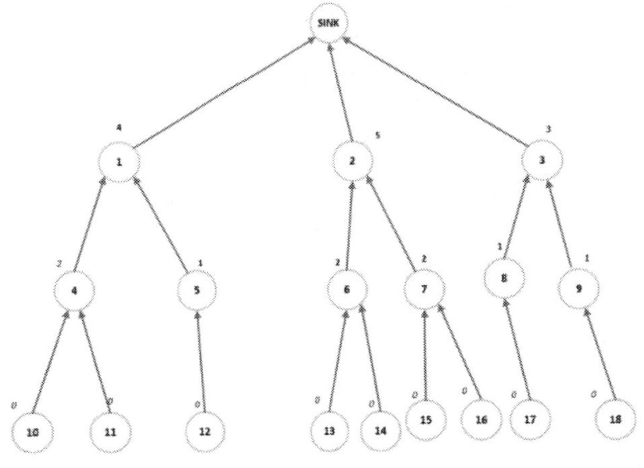

Fig. 2: Network exploiting the number of children metric

TABLE I: LOAD OF DIFFERENT NODES ACCORDING TO ROUTING APPROCH

Nodes/Protocols	ETX	Number of children	Node Weight
1	4 α	6 α	6 α
2	11 α	7 α	6 α
3	3 α	5 α	6 α

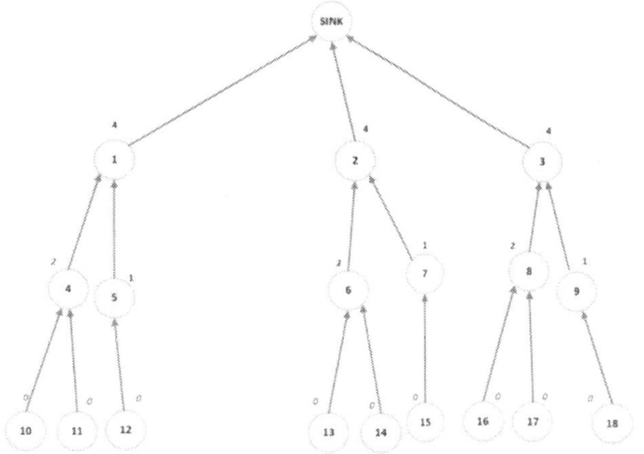

Fig. 3: Network exploiting the number of children of child metric

For simplicity and ease of understanding, we assume in our scenario that each node periodically sends 5 packets each 10 minutes during 30 days. Also, in the current scenario, packets are not treated by intermediate nodes, they are directly forwarded to the sink node. During the evaluation period, each node generates 21600 packets ((5 packets$*$ 30 days$*$ 24 hours$*$ 60 minutes)/ 10 minutes = 21600 packets) that we call α. The Table 1 presents analytical result according to the presented packet generation rate. According to the results presented in Table 1, we notice that with ETX metric node 1 has receive 4α packets while node 3 has 3α and node 2 has 11α. So, node 2 need to transmit three times more than node 1 and 3, thus it will run out of energy more quickly than the two other. This will create the network partitioning. If we consider the number of children protocol we find a slight improvement compared to the ETX metric. Node 1 has to transmit 6α data packet, node 2 has 7α data packet to transmit and node 3 has 5α data packet. However, with our approach, nodes 1, 2, 3 transmit approximately the same amount of data packet, which is 6α. As the energy consumption is proportional to the number of data transmitted. Our proposal is better because in the same time period the nodes consumed the same amount of energy.of the network.

V. CONCLUSION

WSNs are increasingly being used in everyday life and are proving to be an effective solution for data collection. But, the fact that sensors nodes are powered by low capacity batteries limits network lifetime. Also, for the reason that these nodes communicate with the sink on multiple hops, lead to an inequitable energy consumption. Nodes near the sink wastage their energy faster.

Effective energy consumption optimization solution constitute a real challenge for the efficiency of these networks.

In this paper, we first highlighted the shortcomings of works on traffic load optimization in WSNs. Then, we proposed a new approach for parent selection mechanism. In our approach, a node takes into account all other nodes soliciting intermediate services from the target parent in its next-hop selection process. Finally, we performed an analytical evaluation on a given scenario. The results show that our approach improves load balancing in these networks.

In future work, we will carry out an exhaustive evaluation with several parameters and embedded tests in various scenarios to confirm these trends and the impact on performance parameters such as PDR, end-to-end delay.

REFERENCES

[1] T. Winter et al., "RPL:IPv6 Routing Protocol for Low-Power and Lossy Networks," rfc 6550, 2012, pp.1-157.

[2] N. Guan et al., "Delay compensated asynchronous adam algorithm for deep neural networks," 2017 IEEE International Symposium on Parallel and Distributed Processing with Applications and 2017 IEEE International Conference on Ubiquitous Computing and Communications (ISPA/IUCC), IEEE, 2017, pp. 852-859,.

[3] P. Levis et al., "The trickle algorithm," Internet Engineering Task Force, RFC6206, 2011.

[4] Thubert and Pascal, "Objective function zero for the routing protocol for low-power and lossy networks (RPL)," pp. 1-14, 2012.

[5] O. Gnawali et al., "The minimum rank with hysteresis objective function," RFC 6719, 2012, pp. 13.

[6] F. H. Bijarbooneh et al., "Energy-efficient sensor selection for data quality and load balancing in wireless sensor networks," 22nd International Symposium of Quality of Service (IWQoS), IEEE, 2014, pp. 338-343.

[7] B. Ghaleb et al., "Load Balancing Objective Function in RPL draft-qasem-roll-rpl-load-balancing-00," 2017, pp.16.

[8] O. Iova et al., "Exploiting multiple parents in RPL to improve both the network lifetime and its stability," International Conference on Communications (ICC), IEEE, 2015, pp. 610-616.

[9] O. Iova et al., "Improving the network lifetime with energy-balancing routing: Application to RPL," 7th IFIP Wireless and Mobile Networking Conference (WMNC), IEEE, 2014, pp. 1-8.

[10] H. Lamaazi et al., "A comprehensive survey on enhancements and limitations of the RPL protocol: A focus on the objective function," Ad Hoc Networks 96, 2020, pp. 102001.

[11] E. M. Ahrar et al., "RPL: IPv6 Routing Protocol for Low-Power and Lossy Networks," rfc, 6550,2012, pp.1-15.

[12] H. Pereira et al., "Increased Network Lifetime and Load Balancing Based on Network Interface Average Power Metric for RPL," IEEE Access 8, 2020, pp.48686-48696.

[13] S. R. Samal et al., "An Energy Efficient Head Node Selection For Load Balancing In A Heterogeneous Wireless Sensor Network," 52nd Asilomar Conference on Signals, Systems, and Computers. IEEE, 2018, pp. 1428-1433.

[14] K. Hoff et al., "Interactive motion planning using hardware-accelerated computation of generalized Voronoi diagrams," Proceedings 2000 ICRA, Millennium Conference, IEEE International Conference on Robotics and Automation, Symposia Proceedings (Cat. No. 00CH37065), Vol. 3. IEEE, 2000, pp. 2931-2937.

[15] Sampayo, L. Sebastian , Julien Montavont, and Thomas Noël, "LoBaPS: load balancing parent selection for RPL using wake-up radios," 2019 IEEE Symposium on Computers and Communications (ISCC), IEEE, 2019, pp. 1-6.

[16] B. Shah et al., "Guaranteed lifetime protocol for IoT based wireless sensor networks with multiple constraints," Ad Hoc Networks, Vol.104, 2020, pp. 102158.

[17] F. Wang et al., "SL-RPL: Stability-aware load balancing for RPL," Trans. Mach. Learn, Data Min, 2020, Vol.13, pp.27-39.

[18] C. Ji et al., "TAOF: Traffic aware objective function for RPL-based networks," 2018 Global Information Infrastructure and Networking Symposium (GIIS), IEEE, 2018, pp. 1-5.

[19] D.S.J. De Couto et al., "High-throughput routing for multi-hop wireless networks, Diss," Massachusetts Institute of Technology, 2004.

[20] B. Ghaleb et al., "A new load-balancing aware objective function for RPL's IoT networks," 2018 IEEE 20th International Conference on High Performance Computing and Communications, IEEE 16th International Conference on Smart City, IEEE 4th International Conference on Data Science and Systems (HPCC/SmartCity/DSS), IEEE, 2018, pp. 909-914.

On Achieving High Capacity using Small Cells in Multistory Buildings: A Review

Rony Kumer Saha
Radio and Spectrum Laboratory
KDDI Research, Inc.
2-1-15 Ohara, Fujimino-shi, Saitama, Japan
Email: ro-saha@kddi-research.jp

***Abstract*—In this paper, we review the state-of-the-art research studies to present the potential of small cells to address the high capacity demands of in-building users in mobile networks. In doing so, we explore existing works in three major directions toward improving the network capacity, including spectrum accessibility, spectral efficiency improvement, and network densification. It is shown that the exploitation of the Cognitive Radio technology to improve spectrum utilization and the 3-Dimensional (3D) spatial reuse of millimeter-wave spectrum with in-building multiband-enabled ultra-dense small cells to avail additional spectrum using Dynamic Spectrum Sharing can address enormous capacity demand in indoor mobile networks.**

***Keywords*—3D; small cell; network capacity; in-building; millimeter-wave; review; mobile network.**

I. INTRODUCTION

A. Background

In typical cellular mobile networks, a major portion of the data is generated by indoor users at high data rates to support rich multimedia services on mobile phones, particularly in urban high-rise buildings, many of which encompassing several hundreds of apartments. Due to the presence of high external wall penetration loss of a building, the scarcity of available system bandwidth below 3 GHz, and a limit to the maximum transmission power to avoid excessive interference, serving this large amount of indoor data at a high rate with an outdoor Macrocell Base Station (MBS) is difficult. Hence, it now becomes inevitable how to address indoor high data rates and enormous capacity demands.

The received signal capacity at a receiver is a function of the distance from the transmitter and available spectrum bandwidth. The lower the distance and higher the spectrum bandwidth, the better the received signal capacity. The distance can be lowered by reducing the cell size so that the transmitter and receiver are as close in distance as possible. Figure 1 shows the formation of small cells each having a radius r operating at the spectrum bandwidth of b from a large macrocell having a radius R operating at the spectrum bandwidth of B.

Clearly, it can be observed that the reduction in the macrocell coverage into a number of smaller ones allows reusing the same spectrum (B where B=b) spatially (an indirect impact toward the spectrum extension), resulting in achieving more capacity over a certain area (i.e., $C_S = x \times C_M$ where C_M and C_S denote, respectively, the macrocell capacity and the total small cell capacity, and x denotes spectrum reuse factor, which is 7 in Fig. 1), assuming that the Signal-to-Interference-plus-Noise-Ratio (SINR) is the same for both the macrocell and small cells.

Note that a small cell is a cellular radio access node that provides small coverage (typically in the order of 10 meters) at

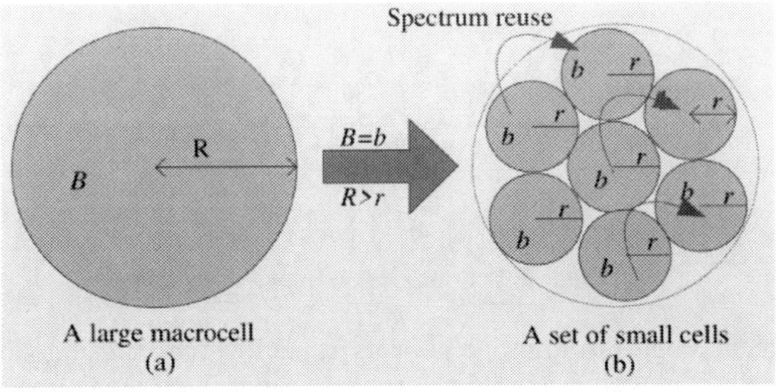

Figure 1. Formation of small cells from a large macrocell.

low power in both licensed and unlicensed spectrum bands to serve its users' mobile and Internet services. Small cells can be deployed by either users or network operators. Operators use them to extend their networks, particularly, to cover dense urban areas, where the presence of several high-rise buildings is a usual scenario, to provide a good signal quality. Femtocells are examples of small cells, and we use the terms "small cell" and "femtocell" interchangeably. Hence, because of a small coverage and a low transmission power, deploying Small Cell Base Stations (SBSs) within buildings as shown in Fig. 2 is considered an effective approach to serve such a large amount of indoor traffic at a high data rate.

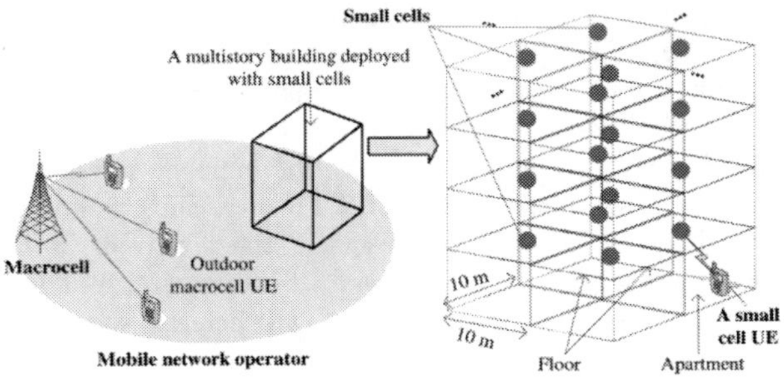

Figure 2. In-building small cell networks.

From Shannon's capacity formula given in (1), it can be

$$C_L = \Phi \times B \,\mathrm{Log}_2\left(1+\left(\frac{P_r}{N+I_T}\right)\right) \qquad (1)$$

where C_L, Φ, B, P_r, N, and I_T denote, respectively, achievable capacity, spectrum reuse factor, available spectrum bandwidth, received desired signal power, noise, and received total interference signal power.

observed that the network capacity can be improved mainly by addressing three directions, including spectrum accessibility, spectral efficiency improvement, and network densification. These are shown in a network capacity improvement triangle in Fig. 3 along with three directions. Corresponding enabling

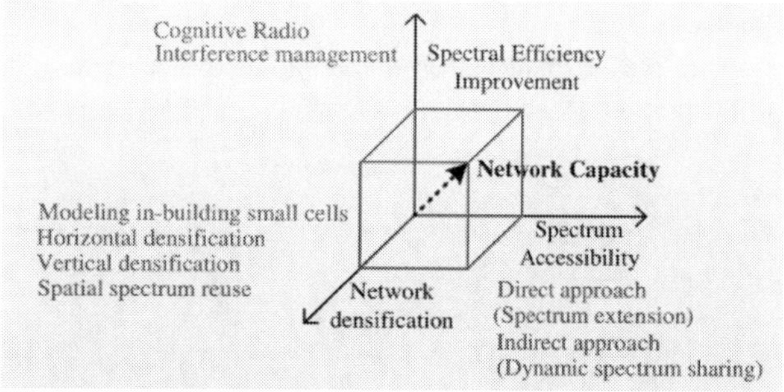

Figure 3. Network capacity improvement triangle.

technologies to improve network capacity indoors using small cells deployed in a building are also shown along each direction.

B. Related Work

Numerous existing research studies have already addressed the enabling technologies along with the three directions [1]-[13]. For example, Saha [1] and Saha and Aswakul [2] have addressed the modeling of in-building small cells in the Millimeter-Wave (mmWave) and microwave spectrum bands, respectively. By deducing the minimum distance between co-channel small cells in both intra-floor and inter-floor levels subject to satisfying predefined interference thresholds, a 3-Dimensional (3D) cluster of small cells has been defined such that the same spectrum can be reused in each 3D cluster of small cells within a building. It has been shown that both horizontal densification of small cells on each floor between adjacent buildings, as well as vertical densification of small cells between floors within each building, can achieve high capacity and Spectral Efficiency (SE) indoors.

Further, Saha [3] has presented how to realize numerous in-building SBS architectures to enable numerous Dynamic Spectrum Sharing techniques by varying the number of physical transceivers as well as the number, amount, and characteristics of spectra per SBS. Further, using game theory, Kamal et al. [4] have presented inter-operator dynamic spectrum access (DSA) algorithms. Furthermore, by allowing both operators to share a fraction of their licensed spectra, Joshi et al. [5] have presented DSS with a view to improving their profit gain, as well as fairness.

Besides, the authors in [6]-[13] have addressed Cognitive Radio technology to address spectrum utilization. More specifically, Saha [6] has addressed an interweave spectrum access technique. Moreover, underlay spectrum access techniques by Saha [7], Khoshkholgh et al. [8], and Liang et al. [9], whereas hybrid interweave-underlay spectrum access techniques by Saha [10], Khan et al. [11], Zuo et al. [12], and Mehmeti et al. [13], have been addressed. It has been shown in [6]-[7], [10] that each spectrum access can improve the average capacity and SE when operating individually, and the hybrid interweave-underlay technique provides the best average capacity and SE performances of all [10]. Hence, though studies in the context of in-building small cells that explore the above three directions of network capacity improvement are essential, no such study is not obvious in the existing literature.

C. Contribution

In this paper, we address this gap by exploiting in-building small cells along these aforementioned three directions to achieve the high indoor capacity demand of existing and upcoming mobile networks. In doing so, we consider reviewing mainly the research works in [1]-[3], [6]-[7], [10]. Consequently, contents in this paper, in terms of texts, figures, equations, and other forms, can be found merged partly or fully with the above works. For interested readers, please refer to the relevant works for any sort of further information. References other than the above works are cited in the appropriate places, wherever used.

D. Organization

The paper is organized as follows. In Section II, spectrum accessibility is discussed under both direct and indirect approaches. Section III covers spectral efficiency improvement techniques, particularly, interweave, underlay and hybrid, spectrum access approaches. In Section IV, in-building network densification and spectrum reuse strategies are presented. Performance results based on [1]-[3], [6]-[7], [10] along three directions toward achieving high in-building capacity are evaluated in Section V. We conclude the paper in Section VI. A list of abbreviations is given in Appendix I.

II. SPECTRUM ACCESSIBILITY

Because spectrum bands below 3 GHz are almost occupied, the high-frequency mmWave spectrum bands have already been considered to address the high capacity demand of Fifth-Generation (5G) and beyond mobile systems, particularly, indoors within multistory buildings. In this regard, to address the massive deployments of small cells to provide high data rates at a short distance, the short-range and the availability of a large amount of mmWave spectrum are promising, particularly in urban indoor environments. Available spectrum for a Mobile Network Operator (MNO) can be increased in two major ways as follows:

- Direct approach: by adding (licensing) new spectrum statically and
- Indirect approach: by sharing used spectrum dynamically/ opportunistically.

In the *direct approach*, a new licensed spectrum can be added directly to a mobile system using techniques such as Carrier Aggregation (Fig. 4), be it contiguous or noncontiguous. However, the traditional direct approaches to extend spectrum are no more effective due to the scarcity of radio spectrum availability, particularly below 3 GHz [14], as well as a huge cost of licensing spectrum. This asks for exploiting indirect approaches to address ever-increasing indoor high data rates and capacity demands for MNOs.

In the *indirect approach*, the spectrum already used by a system (primary) can be shared dynamically or opportunistically by another system (secondary) subject to

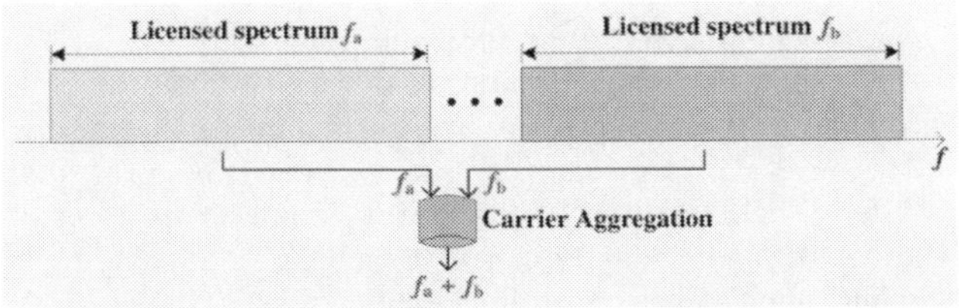

Figure 4. Spectrum access using the Carrier Aggregation approach.

satisfying the condition that the primary system is not affected due to sharing. Such an approach can be termed Dynamic Spectrum Sharing (DSS). Small cells indoors can play a crucial role in DSS.

Based on the number of physical transceivers as well as the number, amount, and characteristics of operating spectra of an SBS, several small cell base station architectures can be realized to address numerous DSS approaches [3]. More specifically, in [3], by enabling SBSs with a single-/multiple-transceiver and operating them at either a single or multiple licensed/unlicensed spectra of homogeneous/ heterogeneous systems, a total of nine SBS architectures are exploited to realize numerous DSS approaches, including Co-Channel Shared Access (CSA), Licensed Shared Access (LSA), Unlicensed Shared Access (ULA), Authorized Shared Access (ASA), Co-primary Shared Access (CoPSA), and Licensed Assisted Access (LAA).

For convenience, a multi-transceiver multiband enabled SBSs operating in the licensed and unlicensed spectrums is shown in Fig. 5. One of the transceivers of an SBS operates at

Figure 5. Type 9 SBS. $F_{l,x} \in \boldsymbol{F}_{l,x} = \{F_{l,1}, F_{l,2}, \ldots, F_{l,\mathrm{xm}}\}$ and $F_{ul,x} \in \boldsymbol{F}_{ul,x} = \{F_{ul,1}, F_{ul,2}, \ldots, F_{ul,\mathrm{xm}}\}$ denote, respectively, a set of licensed spectra of other systems than any mobile system (e.g., satellite systems) and a set of unlicensed spectra (e.g., 60-GHz, 5-GHz, and 2.4-GHz) [3].

the spectrum of its own MNO, the second transceiver operates at the licensed spectrum of a heterogeneous system (e.g., a satellite system), and the third transceiver operates at an unlicensed spectrum (e.g., 60-GHz unlicensed spectrum) using multiple transceivers. Hence, transceiver 1 of an SBS and the spectrum of the MBS of its MNO can realize CSA, transceivers 1 and 2 of the SBS can realize LSA, and transceivers 1 and 3 of the SBS can realize LAA [3].

To avoid Co-Channel Interference (CCI) when sharing the licensed spectrum of homogeneous/ heterogeneous system, Almost Blank Subframe (ABS) based Enhanced Intercell Interference Coordination (eICIC) based on the following principle: *An SBS architecture can be configured such that it can operate only during non-ABSs per ABS Pattern Period (APP)* as shown in Fig. 6 is applied to any transceiver of an SBS depending on its operating spectrum. An ABS is a Transmission Time Interval (TTI) during which no data signal is transmitted

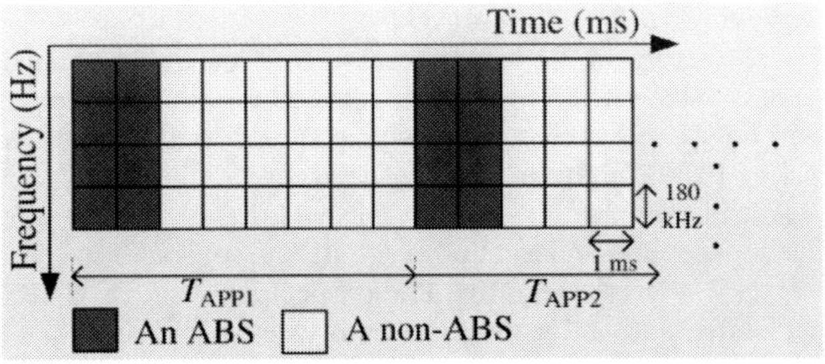

Figure 6. An illustration of the ABS-based eICIC technique [3]. T_{APP1} and T_{APP2} denote APP 1 and APP 2, respectively.

except for some control signals such as broadcast and synchronization signals. An SBS can be scheduled at the same frequency as that of another system only during non-ABSs per APP [3]. Note that for an unlicensed band, no CCI is considered.

III. SPECTRAL EFFICIENCY IMPROVEMENT

MNOs in a country facing challenges from enabling efficient utilization of its available licensed spectrum. This is because the user traffic demand of different MNOs in a country varies abruptly over time and space such that the demand for the required amount of spectra for different MNOs varies accordingly. This causes a great portion of the available spectrum allocated to each MNO in a country to be left unused or underutilized either in time or space. In recent times, Cognitive Radio (CR) has appeared as an enabling technology to address this spectrum under-utilization issue. In CR, spectrum access is a major function, which prevents collisions between primary User Equipments (UEs) and Secondary UEs (SUs) to allow sharing the licensed spectrum of one MNO with another to increase its effective spectrum bandwidth, resulting in improving its spectral efficiency to serve high capacity. Based on how the collisions between primary and secondary UEs are prevented while accessing any spectrum, there are three major categories of spectrum access techniques in CR systems, including interweave, underlay, and overlay. In this paper, we limit our focus on studying interweave and underlay spectrum access techniques.

In the interweave model, the unused spectrum in time, frequency, and geographic location of licensed primary UEs

(PUs) can be shared opportunistically by SUs in a dynamic shared-use basis without interfering PUs, for example, when PUs are inactive [15]. To find an idle spectrum of PUs, SUs need to be able to sense the used spectrum of PUs. Once sensed idle, SUs can transmit at the maximum power. In [6], an Interweave Strategy Based Shared-Use (ISSU) model for the dynamic spectrum access of licensed 28-GHz mmWave spectrum of one MNO to another under an in-building small cell scenario in a country has been proposed and stated as follows. *The licensed mmWave spectrum of one MNO, i.e., primary-MNO (p-MNO) can be allowed to share with small cells in a building of another MNO, i.e., secondary-MNO (s-MNO) only if no UE of p-MNO is present inside the corresponding building of small cells of s-MNO to avoid co-channel interference between UEs of p-MNO and s-MNO. If otherwise, no spectrum of p-MNO can be shared with in-building small cells of s-MNO* [6].

However, in underlay access, SUs can simultaneously access the spectrum of PUs at a reduced transmission power to serve its users subject to satisfying the interference threshold set by PUs. Unlike the interweave access, the underlay access does not need any spectrum sensing. However, it suffers from the reduced transmission power of SUs to limit CCI to PUs. In [7], an Underlay Cognitive Radio Spectrum Access (UCRSA) technique for the dynamic spectrum access of licensed 28 GHz mmWave spectrum of one MNO to another under in-building small cell scenario in a country has been proposed and stated as follows. *The licensed 28 GHz mmWave spectrum of one MNO (i.e., p-MNO) can be allowed to share with small cells in a building of another MNO (i.e., s-MNO) subject to operating each small cell of the s-MNO at a reduced transmission power at any time irrespective of the existence of a UE of the p-MNO within the coverage of the corresponding small cell. The reduced transmission power is varied in accordance with the predefined interference threshold set by the p-MNO* [7].

Though both interweave and underlay have pros and cons as aforementioned, the combination of these two spectrum accesses can maximize the SE. More specifically, SUs can explore interweave access when the spectrum of PUs is idle and the underlay access when the spectrum of PUs is busy. In [10], a hybrid interweave-underlay spectrum access technique for the dynamic spectrum access of the licensed 28 GHz mmWave spectrum of one MNO to another under an in-building small cell scenario in a country is proposed and stated as follows. *The licensed 28 GHz mmWave spectrum of one MNO (i.e., p-MNO) can be allowed to share with small cells in a building of another MNO (i.e., s-MNO) subject to operating each small cell of the s-MNO at the maximum transmission power if no UE of the p-MNO is present, but at a reduced transmission power if a UE of the p-MNO is present [10]. The reduced transmission power is varied in accordance with the predefined interference threshold set by the p-MNO.*

IV. NETWORK DENSIFICATION

SBSs can be deployed both in the intra-floor, as well as the inter-floor, level of a building, resulting in an ultra-dense deployment of SBSs over a certain area of 2-Dimensional (2D) physical space within the coverage of a macrocell. Moreover, due to the high penetration losses of mmWave bands through external and internal walls and floors in any multi-story building compared to low-frequency microwave bands, the reuse of mmWave bands can be explored in the third dimension (i.e., the height of a multistory building), which results in reusing the same mmWave band more than once at the inter-floor level. In addition, the conventional spectrum reuse techniques at the intra-floor level in a multistory building can be used to facilitate the reuse of mmWave spectra in ultra-dense deployed small cells within the building.

In [1], a minimum separation distance for the intra-floor level and inter-floor-level are expressed numerically for the 28 GHz mmWave spectrum to define a set to SBSs (also called a cluster of SBSs) corresponding to the minimum distances both intra-floor and inter-floor levels subject to satisfying co-channel interference constraints in both levels. The size of a 3D cluster of SBSs is then defined such that the same spectrum bandwidth can be reused in each cluster of SBSs. Figure 7 shows an example minimum distance constraint-based 3D cluster of SBSs with respect to floor $n+1$. Region of Exclusions (RoEs) for both intra-and inter-floor levels are shown with red color lines. Green color circles represent Co-channel SBSs (cSBSs) and ash color circles represent non-cSBSs. Hence, resources can be reused in every 3 SBSs intra-floor level and every alternate floor inter-floor level such that a 3D cluster consists of 18 SBSs [2].

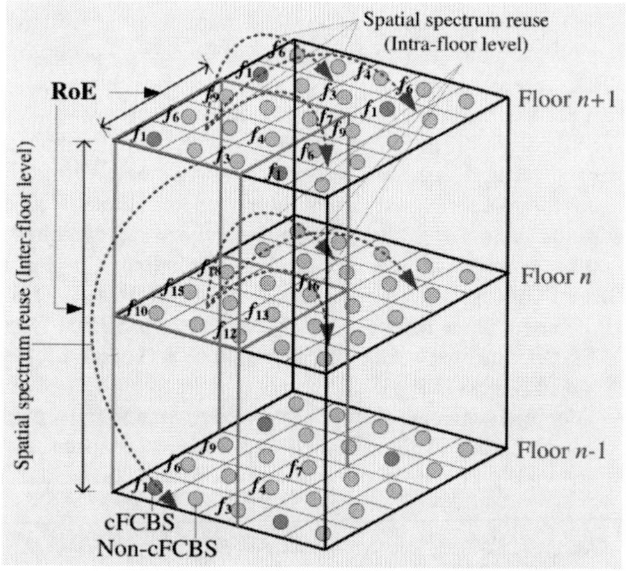

Figure 7. Formation of an in-building 3D cluster of SBSs subject to satisfying the minimum distance constraints in both intra-and inter-floor levels to reuse the same spectrum in a 3D in-building scenario [2].

V. PERFORMANCE RESULTS

Default parameters and assumptions used for generating the following performance responses can be found in the respective references cited (i.e., [1]-[3], [6]-[7], [10]). Hence, regarding spectrum accessibility, with extensive simulation and numerical results and analyses, it is shown in [3] that the network capacity and SE (Fig. 8) can be improved by exploiting an SBS architecture to allow more spectrum to be available using the DSS technique. SBS architectures, including Types 9, 8, 7, and 3, give better SE responses than others due to operating in the

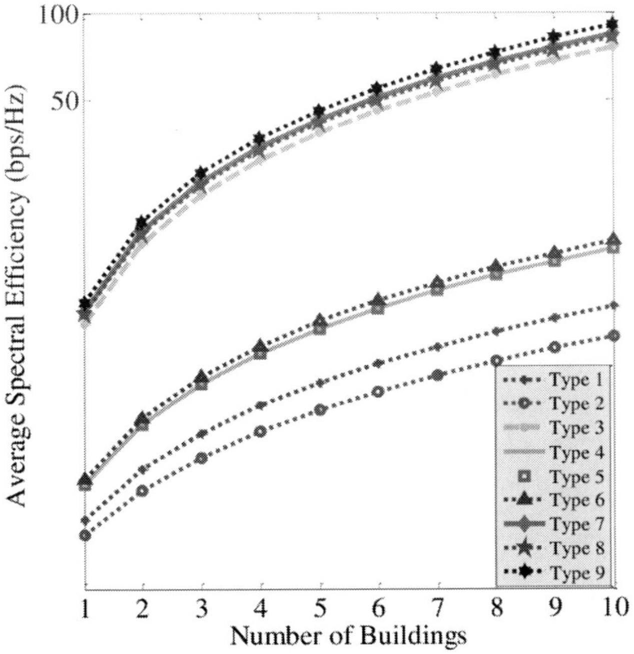

Figure 8. SE responses of numerous SBS architectures [3].

60-GHz unlicensed spectrum providing better channel responses than that of other licensed spectrums. For further information, please refer to [3].

Regarding SE improvement, by applying the ISSU model in [6], it is shown that the average capacity, as well as the SE, performances of an MNO (i.e., an s-MNO) are improved by about 150% as shown in Fig. 9. Further, by limiting the

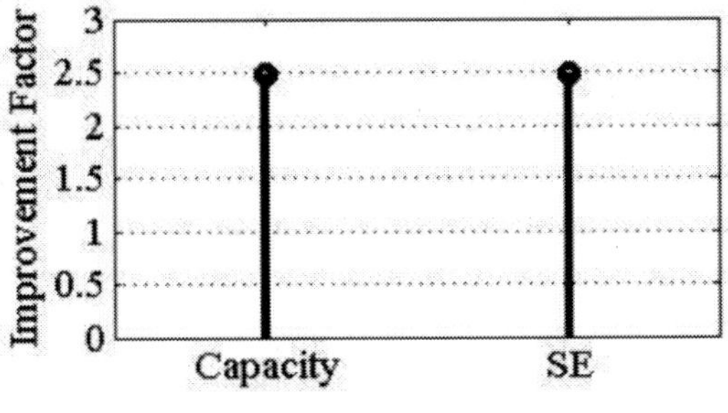

Figure 9. Average capacity and SE performance improvement factors for an s-MNO with applying ISSU for a single building of small cells [6].

transmission power of an SBS to 20% of its maximum power, it is shown in [7] that the proposed underlay technique (i.e., UCRSA) can improve the average capacity and SE of an MNO by about 2.67 times what can be obtained by the traditional Static Licensed Shared Access (SLSA) where each MNO is allocated exclusively to an equal amount of the licensed spectrum as shown in Fig. 10 [7]. Furthermore, as shown in Fig. 11, by limiting the transmission power of an SBS to 20% of its maximum power, it is shown in [10] that the hybrid technique outperforms both the interweave and underlay techniques when each operating individually in terms of SE of an MNO.

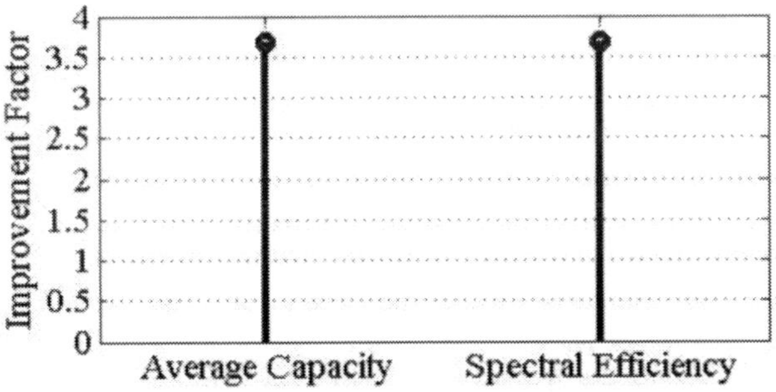

Figure 10. Average capacity and SE improvement for an MNO due to applying the UCRSA technique over that of the SLSA technique for a single building of small cells [7].

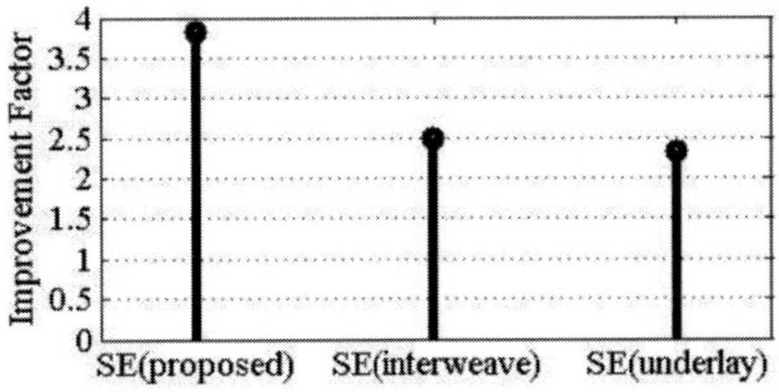

Figure 11. SE improvement factors for an s-MNO due to applying, interweave, underlay, and the proposed hybrid inter-weave-underlay techniques for a single building of SBSs [10].

Finally, regarding the network densification, with extensive simulation results in [2], it is shown in Fig.12 that the SE increases significantly when employing 3D spatial reuse of the

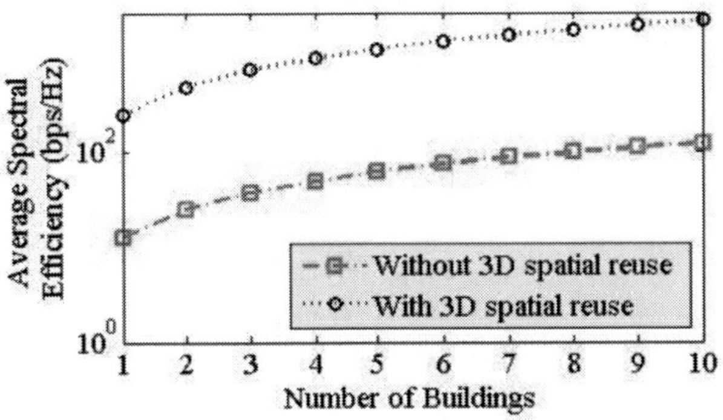

Figure 12. Impact of applying 3D spatial reuse of mmWave spectra to in-building small cells on the average SE [1].

same spectrum (i.e., Vertical Reuse Factor (vRF)) to small cells within each building as compared to when no reuse is considered. Also, in Fig.13, it is shown that the SE improves

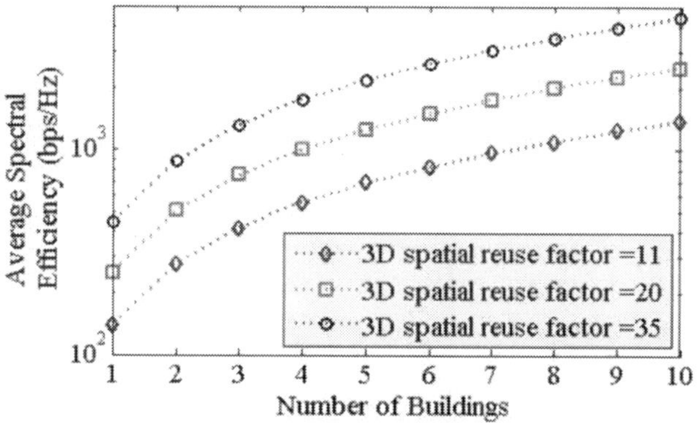

Figure 13. Average SE response for numerous 3D spatial reuse factors per building with a variation in the number of buildings of SBSs (i.e., hRF) [1].

linearly with an increase in Horizontal Reuse Factor (hRF) for any value of vRF such that the overall SE improves by a factor defined as the product of vRF and hRF, i.e., (vRF×hRF).

VI. CONCLUSION

In this paper, we have provided a review on how to explore small cells to address the ever-growing high capacity demands of indoor users, particularly, in dense urban in-building scenarios. In this regard, we have considered exploring major three directions toward achieving high network capacity, including spectrum accessibility, spectral efficiency improvement, and network densification. A set of existing papers [1]-[3], [6]-[7], [10] highly relevant to the enabling technologies along each direction have been reviewed under an in-building scenario to present the potentiality of small cells in achieving high capacity indoors. Relevant theoretical background in the context of in-building small cells has been discussed followed by the performance evaluation of major enabling technologies along each direction.

It has been shown that the following approaches along three directions can help achieve an enormous amount of in-building capacity, required by the existing, as well as future mobile networks.

- Multi-band multi-transceiver enabled small cells operating in the high-frequency millimeter-wave licensed or unlicensed spectrum to realize dynamic spectrum sharing techniques by exploiting small cell base station architectures subject to satisfying co-channel interference threshold for the spectrum accessibility,
- A hybrid spectrum access model (i.e., interweave-underlay spectrum access) in Cognitive Radio Networks for the spectral efficiency improvement, and
- Exploiting both the vertical and horizontal spectrum reuse in small cells deployed densely within buildings for the network densification.

APPENDIX I

A LIST OF ABBREVIATIONS

Abbreviation	Description
2D	2-Dimensional
3D	3-Dimensional
5G	Fifth-Generation
ABS	Almost Blank Subframe
APP	ABS Pattern Period
BS	Base Station
CCI	Co-Channel Interference
CR	Cognitive Radio
CSA	Co-channel Shared Access
cSBS	Co-channel SBS
DSS	Dynamic Spectrum Sharing
eICIC	Enhanced Intercell Interference Coordination
hRF	Horizontal Reuse Factor
LAA	Licensed Assisted Access
LSA	Licensed Shared Access
MBS	Macrocell Base Station
mmWave	Millimeter-Wave
MNO	Mobile Network Operator
p-MNO	Primary MNO
PU	Primary UE
RoE	Region of Exclusion
SBS	Small Cell Base Station
SE	Spectral Efficiency
SINR	Signal-to-Interference-plus-Noise-Ratio
SLSA	Static Licensed Spectrum Allocation
s-MNO	Secondary MNO
sSBS	Serving SBS
sSU	Serving Small Cell UE
SU	Secondary UE
TTI	Transmission Time Interval
UE	User Equipment
vRF	Vertical Reuse Factor

ACKNOWLEDGMENT

This is a review paper, which is mainly based on the author's existing research works [1-3], [6-7], [10] mentioned in the reference section below. Consequently, contents in this paper, in terms of texts, figures, equations, and other forms, can be found merged substantially with that in [1-3], [6-7], [10]. For interested readers, please refer to the relevant works for any sort of further information. References other than these are cited in the paper in the appropriate places, wherever used.

REFERENCES

[1] R. K. Saha, "3D Spatial Reuse of Multi-Millimeter-Wave Spectra by Ultra-Dense In-Building Small Cells for Spectral and Energy Efficiencies of Future 6G Mobile Networks," Energies, vol. 13, no. 7, art. no. 1748, 2020. doi: 10.3390/EN13071748.

[2] R. K. Saha and C. Aswakul, "A Tractable Analytical Model for Interference Characterization and Minimum Distance Enforcement to Reuse Resources in Three-Dimensional In-Building Dense Small Cell Networks," Int. J. Commun. Syst., vol. 30, no. 11, pp. 95-118, July 2017, doi: 10.1002/DAC.3240.

[3] R. K. Saha, "A Tactic for Architectural Exploitation of Indoor Small Cells for Dynamic Spectrum Sharing in 5G," IEEE Access, vol. 8, pp. 15056-15071, January 2020, doi: 10.1109/ACCESS.2020.2966230.

[4] H. Kamal, M. Coupechoux, and P. Godlewski, "Inter-Operator Spectrum Sharing for Cellular Networks Using Game Theory," Proc. 2009 IEEE 20th International Symposium on Personal, Indoor and Mobile Radio Communications, Tokyo, 2009, pp. 425-429.

[5] S. K. Joshi, K. B. S. Manosha, M. Codreanu, and M. Latva-aho, "Dynamic Inter-Operator Spectrum Sharing via Lyapunov Optimization," IEEE Trans. Wirel. Commun., vol. 16, no. 10, pp. 6365-6381, Oct. 2017, doi: 10.1109/TWC.2017.2722999.

[6] R. K. Saha, "Interweave Shared-Use Model for Dynamic Spectrum Access in Millimeter-Wave Mobile Systems for 6G," Proc. 2020 IEEE 92nd Vehicular Technology Conference (VTC2020- Fall), Victoria, BC, Canada, 18-Nov.-16 Dec., 2020, pp. 1-6, doi: 10.1109/VTC2020- Fall49728.2020.9348671.

[7] R. K. Saha, "Underlay Cognitive Radio Millimeter-Wave Spectrum Access for In-Building Dense Small Cells in Multi-Operator Environments Toward 6G," Proc. IEEE 23rd International Symposium on Wireless Personal Multimedia Communications (WPMC), Okayama, Japan, 19-26 Oct. 2020, pp. 1-6, doi: 10.1109/WPMC50192.2020.9309471.

[8] M. G. Khoshkholgh, K. Navaie, and H. Yanikomeroglu, "Interference Management in Underlay Spectrum Sharing Using Indirect Power Control Signalling," IEEE Trans. Wirel. Commun., vol. 12, no. 7, pp. 3264-3277, July 2013, doi: 10.1109/TWC.2013.052813121110.

[9] W. Liang, K. D. Wang, J. Shi, L. Li, and G. K. Karagiannidis, "Distributed Sequential Coalition Formation Algorithm for Spectrum Allocation in Underlay Cognitive Radio Networks," IEEE Access, vol. 7, pp. 56803-56816, 2019, doi: 10.1109/ACCESS.2019.2910720.

[10] R. K. Saha, "Hybrid Interweave-Underlay Millimeter-Wave Spectrum Access in Multi-Operator Cognitive Radio Networks Toward 6G," Proc. Fifteenth International Conference on Systems and Networks Communications (ICSNC), Porto, Portugal, 18-22 Oct. 2020, pp. 42-48.

[11] A. U. Khan et al., "HBLP: A Hybrid Underlay-Interweave Mode CRN for the Future 5G-based Internet of Things," IEEE Access, vol. 8, pp. 63403-63420, 2020, doi: 10.1109/ACCESS.2020.2981413.

[12] P. Zuo, T. Peng, W. Linghu, and W. Wang, "Optimal Resource Allocation for Hybrid Interweave-Underlay Cognitive Satcom Uplink," Proc. The 2018 IEEE Wireless Communications and Networking Conference (WCNC), Barcelona, Spain, April 2018, pp. 1-6.

[13] F. Mehmeti and T. Spyropoulos, "Performance Analysis, Comparison, and Optimization of Interweave and Underlay Spectrum Access in Cognitive Radio Networks," IEEE Trans. Veh. Technol., vol. 67, pp. 7143-7157, Aug. 2018, doi: 10.1109/TVT.2018.2828090.

[14] R. K. Saha, "A Technique for Massive Spectrum Sharing with Ultra-dense In-building Small Cells in 5G era," Proc. IEEE 90th Veh. Technol. Conf. (VTC-Fall), Honolulu, HI, USA, Sep. 2019, pp. 1-7.

[15] M. R. Hassan, G. C. Karmakar, J. Kamruzzaman, and B. Srinivasan, "Exclusive Use Spectrum Access Trading Models in Cognitive Radio Networks: A Survey," IEEE Commun. Surv. Tuts., vol. 19, no. 4, pp. 2192-2231, Fourth quarter 2017, doi: 10.1109/COMST.2017.2725960.